C000218685

Fits & Starts

Also by Maurice Richardson

EXPLOITS OF ENGELBRECHT
THE FASCINATION OF REPTILES
LITTLE VICTIMS

Fits & Starts

Collected pieces by
Maurice Richardson

Introduction by Julian Symons

LONDON
MICHAEL JOSEPH

First published in Great Britain by Michael Joseph Limited
52 Bedford Square, London WC1
1979

© This collection by the Estate of Maurice Richardson 1979

All Rights Reserved. No part of this publication
may be reproduced, stored in a retrieval system,
or transmitted, in any form or by any means,
electronic, mechanical, photocopying, recording
or otherwise, without the prior permission
of the Copyright owner.

ISBN 0 7181 1821 9
Photoset by D. P. Media Ltd, Hitchin and printed and bound
by Redwood Burn Ltd, Trowbridge and Esher

Author's Foreword and Acknowledgements

This collection of short stories, reportage, essays and reviews covers the last forty years. I do not think any further comment from me is needed.

My relations with editors have been almost entirely harmonious, often euphoric. I should however like to express particular thanks to Richard Bennett, Editor of *Lilliput* 1947–50; to David Astor of *The Observer*, to my old friend, Terence Kilmartin, his literary editor – also to the late Viola Garvin, Terence's predecessor; and, more recently, to Willy Landels of *Harpers & Queen* and his infinitely sympathetic assistant editor, Ann Barr. I must also thank John Gross of *The Times Literary Supplement* and his assistant editor, Mary-Kaye Wilmers – she of the therapeutic personality – for feeding me with books to review on which I could spread myself.

1978

Much of the material in this book originally appeared in newspapers or journals, and, in addition to those mentioned in the author's acknowledgements above, the publishers would like to express their thanks to the following: *The Times, The Financial Times, The Daily Telegraph, New Statesman, Punch* and *Books and Bookmen*.

Contents

Introduction

One of the attractive, although at times infuriating, things about Maurice Richardson was that he embodied in himself so many contradictions. A prime example can be found in his attitude towards luxurious living. True luxury, of the Edwardian kind that implies excess, was a way of life into which he sank with the ease of somebody entering his natural element. Read the loving account in *Doucer de Vivre* of the breakfast table at Ernest Mocatta's house, which contained 'dishes of sole, salmon kedgeree, fried eggs, scrambled eggs, kidneys, a blushing York ham, a glazed tongue', all, as he says, 'for two of us only and Ernest never ate more than one boiled egg.' But excess means waste, and one of Maurice's many selves disapproved of waste, so that he was for years a member of the Communist Party which stood – among other things – for the elimination of Mocattan luxury.

Many other contradictions made up his complex personality. He drank a great deal and then went on the wagon, taking no liquid but soda water. He was a sceptical humanist fascinated by freakish religions, and even more by the odd characters connected with them, like Aleister Crowley the self-styled Beast 666, and the Yorkshire Yogi, Dr Alexander Cannon, both of them described here. A believer in the healing powers of psychoanalysis, he was himself a difficult and unrewarding patient; an intellectual whose 'reading was very wide, his versatility formidable' as he says of Baron Munchausen's biographer, Rudolf Erich Raspe, he had also the journalist's magpie quality of pecking quickly at a subject and flying away. He was a persistent teller of autobiographical tales, among them luncheons with Beast 666, Irish misadventures with Professor Dawkins and a lively East End evening with Virginia Bath, yet he remained in many ways a man resolutely reticent about his own personality and beliefs.

My own friendship with Maurice was warm but not deep. We met first in the course of some Soho pub evening before the War, and saw quite a lot of each other for a period of ten years or so ending in the middle fifties, after which we met much less often. We had in common a devotion to crime stories and to real life crime, but in addition Maurice was a splendid pub companion, full of good stories which began realistically but spiralled up into fantasy. The stories in the Profiles section of this book are admirably told, but they are still only shadows of his conversation at its most vivid. He had a sense of style in relation to clothes and conversation, as well as in his writing, and the kind of charm in talking to women that makes them feel that their appearance is of even more interest to their companion than what they are saying.

Maurice had a chunky, broad-shouldered boxer's build (he had been in fact a good amateur boxer), and when I first knew him looked distinctly like the American player of tough parts, Chester Morris. Later, when he put on weight, his features took on a Churchillian cast – Randolph, not Winston. His boiled blue eyes, slightly protuberant, had often a glare or glaze of what looked like hostility. I have known people who found him frightening, and there is no doubt that he could be aggressive in the company of those he disliked or found boring. He shared this aggressive quality with his friend John Davenport, who is mentioned in one of these pieces, and also appears fictionally in the first of them as a headkeeper, described accurately in relation to the real Davenport as 'a powerful man with a figure like a sawn-off Hercules.' John must have held the record for being thrown physically out of London clubs. Maurice could not have matched this, but had trouble enough while in his cups. I never myself had any greater difference with him than a brisk exchange of verbal abuse in which he called me an academic prig and I said that he was a snob fascinated by the rich. Both accusations had, I daresay, elements of truth.

I can see that I am in danger of putting in 'what is known in the trade as the Acid Drop', as Maurice wittily puts it in a short article about obituary habits. But I take heart from his endorsement of a Cromwellian 'warts and all' approach in the last line of that article, and in Maurice's case nobody would write truly about him without taking some account of his shortcomings. *The Times* could find nobody ready to write an orthodox anonymous obituary notice, and publishers and editors particularly needed all the tolerance at their command in dealing with him. Maurice was a manic depressive, and by all accounts could be awkward to deal with when manic, and simply unproductive while in deep depression. Editors suffered emotionally, publishers financially, at his hands. The list of those who made advances on books he never produced would have to be numbered on more fingers than ordinary humans possess.

That was the dark side, the side on which idle, luxury-loving Maurice might say how detestable it was for a gentleman to be pestered by literary tradesmen. The compensations are expressed by the pieces in this book, which testify to the fact that Maurice was the most imaginative and most wide-ranging literary journalist in Britain. He was interested in anybody and anything unusual, and had remarkable powers of sympathy in talking to burglars, boxers, wrestlers. He could empathise with everybody except Mr and Mrs Everyman. He was fascinated by snakes and insects, and by any other natural phenomenon that enlarged his knowledge of human behaviour.

At his best he was also a brilliant observer and analyst. Nobody has written better, more perceptively and less sensationally, about the Moors Murders, has pinned more certainly the barrack-room lawyer quality in Brady, or examined with equal skill the subtleties of the Brady-Hindley relationship. The piece is so good that one is left wishing he had written a book about the case. But although Maurice wrote more between covers than is generally known, including three novels, the recently reprinted science fiction stories called *The Exploits of Engelbrecht*, an account of his experiences in the Fire Service and a short book about prep school life, his talent was most truly expressed in the article written to order and with a deadline, and in his weekly articles on TV and his crime reviews.

My only regret about the present excellent collection, which ranges back over rather more than the forty years mentioned in the foreword – 'Way Out in the Continuum' I think appeared in *Horizon* during the War – is that it includes no TV or crime pieces. Maurice invented the telegraphically brief crime review, and practised it brilliantly. I suppose these very short pieces with their stunning similes would be out of place in a book, but there are longer pieces about Ambler and Simenon that would be worth reprinting. And the wit and style of his TV reviews transcends the ephemeral nature of what he called the repertory of rot.

His attitude towards the square eye in the living room was typically ambivalent. Part of him disapproved the time wasted, his own time and that of others, on pernicious or mind-rotting rubbish; another part was fascinated by the rubbish and devoted to it, as some people treasure the badness of truly bad films; and a third Maurice applauded TV as informer, liberator, potential influence in raising mass standards. The combination was unique, and the high standard of TV critic-ism in Britain today is at least in part because of his example. Perhaps another selection of reviews and articles – I have the impression that there is plenty to choose from – will prove the point.

I last saw Maurice a few years back, when we met unexpec-tedly in a Westminster street. He advanced on me with a wide smile on his face, and his arms flung out in greeting. His death last year, at the age of seventy-one, came at the house of a friend where he was staying for a weekend. One of the several pub-lishers he knew came over, and found him in fine conversa-tional form. Maurice had wanted to see him particularly to talk about a book for which he had signed a contract. They agreed to change the book for another title, which the publisher felt fairly certain would also not be produced. Maurice went cheer-fully to bed. His host took up a cup of tea in the morning, and found him dead. He had suffered a coronary in the night. It was a peculiarly appropriate easing out of life for one whose charac-ter and beliefs were, upon the whole, so deliberately Epicurean.

Julian Symons

Short Stories

One Gun Short

'What a perfectly delicious morning.'

Sir Edwin Dalby strode over to the far end of the dining-room of Ockley Park, his house near Dorking, and threw open the French windows. Then he came back to the sideboard and helped himself to coffee and salmon kedgeree.

'Yes, isn't it,' said his son Harry, draining his coffee cup. He leaned back in his chair and put his thumbs in the pockets of his leather waistcoat. 'You know what the temperature is on the thermometer on the terrace? Sixty-nine. And it's only,' he fished out a half-hunter and touched the spring to open it, 'three minutes past eight. That means it'll be well up in the high seventies by midday and . . .'

'And it's the eleventh of October, and you're going to shoot pheasants and it doesn't seem natural,' said his sister Gertrude sharply, finishing his sentence for him. She was by way of being a new woman.

'I don't suppose,' said Lady Dalby dreamily, 'that the pheasants find one day any more natural than another to be shot on. Poor dears, they'll be looking so exquisite in this weather. Couldn't you shoot' – she lowered her voice – 'blue monkeys instead?'

'You know you'd never allow, it, Chloe, don't be absurd,' said Sir Edwin. The Blue Monkey was the nickname of one of their guests, the Marquis de Soveral, the Portuguese Ambassador, a bosom friend of the King's and a most popular institution in Edwardian society.

It was a custom of the Dalbys that on shooting mornings they all got up early and formed what Sir Edwin called *un bloc de famille,* not that this implied any lapses in hospitality, merely that there were some moments when families must be more united than others and a shooting morning was one of them.

Sir Edwin held a final check-up with his wife about luncheon and who was going to look after the ladies, and how. Then he nodded to his son.

'Come on Harry. I told Davenport to be round at a quarter past eight.'

Father and son sat sprawling in leather armchairs in the gunroom confronting the estate map on the wall. Sir Edwin took from its leather case a cigarette-holder with an amber mouthpiece, and a meerschaum front piece made to take oval cigarettes. He fitted in a fat oval Ottoman Empire cigarette and lit it with a gold spirit lighter. The fastidious routine took some little time. It was typical of him and his period. He used to say: 'I'm the only Englishman who knows how to live as well as the rich Jews. I pride myself I have an eye for detail.'

His house was unique: a delightful compromise in yellow stone between an oriental palace and a regency mansion with domes and turrets and minarets; but with large windows that made for light airy rooms, as if the Brighton Pavilion had gone rural. It was set on a plateau on the southern slopes of the 'Surrey Alps'. It was from here, only a few years later, that a young writer named Ronald Firbank was to coin the phrase 'the blue doom of summer'. It reminded you a little of John Martin's picture 'The Plains of Heaven'.

There was a knock at the door and Davenport, the head-keeper, came in; a powerful man with a figure like a sawn-off Hercules. He was regarded as a treasure in his profession in which eccentricity can be an asset. He had more than once snatched away the gun from a mediatised prince who was plainly a danger to life and limb.

The Dalbys got up and came over to the estate map. There would be nine guns, but the strategic placing was important as some of the drives involved precipitous woodland. The stands were allotted so as to give the easiest to the Marquis de Soveral and the hardest to Harry.

Sir Edwin glanced at the clock over the gunroom mantel-piece. 'You're meeting Grubby Greville at Dorking, aren't you, Harry?'

'Yes, Daddy. I'm taking the dogcart and Tim the tiger. Can't always trust the motors.'

'Off you go, then.' Sir Edwin fitted another fat Turk into his amber and meerschaum holder.

About half an hour before the conversation in the gunroom, a couple had alighted from an earlier London train at Dorking station and fetched their bicycles from the guard's van. The man was short, sturdy and compact with rather small eyes and a reddish face. He had a short russet beard and wore a cap and a soft collar. His clothes were shabby. The woman had a long face with protuberant, rather sad eyes, and her clothes were shabby. They spoke Russian which I will interpret, cutting out the names and patronymics.

'You know,' she said, as they wheeled their bicycles out into the station yard, 'it's awfully hilly country for bicycling.'

'You know what Hegel would have said if he'd had a bicycle? You've got to go up to come down.' He took a map from his pocket. 'Now this is where we are, and where we want to get to is *there*. Right! *En avant. Encore de l'audace.* And, for today at least, to hell with politics. I'll lead the way.' He sprang on to his bike and pedalled off singing in a faintly cracked baritone.

Harry met Grubby Greville, complete with gun cases and his soldier servant, Wrykin, who was to load for him, at Dorking station.

'I say, old man, you're looking a bit green about the gills.'

'So would you if you'd been standing bolt upright in a wardrobe half the night with your mouth full of feather boa.'

'Good God! What happened?'

'We'd just finished round one and I was opening a bottle of fizz when her maid rushed in to say his nibs had arrived back. Changed his mind about going to Hamburg. I just had time to hop into my clothes and hide in the wardrobe until the coast was clear.'

'Well, if you will have affairs with married women you must expect that kind of thing. Hope it won't put your eye out.' They climbed into the dogcart and Harry took the reins from Tim the tiger.

'What's the form?' Grubby asked as the dogcart bowled out of the station yard.

Harry began ticking the guns off on his fingers. 'There's you, me, Papa, the Blue Monkey, Crofton-Atkins, Vincent Jacques, the Duke. . .'

'Which Duke is that?'

'Dorset.'

'Have they all brought their wives?'

'All except the Blue Monkey and Bones Barlow. His has bolted.'

'Anything unmarried?'

'Only my sister Gertie.'

'She still a new woman?'

'Newer than ever.'

'Any suggestions as to where I should direct my attention?'

'If I were you I'd try the Duchess. Better than evens, I'd say.'

'What about the Duke?'

'Only interested in port and brandy.'

Grubby stroked his moustache. 'I say,' he said, 'I believe this is going to be a rather jolly party.'

'You never know,' said Harry.

They had nearly reached the lodge gates when two bicyclists emerged without any warning, on the wrong side of the road, from a side turning. Harry pulled hard on the reins. He just managed to avoid the man but the woman fell off her bicycle and lay in the road. The dogcart tipped over and Harry, in trying to save himself, fell on his wrist.

It was quite a nasty little spill. When it had been sorted out the Russian lady didn't seem to have any bones broken but was suffering from shock. Harry had a badly sprained wrist, which put holding a gun right out of the question. Grubby, the little bearded Russian gent, Wrykin and Tim the tiger were intact. Harry telephoned his father from the lodge to send a motor along. Five minutes later, during which the Russian admitted that they had been on the wrong side of the road, Sir Edwin arrived in the most capacious of the De Dion Boutons. They were all driven up to the house, the Russians' bicycles being left at the lodge. The Russian lady was taken upstairs to a bedroom and told she must rest. The blinds were drawn. Lady Dalby tucked her up with a hot-water-bottle and ordered her Russian husband downstairs. On the way he passed the doctor, a fussy little person who had just finished strapping Harry's wrist, coming up to attend his wife. In the hall he found Sir Edwin smoking another of his fat Turks through the amber and meerschaum holder. 'What worries me, Harry,' he was saying, ' is we're one gun short.'

'How about the doctor?'

'My dear boy! Has pain rendered you insane? Don't you remember last year when only swift intervention by Davenport prevented a regicide?'

'I was in Cairo.'

'And I was damn nearly in eternity. H'm, yes. Well. I wonder. Most improbable, of course, but you never know.'

He turned suddenly to the Russian who was looking at a Canaletto that hung above the hall fireplace.

'I suppose, sir, you're not by any chance a game-bird shot?' He repeated his question in very fair Russian.

'Oh yes, indeed. It is my very favourite recreation. I have shot in Siberia. Duck, pheasant, snipe.' He made the movements of a man holding a gun and swinging it through the air after a bird in flight. 'Here you shoot pheasants battus flying high over, do you not?'

'By George, this could be the solution,' said Sir Edwin. 'Harry, he's about the same size as the Blue Monkey, ain't he? Run upstairs, there's a good boy, and ask him for some kit and then get his man to ferret it out. He always travels with at least two of everything. You'd think he was a pair of Siamese twins. Now, sir, I'm going to ask you as a great favour whether you will join our shooting party as we're one gun short.'

The Russian's face lit up. You could see the idea appealed to him enormously. Then he frowned and screwed up his eyes.

'You're thinking of your wife, of course,' Dalby said. 'We'll take good care of her, never fear.'

The doctor came trotting down the broad, shallow staircase. 'Are you the lady's husband, sir? Well, I don't think your wife has any concussion. All she needs is rest. If you'll just go up and speak to her for a moment and tell her again what I've said . . .'

'That settles it,' said Sir Edwin. And to Harry, who had appeared at the top of the stairs, he called: 'Harry, as soon as this gentleman has had a word with his wife, show him somewhere he can change and then bring him to the gunroom. And Harry, here, I say, come down a minute.' Harry obediently came down. 'Harry,' said Sir Edwin into his ear. 'Don't ask him any questions. I'm pretty sure he's a political exile. I can smell'em a mile off. And I don't want him scared.'

'I hope you know what you're doing, Sir Edwin,' said Davenport, accepting a cigarette from Dalby's heavy striped gold and white-gold Fabergé case.

'I hope I do, too, Davenport. I tell you there's something very impressive about this chap. Makes you feel he's a man of his word. Now, have you looked him out a pair of guns? Good man. Ah, here they are.' Harry and the Russian came into the gunroom. 'Come over here, sir. This is my headkeeper, Mr Davenport. Now, try this pair of guns.'

In a heather mixture knickerbocker suit, stockings, stout shoes and shooting spats, the Russian looked, as Harry expressed it, just the ticket. Davenport handed him a gun and he broke it with a light, firm, accustomed touch, snapped it shut and raised it to his shoulder. His face lit up.

The Blue Monkey strolled in, smoking a cigar almost as big as himself. Harry introduced them. 'This is the Marquis de Soveral, who's lending you some shooting kit.'

The Russian made a little bow. 'I am very obliged.'

'Not a bad fit, are they, by Jove,' said Soveral, 'but your head'll be too big for my cap. More brains in it, I expect. Alright, my boy,' he wagged a finger at Harry, 'I got it in first.'

Sir Edwin rummaged in a cupboard. 'Here, what about this? It's an old deerstalker of my father's. He had a head the size of the Albert Hall. Now, it's time we were moving off. The others are round on the terrace. Davenport, you'll look after the Russian gentleman.'

It was evident from the very first drive that the Russian was safe as a house. He refrained from swinging round at shoulder level like a naval gun turret, and kept his gun well up. He was a bit slow at changing guns at first, but he soon got the hang of it. His excitement when he brought off a left and right in front and a third bird behind, was infectious.

Davenport, strolling round the stands, reported to Sir Edwin. 'You were quite right, sir. He's perfectly safe and sensible and he's got the making of a good shot.'

They shot the home coverts and went back to the house for lunch. The Russian trotted upstairs. He found his wife sitting up in an armchair eating lunch off a tray. 'I must say,' she said, 'they are very considerate. Did you have a good shoot?'

'It was wonderful. Ecstasy. The woods were all brown and blue and gold, the pheasants flying high overhead like in a picture. I must go down now. There is a *déjeuner de chasse*. Will you be fit to to travel back this evening? They will drive us to the station, and our bicycles.' He bent and kissed her forehead. 'I feel in danger of being politically corrupted and compromised, like a young girl who wakes up in a house of ill fame.'

'Don't worry,' she said. 'Why shouldn't you have a holiday?'

In the dining-room he was congratulated on his shooting and made to sit on his hostess's right. He would only drink a glass of light beer.

'A very sporting effort, if I may say so, sir,' said the Duke, swallowing half a claret glass of brandy.

Lady Dalby turned her charm full on. 'When we were *en poste* in Petersburg,' she said, 'my husband used to say every morning when he got up, and every night when he went to bed: "There'll be a revolution in this country some time in the next fifteen years." What do you say? Speak your mind. We're liberals here. At least, Edwin and I are.'

'I would say husband's estimate is correct, but on one condition: this is that there is a European war.'

'And you think there will be one?'

'It is certain, as certain as, how do you say, eggs is eggs.'

'But why is it so certain?' asked the Duke.

'Excuse for talking politics, but you ask the questions . . .'

'My dear fellow, of course. Pray continue.'

'It is because the whole economic social and political system under which we live contains and creates ever mounting tension and international rivalry which can only be resolved by war. In addition to which, I am sorry to say this, your Foreign Office has a policy of building up power blocs which is having effect of bringing war nearer.'

'I often think,' said Lady Dalby, 'that there ought to be a society which everybody could join called the Enemies of Human Suffering.'

The Russian nodded. 'Not such bad idea. Not at all. But you would find yourself in association with all kind of desperate characters, socialists, revolutionaries . . .'

'Oh, I shouldn't mind that in the least. I always get on with Frances Warwick like a house on fire.'

'And what do you think of the prospects of a revolution in this country?' asked Gertie Dalby, the New Woman.

The Russian smiled. 'My dear young lady,' he said, 'if you want a really difficult tough place for revolutionary, it is England.'

'Do you think the fact that we're nicer has anything to do with it?' said Lady Dalby.

'Oh Mummy, really! It depends on who's being nice to whom.'

But it was time for the afternoon drives to start.

'What did you think of him, Mummy?' asked Gertie after the men had gone. 'I thought he was sweet.'

'Yes, I thought he was a dear little man and so clever, but I wouldn't like to cross his path.'

'What class would you say he came from?'

'Oh, quite respectable. What they call junior nobility. Equivalent to upper middle class here.'

The little Russian didn't shoot quite so well in the afternoon but he didn't disgrace himself. He rather surprised his loader by asking how much he earned. At tea, having changed back now into his own clothes, he was joined by his wife. Lady Dalby made a great fuss of her and introduced her to the Duchess who was wearing a tea-gown with cascades of lace designed to draw attention to her breasts, which Grubby had already begun privately calling the Surrey Alps. Catching his eye, she asked:

'What are you giggling at?'

'Oh, nothing special. I was just thinking of ways and means to avert a revolution.'

The butler came to say the motor was at the door. It was time for them to leave for the station.

Sir Edwin and Lady Dalby saw them to the front-door with perfectly sincere protestations about pleasant surprises and all's well that ends well. 'Your bikes are strapped on the back,' said Sir Edwin, 'and the chauffeur's got a couple of brace of pheasants for you. Bon voyage, and again thank you so much for helping us out. Oh, I say, I'd forgotten. Just a moment, you must sign the visitors' book.'

The little Russian took up the pen and wrote: 'N. C. & V. I. Ulyanov'.

Then, shrugging his shoulders and smiling as if at some private joke he added, in brackets, '*(Lenin)*'.

Tower of Silence

I'm fond of my club. There is something deliciously reassuring in its leathery eunuchoid cosiness and all-male meals . . . Yes, yes, I know waitresses have taken over; but ours are the right type, respectable old nannies, not those menopausal Medusas wafting scent over your game pie.

Of course it has its defects. One of them is a convention of mateyness that makes it difficult to escape bores, but it's extremely comfortable and has a good library. I only wish I could spend more time in it, but as a budding psychiatrist, registrar at a large suburban mental hospital, I'm lucky to get half a day a fortnight.

This day I was cosseting myself. I'd just shaken off an attack of 'flu and felt I deserved a treat. I lunched alone, an invalid's lunch of foie gras, chicken fricassee, and claret. Then I retired with a large glass of tawny port and coffee to the red leather sofa in the bow window of the smoking room, to the most euphoric sofa I know.

There are several doctors among the members. We've quite a medical tradition. I was once told this was the only club in London where you would find two venereologists giving the under porter a free consultation on the billiard table. And we include a sprinkling of psychiatrists, among them two analysts who started as Freudian and Jungian enemies and have now become bosom chums in some nebulous doctrinal half-way house and are rumoured to exchange patients every leap year. All of us refrain from talking shop, all of us with one exception. And now, as I opened my eyes from my post-prandial coma I found him sitting beside me: the one and only Dr Gilhooley, the Ancient of Days or, as some call him, the Ancient Mariner. He's certainly the oldest member, but it's incorrect to call him the Club Bore because he can be extremely interesting. However, he likes to take his time over it, and unless I've got an afternoon off I prefer not to be one of the three that he stoppeth.

He is a small, well-proportioned man of the type whose heart doesn't have to do much work. His face has wizened into a faintly reptilian cast but his hazel eyes still shine and his movements have a lizard-like agility. He always wears comfortable-looking, well-cut flannel suits, and soft silk shirts with flapping collars.

'I was hoping you would wake,' he said. 'I wanted to congratulate you on your DPM.'

The Diploma in Psychological Medicine is a compulsory hurdle in the career of the budding psychiatrist. It was acute of him to know that I'd passed it.

'I hope,' he said, with an old man's cackle that was meant to signal a joke, 'that you haven't overstrained your cerebral cortex. You remember Batty Tuke's hypothesis?'

'I'm afraid I don't,' I said. 'I think he was a bit before my time.'

'He was indeed. Sir J. Batty Tuke. That was his real name. He was a big noise in Edwardian psychiatry. He held that over-exertion of the brain was a frequent cause of insanity. One of his ideas was – whisper it – that many a young doctor never recovered from passing his examinations.'

I ordered two more glasses of port. Dr Gilhooley approved of tawny as less onerous on arteries and alimentary canal than vintage, and I sat back at ease ready for more curiosities of Edwardian psychiatry. But with the lability of old age, his mood changed abruptly. He was off on a detailed description, not far short of total recall, of the film of *Murder On The Orient Express*.

'Now tell me,' he said, 'would you say that a situation, in which a dozen people conspire together to murder one individual in such a way that suspicion cannot fall on any one of them, is likely to be found in real life?'

I said I thought it must be very rare, though I supposed you might find it in a closed institution like a prison or a ship or a barracks.

'But not, you would think, in a mental hospital?'

'Good heavens, no. At least I should hope not.'

'And yet such a murder was committed in Wendover

which, if I mistake not, is where you are at present a registrar.'

'Is that really true? It must have been a very long time ago.'

'It was. Considerably before you were born. Would you like to hear the story? Of course, if one were telling it to a lay audience, one would set the scene. For you that's not necessary . . .'

No, it most certainly wasn't. Wendover loomed large in my life at that time; one of those huge mental hospitals, like Hanwell and Friern, which were built in the middle of the last century. A Betjemanic architect's nightmare in greyish yellow brick. Only in the last fifteen years or so has it become decongested and even partly modernised. It still leaves an enormous amount to be desired, but compared to what it was I daresay it's a demi-paradise.

Dr Gilhooley took a large swig of port and licked his lips, which I noticed were bluish and faintly mottled like an orchid.

'I will now proceed with this atrocious history,' he said. 'The period is about the turn of the century. The hospital looked much the same then as it does now. But there was one feature you will not have seen because it has been pulled down. That was the tower which commanded a view of the entire hospital grounds. It was a watch tower. In those days nearly all patients were certified and the authorities were obsessed with escapes. Bear this tower in mind . . . I hardly know how to convey to you the difference between mental hospitals then and now. Let me see, when did you qualify?'

'Seven years ago.'

'In that case you've never experienced a male refractory ward in the days before the Chlorpromazine revolution. There were fights and tussles the whole day long. Patients in states of acute catatonic excitement would be confined to the padded rooms. Hypomanics would pester and incite the others until trouble started.'

'Of course,' I said, 'only a small proportion of patients were excitable at the same time.'

'True enough. But the role of the staff, both doctors and nurses, was largely custodial. Bless my soul; why, when I was a young man, the male nurses wore dark blue uniforms and peaked caps like prison warders. And a lot of them ate their dinners off newspaper. Not that they were any the worse for that. Some of the unlettered types made good nurses. They had a kind of natural animal sympathy.'

I said I wondered what they would have thought of a really modern mental hospital run on therapeutic community lines with daily group meetings of doctors, patients and nurses.

'They'd have had a fit,' Dr Gilhooley said.

'Mind you, ' I said, 'even in our enlightened days you sometimes get a lot of opposition. When ward community methods were first introduced there was often bitterness among the staff. They felt insecure, not so much afraid, if you follow me, but anxious lest their authority was going to be taken away from them.'

Dr Gilhooley pressed his lips together. 'Do you know what a bear pit is?' he said. 'I don't mean what the Elizabethans had instead of television. A bear pit in old-fashioned mental hospital parlance was a field about a hundred yards square surrounded by high wooden palings. There might be a few trees growing in it and there would certainly be some seats. Every fine afternoon some two hundred of the more severely ill mental patients would be turned loose in the bear pit for their daily exercise. You might see a young man writing on a tree with a stick like Orlando in *As You Like It*, only he would be chasing his writing round the trunk. There would be catatonics standing about in odd stereotyped positions. Some would be stalking round and round at a furious pace. Nobody spoke to anybody. Nurses in uniform sat on the seats. Bear pits were not uncommon until right up to the last war. That gives you some idea of conditions. Of course there was a lot of variation between hospitals. But they were hopelessly understaffed. You hear a lot about that today, but when Wendover held 2,600 patients there was one medical superintendent and four medical officers. The superintendent was a law unto himself. If he was slack and the atmosphere flaccid, the medical officers might degenerate. In one or two hospitals I've known they did nothing but drink and play snooker.'

'Booze and billiards,' I said. 'The occupational diseases of primitive psychiatry. But aren't you laying it on a bit thick, Dr Gilhooley?'

'No, my dear, boy, I promise you I'm not. There were spots of enlightenment here and there, but as I say everything

depended on the superintendents. These had their eccentricities. There was one I served under who was mad about
cricket and believed it had special therapeutic virtues. When he
advertised for a medical officer he used to put SLOW BOWLER
PREFERRED. Then there was dear old Chesney who was superintendent at Coverdale. He was crazy about hydrotherapy. The
continuous bath. It used to be very popular at one time, especially for manic depressives. If you look up 'Baths' in the
standard *English Dictionary of Psychological Medicine* for 1892
you'll find sixteen different varieties. That's as true as I'm
sitting here. Of course facilities were limited so Chesney had a
gigantic shallow tank constructed . . .'

I looked at my watch. Nearly time for strong tea and anchovy
toast. Dr Gilhooley was delighted at having a captive audience
for so long. He snapped his fingers with pleasure. Still fully
wound up, he let loose a string of bizarre anecdotes. At a mental
hospital in the Channel Islands there had been a schizophrenic,
a man of no education who, if you handed him a fossil, would
give you a most vivid description of the landscape of its period.
The superintendent used to show him off to visitors. At another
hospital a Scandinavian sailor had passed at one single evacua-
tion a pound and three quarters of pebbles. In 1931, Dr Alexander Cannon, a medical officer on the staff of Colney Hatch,
had been requested to resign his appointment because he had
written a book called *The Invisible Influence* in which he claimed
to have levitated together with eighteen pieces of luggage across
a chasm in Tibet. . . .

'But I am digressing,' Gilhooley said. 'Now, I was about to
tell you a horrible story, wasn't I? What was it about?'

'It happened at Wendover in the old days. Something to do
with a tower.'

'Of course, of course. Well, now, it all began with the reign of
a new superintendent. Wantage. the old superintendent who
retired, had been one of the passive custodial type. "Let's have
a quiet peaceful hospital," he used to say. There was always a
strong smell of Paraldehyde in his wards. He was bone lazy. He
was a member of the Garrick and used to play bridge there a lot.
It got so that when they wanted him to attend to hospital
business they would telephone the club and say; "urgent message for Dr Wantage. Patient's escaped." When he got back

breathless to Wendover they'd greet him with: "It's alright, doctor. Patient's been recaptured. But while you're here would you mind signing these forms."

'Well, the new superintendent, Dr Makins, was the exact opposite of old Wantage, burning with reformist zeal. And of course all his reforms meant more work for the staff. He insisted that terminal schizophrenics, who had been left to vegetate, should be taken for walks every day. He stalked through the hospital regrading patients, unlocking locked wards. In no time he had the staff loathing his guts.'

'What about the medical staff?' I asked.

'They had to toe the line, of course. They didn't like it but there was nothing they could do about it. Anyway, they weren't so far gone in sloth that they couldn't respond to Makins' therapeutic enthusiasm. All might have been well if it hadn't been for the tragedy which I'm just coming to.'

Dr Gilhooley broke off to offer me a fat Turkish cigarette from an elderly but still posh-looking leather case. He followed up with a history of cigarette smoking in England, from the Crimean War onwards, with special reference to the virtues of Macedonian as opposed to Virginian tobaccos. I steered him back to Wendover by tapping the glass of my watch.

'You are eager for the denouement, what I believe is known as the pay-off. Very well. Now among the patients Dr Makins had upgraded was a man named Beavis. When Makins first examined him he was in the refractory ward. He'd been diagnosed as a manic depressive; manic phase with distinct paranoid tendencies. This of course can lead to very uncertain and aggressive behaviour. Beavis was a middle-aged man of some intelligence and education. He made a favourable impression on Makins, was quiet and orderly and free from any signs of delusions. He complained that he was being kept strictly confined to the ward and not allowed to go out or occupy himself in any way. Makins asked him if he had any particular occupation in mind and he said he had, yes, carpentry. Makins discussed his case both with the medical officer in charge of the male side, and with the ward charge in attendance. He told them that in his opinion Beavis had recovered from his manic attack and should be upgraded with a view to possible discharge in a matter of weeks. The ward charge begged to differ.

He said Beavis was a very tricky patient, given to sudden fits of violence. "I warn you, Dr Makins, sir," he said respectfully. "He's very deceptive. He'll be good as gold for days at a time and then, without any warning, he'll turn nasty. And of course when the moon's at the full there's no holding him."

'Makins wasn't standing for this. "Don't give me that superstitious rubbish, my man," he snapped. "It's not surprising if a patient of his intelligence gets irritable when he's kept cooped up like this. I'm regrading him to Ward 3 as from today until further notice. See that he's taken over there before dinner time."

'So Beavis was upgraded to Ward 3 and there was more muttering among the male nurses. I always say that if you take your hospital nursing staff, by and large you'll find a small proportion of saints, a more or less average collection of people who'll be both nice and nasty, and a small proportion of sadists. Among the average bunch there may be not a few who'll swing one way or the other, according to the general tone of the place. And that comes from the top.'

Dr Gilhooley darted me one of his bright lacertian glances to make sure I was listening, and poured us out two cups of dark brown tea strong enough to induce an attack of anxiety neurosis.

'Of course,' he said, 'it must be admitted that Makins was not a tactful man. Reformers seldom are. He was a congenital fusspot and he had a genius for putting people's backs up. But he is not to be blamed for what happened. No, he is not to be blamed. For a little while all went well. Beavis' equilibrium remained undisturbed. He worked long hours in the carpenter's shop making a model of a Roman galley and gave no trouble in the ward. And then the precipitating factor arrived on the scene. You may say that with psychotics there is always a precipitating factor ready to hand. That may or may not be so. It doesn't alter the fact that this was a piece of damned bad luck. In the course of his reforms Dr Makins, as well as regrading patients, had been shifting some of the nurses around; for he thought, rightly no doubt in some cases, that several of them had been too long in the same ward. The changes were made after a confabulation between Makins and the head male attendant, Tunstall. This official, equivalent to the matron on the female side, was a very powerful figure in the hospital hierarchy of those days. He was allowed the dignity of wearing a swallow-tail coat at hospital functions. Tunstall was very jealous of his own personal authority, and opposed to any libertarian reforms on principle; but being a Pecksniffian hypocrite, as well as a man of considerable natural organizing ability, he'd managed to keep up a suitable façade of cooperation in front of the new superintendent. Now, one nurse, who had been moved from the refractory ward, was a certain Birkbeck, a youngish man from the north. A bit of a rough diamond. Like not a few male nurses, he'd been a soldier. He was genial on the surface and popular with his colleagues, but he was inclined to be rather a bully. And between him and Beavis there was a long-standing feud. Beavis had sneered at him and touched him on the raw with that intuitive feeling for the weak spot which paranoid manics possess. There had been one rough house between them and the ward charge had accepted Birkbeck's version. And now Birkbeck was moved to Ward 3 and the first patient he saw was Beavis.

'You might think that the appearance of his deadly enemy would depress Beavis, like a prisoner who's been recaptured; and that at first was what it seemed to do – but only at first. You can imagine the tension that was generated between these two: the intelligent, educated, imaginative patient and the ignorant, loutish male nurse. It was like a thunderstorm piling up in stages. One stage was when Birkbeck persuaded Oakes, the ward charge in 3, that Beavis should be searched every time he came back from his carpentry.'

'Not,' I said, 'an altogether unreasonable suggestion, surely?'

'Possibly not. But the searching, I understand, was carried out by Birkbeck with the minimum of dignity. Beavis retaliated by compiling a notebook which he called "Crimes of the Male Nurse Henry Birkbeck". It was found afterwards in his locker. The final stage was reached when a mischievous patient told Beavis that Birkbeck, the ward charge, the head male attendant, and the medical officer responsible for the ward were all petitioning the superintendent to have Beavis sent back to the refractory ward.

'That afternoon the storm bursts. Beavis comes in from the

carpenter's shop and stands meekly in front of Birkbeck, waiting to be searched. Birkbeck bends forward a little as he runs his hands over him. Beavis whips out a small chisel which he's been hiding up the sleeve of his overalls and drives it into Birkbeck's neck, slap into the carotid. Blood spouts. Birkbeck collapses and is dead in a matter of seconds. Staff come running. Beavis is taken to the refractory ward, and locked up alone in a full-padded room. So that's your first murder for you.'

'No mystery there,' I said.

'No, indeed. And not much about the next, either. Well, as you may imagine, the shock was felt right through the hospital. Beavis, of course, as a certified patient was outside the law. However, there were demands for a detailed investigation from several quarters: the Commissioners, the local police and coroner's office, the Asylum Workers' Federation, and, not least, from the superintendent himself. He didn't exactly improve matters by calling meetings of the male nursing staff, in relays, and telling them that they musn't imagine that what had happened was going to make the slightest difference to his policy of reform. It was very late that night before everyone settled down to sleep and there was a big run on the chloral. And next morning, what do you think they found? Surely you can guess?'

'Oh come now,' I said. 'Even if I could, which I can't, I wouldn't want to spoil your pleasure in telling me.'

Dr Gilhooley rubbed his aged, mottled hands. 'Next morning,' he croaked dramatically, 'on the concrete flooring at the foot of the tower, they found the body of Beavis. His skull was fractured. There were no marks of violence upon him. Now what do you make of that?'

'I suppose,' I said sportingly, trying to keep up the mystery, 'it could have been suicide.'

'Suicide my stethoscope! It was murder, carried out with the precision of a military operation. Motive? Partly vengeance but mainly a demonstration to intimidate the superintendent, a warning to him to drop his reforms. Tunstall, the head male attendant, was the organising genius behind it all. The killing of Birkbeck brought to a head the trouble that had been brewing between him and the superintendent. Tunstall called a meeting of twelve of the male nurses who he thought were most incensed. There was some stump oratory on the lines of: "Our colleague has been foully murdered with deliberate malice aforethought by one who, though he is a certified patient, knew full well what he did, and all because of the new and perilous system of licence and misrule which has been imposed upon us. If we do not take action now, and drastic action at that, our lives will no longer be safe." And so on and so forth. They then put it to the vote and solemnly announced that Beavis was guilty of murder. . .

'They stole quietly along to the refractory ward where Beavis was asleep. They put a strait-jacket on him, and told him he had been tried in his absence and found guilty of the wilful murder of Birkbeck. They were taking the law into their own hands and were going to execute just sentence upon him. Then they gagged him and carried him out of the ward and up the steps of the tower. They removed the strait-jacket and the gag and slung him over.'

'But what about the medical officer on night duty?'

'They hadn't forgotten him. They'd laced his cocoa. They'd thought of everything, even to removing any traces of the gag.'

'But wasn't there a frightful row? You don't mean to say they got away with it?'

'There was hell to pay. But there was absolutely no evidence to show that Beavis hadn't chucked himself off the top of the tower. They'd been very careful how they'd handled him and they'd planted on him a master key which opened all locks in the hospital, making sure that it had his finger prints on it and no-one else's. So the coroner's jury brought in an open verdict. The superintendent swore they were a lot of murdering black-guards. The men threatened an action for slander. The atmosphere got so strained that the authorities transferred the superintendent and appointed a new one.'

'Tell me,' I said, 'were you yourself on the staff at the time?'

'Indeed I was not,' said Gilhooley. 'That would make me a centenarian. I was told the story when I first joined the hospital staff as a very junior medical officer, just qualified. I was told it over cocoa on night duty by an elderly ward charge who had been a young nurse at the time. He took no part in it himself, but he heard all about it. Well, there you are. It's not a nice story but we're not a very nice species.'

I heaved a deep sententious sigh. 'Ah well,' I said, 'in the great global therapeutic community of the future, which is our only salvation . . .'

Dr Gilhooley interrupted me sharply. 'Good gracious! Is that your idea of the millennium? It's not mine . . .'

'What is?' I asked.

'A nice snug club and a captive audience.'

East End Nights

Other possible titles for this story could be 'My Debt to The Kray Twins' or even 'Some Day I'll Find Her', but the reasons for that will come later. It begins quite a long time ago, in October 1929.

The East End then was very different to what it is now. It was yet the most exciting and variegated part of London to anyone with a romantic imagination, but it was still very poor. When, as a West Ender, you went into an East End pub, you were at once conscious that the people looked quite different. A lot of the men wore caps and white mufflers. The girls looked a bit slatternly. The tall men with big bones were tall, but there were a lot of small under-sized men; you couldn't help thinking of them as runts. They hadn't had enough to eat for generations.

Our routine for an East End pub crawl was much the same as it is now. We would start at the Prospect of Whitby in Wapping Wall. This was nothing like so posh as it has become, with its West End prices. Then we would walk on to the Grapes in Narrow Street, famous to Dickensians as the Six Jolly Fellowship Porters in *Our Mutual Friend*. Here you get the best view of the river, which at high tide slaps against the pub's walls. You can see the Isle of Dogs curving out to the south-east, with Rotherhithe opposite and Deptford in the blue evening mist lower down. But in those days the landlord was so oblivious of the touristic possibilities that he didn't bother or couldn't afford to separate the Gents pisser from the riverside balcony.

The next port of call after the Grapes was 'Charlie Brown's' at the end of West India Dock Road on the right. Old Charlie was a wheezy old boy with a scarlet face and scarlet slippers. He had quite a collection of oriental curios and was a bit of a snob. He used to say: 'Everyone is equal in the sight of the Lord and that's how I treat them.' The next moment he would slap a signed photograph of Lady Oxford down on the counter and tell you: 'She was here last night, one of the highest of the land.' In the bar at the back, the long bar where the juke box is now, there were several oddities hanging from the ceiling, a sheep with six legs and a plaster Turk's head, and there was dancing to a gap-toothed piano played by a little fellow with a round baby face and stubby fingers. He was known as Blind Jack because he was stone blind. He was also stone bald.

The girl who carried the cap for Blind Jack was Jean. She was a character and a rather subtle one; in some ways she was a typical East End girl with an independent be-damned-to-you manner; in other ways she was different, with something romantic about her. She was about twenty-six, rather broad in the beam, with brown eyes and lank brown hair, high cheek-bones and faintly slanting eyes. She looked as if she had some Russian and a touch of Jewish in her – a familiar East End mixture. Alan Collard used to say that she was like Pola Negri, the film star, and that after the usual going-over, including a few visits to the dentist, she might have looked terrific.

Jean and I chummed up and whenever I went to 'Charlie Brown's' she would come over and have a drink and we would talk. The maddening thing is that I can't really remember what we talked about. She was certainly tactful and didn't ask a lot of questions; she was also intelligent. I always enjoyed her company. There was something a bit wistful and melancholy about her but she was very much a person in her own right. She generally wore a skirt and a white silk, often slightly grubby, blouse.

When the pub shut we used to go to the big Chinese restaurant in West India Dock Road where Limehouse Police Station now is. This was laid out like a dockside café in a film set, with the floor on two levels; if you sat at a table on the top level you got a fine view of what was going on. There were generally a few fights between the tarts, most of whom were indescribably unappetising old bags. The little Chinese proprietor, squealing like a pig, managed to separate them. Sometimes the law would arrive and cart a couple of them away cursing.

The food wasn't anywhere up to present day Chinese restaurant standards. After dinner we might go and play dice at a Chinaman's house in Pennyfields. This was a tiny little house with a one-candle-lit front room. The dice game was very simple. The Chinaman kept the bank and you bet on an oil-cloth, marked with numbered squares, on the possible combinations of three dice. If you lost too often you had only to say 'Give us a drink, John', and the dear little Chinaman handed you one shilling and sixpence to go on playing with. He was the most benevolent banker-croupier I've ever encountered. The game was absurdly small; the biggest win I remember was thirty-six shillings.

One night there was a sudden bang on the street door. The police. 'Come on,' Jean said, grabbing my hand. I followed her upstairs into the Chinaman's bedroom. We were joined by a slightly drunk Swede, an English girl and a docker. We sat on the bed giggling, while below the Chinaman stoutly denied that he had been gambling. Jean started rummaging under the Chinaman's pillow and produced a pair of long black cotton stockings and a loaf of bread.

I think I assumed then that Jean was a tart. This, as I found out long afterwards, wasn't strictly true. She might go with men but she worked, intermittently anyway. It never occurred to me to go to bed with her. I think because I had an almost obsessional fear of VD; also I was then much more of a snob than I am now; but if she'd asked me to take her 'up West' and give her a meal there, I would have. But she never did. She was never grasping. I used to give her a few bob when we parted and I caught my tram back to Bloomsbury and my fourteen-shillings-a-week room in Doughty Street, where a few years later the collector of literary history would have been able to hear through the wall the young Dylan Thomas retching into a pail.

One evening I went down to Limehouse with a friend I will call H. We were both working in the same office. We met up with Jean and went on with her from 'Charlie Brown's' to another pub, the Commercial, which has since been pulled down. It was very clean and neat, with elaborately arranged flowers. Orientals used to go there. H. was a big drinker and we had been to many pubs on the way. He didn't seem to be very pleased that I'd brought Jean along, and complained that she was a bore. I said she was much less of a bore than he was. I was distinctly tight by this time and I saw, out of the corner of one eye, H. pouring a double gin into my glass of bitter. I drank it, as if under a spell; I suppose I felt, youthfully, that I had to accept the challenge. Why did the amiable H. do this to me? I thought at the time it was a sort of malicious elephantine caprice. Looking back I feel sure there was a deeper reason. H. was queer and had a penchant for young boys. He must have come to an arrangement with someone in the pub and wanted me out of the way.

The next thing I remember is being out in the street, stumbling along having almost lost the use of my legs, with Jean supporting me. She carted me to her room, which was under one of the railway arches of the old Fenchurch Street-Tilbury line. The ceiling was curved; it had been blue-washed. There was an iron bedstead with a white counterpane. I thought with relief that it all looked very clean. Then I more or less passed out. I woke up some time later with Jean beside me. Somehow we'd managed to get my clothes off. She was soft and warm and I rolled over to her and made love too quickly after the way of very young men.

I was woken in the early morning by the crash of the hob-nailed boots of the dockers going to work. Jean made me a cup of tea. I kissed her and dressed. I had about three-and-six to get back to Bloomsbury with, so I gave her a cheap imitation tortoiseshell cigarette case and a white silk handkerchief. It was a blue misty October morning. I had a sharp hangover. Soon I was starting to worry over whether I had caught anything. However I hadn't. I saw Jean several times after that though at quite long intervals. Always she was friendly and smiling whoever I was with. Once she showed me the cigarette case and smiled a secret smile. So foolish are the young that I was embarrassed, and relieved when she shut her bag. Then I moved to the country and never saw her again.

In 1961 I was supposed to be writing for *The Observer* an article on the new style East End pubs. Dan Farson took me on a preliminary tour of some, such as the enormous Iron Bridge in East India Dock Road. I chummed up with landlord, Slim Watts, an ex-merchant seaman, tough and solid and wise, and his wife Queenie, a singer who was then just beginning to make a name for herself. We also went to the Rising Sun in Bow, since pulled down, another East End mecca of jazz in the Sixties.

Later I went down with a photographer, Don McCullen, and a friend now dead, Eric Parr. Eric was driving and I knew from experience that he had absolutely no sense of direction; he had once driven me twice round the Isle of Dogs. I wanted to revisit the Rising Sun, so I asked Queenie Watts if she would come with us and direct us. Queenie said she was sorry she couldn't because there had been a death in her family and, according to local conventions, although it was all right for her to serve behind her own bar, she mustn't be seen out and about in other boozers. However, Slim would take us. So we piled into his car and drove off, arriving at the Rising Sun about twenty minutes before closing time.

The place was packed solid with a very smart Saturday night crowd, in dark suits and Daz-white shirts. A singer on the stage was yelling her head off. I made my way to the bar, and everybody was as polite as they always are in the East End, which is on average a great deal politer than in the West End. Suddenly a space opened before me and I found myself at the bar. I was more than a little high, for I'd been drinking brandy and ginger ale, which is not the drink to go pub crawling on. Standing close by was a tall beautiful dark girl, with long hair down on her shoulders. She must have had some kind of artistic strivings, because her eye make-up was wonderfully complicated, with a pattern of little squares and circles and dots. She had a girl friend with her who had red hair.

Eric Parr had fetched up beside me, and I asked the tall girl if they would like to come up to the West End with us and tell us what they thought of it. I said: 'We've got a car and we'll drive you back to wherever you want to go whenever you say. We won't kidnap you.' She was a bit shy at first. Then she said: 'All right. Why not?'

Presently I noticed something odd in the atmosphere in the pub. My sensibilities weren't at their sharpest owing to so many brandy and ginger ales, but it was unmistakeable. It was very near closing time and a lot of people had left. Over by the door was a knot of a dozen or so young men. Slim Watts was talking to them. The tall dark girl came over to me and said: 'I'm afraid we've changed our minds.' I said: 'Oh well, never mind. I hope I'll see you again some time.' Then I was out in the street getting into Slim Watts' car.

As soon as we started Don McCullen said: 'Jesus, Maurice, you were bloody lucky. If it hadn't been for Mr Watts here you'd have had a kicking.' I said: 'What on earth are you talking about? Why should anyone want to give me a kicking? What had I done? You must be mad.' He said, 'You don't understand. They thought you were coming the West Ender over one of their girls, taking a liberty.' I asked Slim if there was any truth in this. He said: 'Well, there were some rather naughty boys there, but I knew a couple of them so it was all right.'

I still didn't believe it. A few days later I went down to the Iron Bridge, totally sober, and said to Queenie: 'I hear your old man saved me from a kicking the other night, Queen.' 'He did that, Maurice,' she said, 'and he had quite a job too.' Slim came sidling along the bar like a great muscular crab and I put it to him. 'Yes,' he said, 'for a minute or two I didn't think I was going to be able to hold them. Then two more of them came in who knew me, two who sometimes come in here, and it was all right.'

'Well I'm damned,' I said. 'It shows you the dangers of pub-crawling on brandy and ginger ale.'

I asked them about the girl. Queenie said she thought she occasionally came into the Iron Bridge but she didn't know her name. She gave me a quick astute sociologist's account of her background as she saw it: 'Probably married, quite likely to a seaman. Works in a factory. Might go to Majorca for her holiday. Independent when she feels like it.'

Neither Queenie nor Slim knew her name. Then Slim said: 'All I do know is her mother is a rather square-shouldered woman who works on the buses. Her first name is Jean.'

Could it be? I did a lot of totting up of years and dates. It was possible, though if October 1929 was the date of the girl's conception that made her thirty-one. I would have put her at twenty-seven at the most. However . . . Some months later, in summer at home, I got up early to do some work and saw the door of my daughter's room was open. I looked in and saw her lying on her back with her head on the pillow and thought with pride what a pretty girl she was, and instantly her face reminded me a bit of the face of the daughter of Jean who worked on the buses. That didn't prove anything, though.

In 1970 I was down the East End again and got chatting with the landlady of the Oporto in West India Dock Road, a marvellous woman and a blitz heroine incidentally, who remembered Limehouse in the old days. She had known Jean well and remembered her kindness to Blind Jack and how she used to work sometimes in a factory. What had happened to her? Ma shook her head. Suicide; gas; two or three years ago. Had Jean ever had a child to her knowledge? She didn't think so. Couldn't be absolutely certain, because she often hadn't seen her for quite long periods at a time, but she thought it a hundred to one against.

I walked along to The Rose and Crown in Pennyfields, which the Wattses have recently taken over. I chatted with Slim and I reminded him of the night he saved me from a kicking. He said he wouldn't forget that in a hurry. And did I know who had turned the scale? The twins.

'You mean the Krays?'

'That's right, Ron and Reg. They was just beginning to make themselves felt in 1961. They often used to come into the Iron Bridge but they could never put the finger on me because I never gave them the chance. So we were quite friendly in a manner of speaking. Also we were at school together. They liked Queenie's singing. That night they steamed into the Rising Sun at the critical moment and I asked them to tell the others to nark it, and they did.'

'Well, flip me,' I said. 'Whatever they've done since, I'd like to send them a Christmas hamper.'

Way Out in The Continuum

This is decapitated head No 63, Universal Institute of Cerebral Physiology, electrotelepathecasting in all directions in space-time. For the benefit of you earth-dwellers and third dimensionals who think you are living in what you call the past, I will describe my day.

It is hour 1 of day 97 year 3946 – by an odd little concidence just 2,000 years after the outbreak of the First Great Atomic War, but don't let that worry you; it didn't last long and nobody won.

I repeat: it is hour 1 and the artificial blood supply apparatus to which I am attached is standing on its bench in the lab overlooking the Park of Giant Vegetables. The blood pump has just switched over to 'day'; it's working beautifully smoothly, giving me what they call Mild Euphoria, a rich, vital, but not too stimulating mixture. The Lab attendant in whose charge I am is filling in my morning reaction chart, and if I roll my eyes I can just catch sight of her profile. She is a pretty little thing, one of the latest products of the Interplanetary-Racial-Cross Fertilization Institute. On the Earth side her ancestry shows Chinese, West African Negro, Cape Cod and Kentish Weald. The Neptunian comes out strong in her aquamarine skin – I always call her Bluey. From her Venusian mother she inherits the small pomegranate-shaped third breast, and from her Uranian grandfather a striking organic feature which I hardly know how to describe to you listeners because it is, quite literally, like nothing on earth. . .

As soon as Bluey sees I'm awake she gets busy on my breakfast. I'm not fussy like some of these Decaps who are always wanting their schedule changed. I always want the same thing at the same co-ordinate. May be it's because I wasn't decapped until I was what you time slaves would call middle aged; the Lab Super says I'm a grey head on green-painted shoulders and slaps my pressure gauge in a hideously familiar way; but what can one do? *Il faut souffrir pour être immortel.* Anyhow, my breakfast has been the same now for the last two hundred years by your reckoning: oysters washed down with black velvet, followed by durians.

The oysters come along on a conveyor that passes them one by one under the mechanical fork which is geared to an interrupter mechanism that synchronizes with the liquid-intake pipe so that every few mouthfuls there is a pause for a drink. At any moment, in case of accidents, I can interrupt the whole works by putting out my tongue; this breaks a photo-electric circuit. Some Decaps can't stand the mechanical feeder; they insist on being spoon-fed by their attendants. Poor old 33 choked and spluttered fit to burst the first time they tried it on him. He got in such a state they had to black him out altogether; deep unconscious therapy they call that; we get a good deal of it.

I'm reckoned a fast eater, so Bluey sets the dial at 5 and we're off. The motor starts up with a gentle appetizing purr; the fork pricks into the first Colchester – home grown in the Lab's sea-fruit farm – lifts it and pushes it nice and slowly towards my lips. And for the next three hours there's not a happier Decap on the bench.

When breakfast's over, Bluey detaches the rubber bag into which three gross Colchesters, two dozen durians and a gallon of black velvet – I've told you I'm a fast eater – have dropped, and empties them down the chute. She makes a point of doing this in front of me so I'll know there's no deception. There's been a regulation about this ever since 33 complained he was being given food he'd already eaten and bit the Lab Super's thumb as a protest.

Then she slips a milligramme or two of pituitrin B into the bloodstream to counteract any cerebrotonic cortical allergy to nicotine, and fits a big fat juicy Havana into the pink rubber fingers at the end of the cigar arm.

After that we have our regular morning tiff. Bluey, who's always trying to raise what she calls my 'cultural and political level', plugs into the Universal Brain Trust programme.

'For Max's sake turn off that crap and give me my feely set!' I howl.

'Now, 63,' says Bluey, 'you know perfectly well you're not allowed to play with your feely set till after lunch. Lab Super's orders. You wouldn't like to get me into trouble, would you?'

'Yes,' I always come back, 'there's nothing I would like better, and you know it.'

I consider this restriction on the use of feely sets an unwarrantable interference with the liberty of the cerebral hemispheres. If Decaps of pronouncedly thalamotonic type such as 33 and 25 wish to spend eternity in a feely trance, that's their affair. I may attach more importance to consciousness myself, but that doesn't mean I'm not partial to a quarter of an hour's feely-play after breakfast; I find it goes very well with the first cigar of the day. But Lab Super or no Lab Super, I'm not standing for Agit Prop from the Universal Brain Trust. After all, we Decaps have some privileges in exchange for our artificial bloodstreams, that are open for any biochemist with a new molecule to meddle about with, to say nothing of the loss of our trunks and limbs. And not the least of those privileges is : no compulsory Agit Prop.

As usual, Bluey and I compromise. No feelies till after lunch, but instead of UBT a game of four-dimensional chess with Decap 81. Bluey wheels me and my blood supply down to 81's end of the bench. I warn her not to leave my apparatus standing too close to 81, while she and 81's attendant are connecting up the model continuum frame and getting out the space-time counters. You see, 81 is a biter. It's an odd contradiction because not only is he senior Decap, but in other respects he's far and away the most cortical type in the Lab; hyperintellectual, quite rarefied, he looks down his nose at me and calls me the clubman. This snapping must be some sort of nasty little hypothalamic tic, I suppose. One time when something went wrong with the conveyor belt of the skull-scrubbing machine and we all got joggled up much too close together, his teeth met in 33's ear and they had to black him out before they could make him let go. However, nothing can go wrong at four-dimensional chess, unless he spits at me – and that's not so terrible. He can't cheat because the whole thing is electronically controlled.

All is well. We've had a very close game lasting about three weeks by your old earth duration measurements. It's time for preprandial black-out, during which they give our cerebral arteries a high-pressure blow-through with this new peptone-plasma solution the Martian physiologists are so hot on. Then comes lunch.

There's not an awful lot to tell you about lunch except that, as with all our meals, we get the best of everything and as much of it as we like for as long as we like. We Decaps are never bothered by lack of appetite. Our palates, freed from the stomach's and liver's bondage, are ever avid, and we go on champing and swallowing and savouring our favourite dishes for days on end. On special occasions such as Gourmet Club Meets I've known lunch last a month, and it might be going on still if our jaw muscles didn't have to rest. On shellfish day, last Club Meet, I scoffed a hundred-weight of assorted Dublin Bay prawns, scampi, langoustes, écrevisses, durian-fed Venusian landcrabs, and those delicious giant Martian lobsters which you used to get in the Lake of Blood before it was drained by order of the Universal Brain. As for drink, 16, who's of a statistical frame of mind, calculates that at a little six-hour snack affair he drank two dozen bottles of old-fashioned claret, a firkin of Lunar Fungus Vino Fino, and a litre or so of the new Plutonic inorganic liqueur – radio-active but quite harmless. They make it from crystals found in the deposits left by the cosmic ray maelstroms, and it's supposed to stimulate your historical consciousness.

After the usual post-prandial metabolic check-over, and a precautionary electroencephalogram to see that no brain storms are on the way, Bluey fixes the cap with the feely electrodes over my skull, inserts the 'smelly' plug up each nostril, and switches on.

This afternoon the Play Time Station is disseminating a life-size electronic model of θ 5466, the young Mercuric musical comedy actress who made such a smash hit in the spectacular feely revue 'In a Rocket to the Moon with Ashtaroth'. Her feely dialogue is specially written for her by People's Playwright No. 1. She's a very popular number with the Decaps, and as I roll an eye sideways along the bench I catch sight of no fewer than seventeen of her. Personally I'm not very keen on these Mercuric females. I may be old-fashioned; or perhaps it's because I'm very nearly a pure Earth type, although Engels only knows

I'm no snob, I've not a vestige of planet prejudice, but I can't see the point of all these extra limbs and appendages. I like a girl to be a girl – not an octopus. However, I tell Bluey to leave me plugged in.

I must say the kid (after all he's only 300) who wrote that dialogue knew his stuff. Writing feely dialogue is damned difficult. You have to be prepared for all kinds of reaction situations, and have standard pattern alternative lines written ready to answer each one according to the electrotelepathic vibrations registered at the central feely station. No wonder the feely technicians are reputed to be such harassed types.

As a matter of fact, we get an example of how things can go wrong this afternoon. Poor old 33, who never can let well alone, says to his electronic model: 'But θ 5466, how can a lovely stream of quicksilver like you possibly love an old billiard ball like me?'

This, of course, is an easy one for the dialogue writer; he's got it all taped and typed long ago – commonest reaction pattern for all numbers over fifty.

The electronic model of θ 5466 passes a score or two of her silver-gilt antennae lightly over Decap 33's mug and answers pat:

'Because you're wise and chiselled like old ivory, because you're rugged. . .'

But at this moment something goes wrong with the apparatus at the Central Feely Station, the needle sticks in a groove or something, and all poor old 33's electronic model of θ 5466 can say is: 'You're rugged, you're rugged, you're rugged'. And 33 thinks he's being made fun of and tries to savage her. It's a good thing he's only a limbless Decap in the Lab and not an ordinary number in a public feely parlour, otherwise there'd be a scandal and a lot of flashes to the Universal Times about what beasts these old numbers are and how life ought to end at twenty for all outside the physiology labs except prime numbers.

Meanwhile there's hell and damnation to pay on our bench. All the feely dialogue seems to have got jammed and all seventeen electronic models of θ 5466 are squawking, 'You're rugged, you're rugged, you're rugged'. 33's scalp starts to crackle and they have to black him out. They also have to black out 81, who's managed in the confusion to get quite a bit of his θ 5466 between his teeth. Resident physiologists come rushing in and the feely sets are switched off.

However, as I'm so calm and give so little trouble I'm allowed to tune in my telecast set to the new experimental station under the auspices of the Cosmic Historico-Physical Institute. This aims to reconstruct the so-called past by means of trapping and amplifying the electronic vibration reflection patterns. They say it'll be given a public wavelength soon on account of its high educational value, but I don't know so much. It's another of our Decap privileges to tune in on it pretty regularly, and I can tell you they've been having a lot of trouble.

This afternoon they're in a rare state of excitement ; the announcer says they're catching scenes – and picking up the dialogue too – at the court of an ancient British Earth King, Charles II. Well, I'm no great shakes on history, but it all smells faintly phoney to me. First there's a hell of a blur; then we see a redhead in a cartwheel hat upsetting a basket of technicolour oranges which bounce like tennis balls. Where-upon we hear a voice yell: 'Cut', and a notice which says: 'Scene 2, take 96', and it turns out just as I thought all the time: we've got caught up in the twentieth century with a primitive British Earth film outfit making an early squawky about Nell Gwynne, a plucky proletarian girl who, so *we've* always understood, organized the Chelsea Pensioners Union and led them into action at Peterloo.

They've got a long way to go before they perfect this thing. Indeed, from what I've heard I shouldn't be at all surprised if we didn't see some of the research workers of the Cosmic Historico-Physical Institute joining us Decaps on the bench before long. It seems the history they're picking up in space-time doesn't altogether square with the stuff we're taught in poli-class. Take another little episode from Earth history, for instance. The year 1941, in the middle of the second lesser Earth war. Now we've always been taught that it was the German agent, Beelzebub Trotsky, who piloted Hess's plane on his famous flight to Britain, and they'd have made it, too, if Lord Claud Cockburn, the historian, editor of the famous weekly paper *The Truth*, hadn't taken off in a rickety old helicopter from the roof of the *Worker's Times* and shot them down over Buckingham Palace. Well, from what I've heard, and you'd be surprised how rumours get around, the Institute boys have picked up the death scene of Trot and it happened over a year before in another part of the world altogether. Seems he was clocked by a loony, one of his own disciples, in Mexico.

But that's not all. I'm told the Universal Brain has been saying that not only can you rewrite history, but in these days you can also re-enact it. And he's planning to send whole armies of electronic agents out into the continuum – or back into the past as you Earth-dwellers would say – to make bloody well certain, once and for all, that history ran true to text book form. So look out for squalls in the continuous present.

I'm not saying any more about this. Judging by the stuff Bluey's just slipped into my bloodstream, I've said too much already. I don't want to forfeit any privileges. A Decap has nothing to complain of. How can he have? He's only to express his lightest whim for it to be gratified instantly. And he's never anxious or depressed for more than a few seconds before they either black him out or pep him up with an extra dose of Euphoria mixture.

It's evening now. I rather think I've been blacked out for a bit. They're closing the gas-tight roof over the Park of Giant Vegetables, preparatory to pumping in the nitrogen mixture. I sometimes wish they wouldn't grow those Vegetables quite so damned big. It's the first evening they've let it get really dark for quite a time; I remember now, the astronomers are a bit worried about a cluster of white dwarfs way out towards the edge of the galactic disc. They're going to knock hell out of their nuclei around midnight. Proton bombardment. Make space a bit less crowded. Ought to be some classy fireworks.

It's Bluey's night off. She's going to some electrical orgy or other on one of Jupiter's satellites, and is looking very taking dressed in nothing but a swarm of fireflies. I tell her to be careful she doesn't lose her body, and she laughs and hands me over to the tender mercies of my next-door neighbour 64's attendant, who's got a deal too much Martian in her disposition for my liking. 33, who's already had a brush with her, thinks she's a slapper. He suggests I provoke her so she loses her temper and then we can report her to the Lab Super. But

I'm not having any. Me for a quiet time. I shall be quite happy listening in to the latest Universal Sabotage case. A space rocket carrying enough atomic explosive to blow the poor little Earth clean off its orbit, and manned by a crew of Martians disguised as Saturnines, was spotted by the Inter-planetary Security Police lurking in a crater on the Moon. They were immobilized by general paralytic ray and caught absolutely red-handed, just in time. They had Atomic time rockets trained on the Earth and a barrage of leaflets printed in Saturnine to follow. With such strained relations between the Earth and Saturn it would have touched off an inter-planetary war for certain. Typical piece of Martian provocation, heavy handed but effective. We're all wondering what's behind it, and I'm very much looking forward to the trial. The preliminary examination showed that all the accused had been heavily inoculated against truth drug, so the Universal Prosecutor's having their skulls lifted off and electrodes inserted straight into the cortex for direct stimulation. They'll talk.

They've just wheeled back 62, my next-door neighbour on the other side. Been out on one of his high-speed jaunts, attached to the head of a light rocket. He says the sensation is quite extraordinary, and I can well believe it. Damned if I'd go near the things. 64 says three new Decaps are coming in tonight – all from the Cosmic Historico-Physical Institue. What did I tell you? I don't suppose they'll be allowed consciousness for a good many years yet. 64 also says the latest Solar System gossip is that the Universal Brain's decided the Earth has got senile and is due to be retired before long. He thinks they'll disintegrate it. I should worry!

Very bad news. If Bluey was in charge she'd fill me up with Euphoria right away, but this Martian oaf is hopeless and an old-fashioned sadist. The Nazis of the Universe, that's what we call the Martians.

After dinner the Lab Super paid his usual visit. I thought he looked a little odd – embarrassed about something. After he'd trolleyed along the line of benches and glanced at the reaction charts he said he had something rather important to tell us. It appears the Universal Brain Trust has just drawn up a new millennial plan. The meaning of the Martian provocational plot has convinced it of the urgent necessity for a new and far more intense drive for increased and ever-increasing co-operation, collectivity and general oneness. In this drive we Decaps are to play an important part, 'a vanguard role' were the exact words. A research programme has already been drawn up and experimental work is to be begun at once with a view to promoting closer and ever closer biochemical, physiological and ultimately cerebral relationship between Decaps in organized groups. They will begin by blacking us all out and reconnecting our blood supply to large pumps in groups of six, so that every six Decaps will share the same blood supply system.

That's only the beginning. The ultimate aim is total cerebral community. Larger and larger brains, until they get something altogether new. What good that will do, search me; but that won't stop them. They're going to try everything – electrical inter-connection, rays, surgery, cortex grafting, all the -isms and -asms in the ology. As I told the Lab Super, they might just as well bang our heads together and be done with it. And who do you think they're teaming me up with? 33, who's the most troublesome Decap in the whole Lab and a sex maniac into the bargain. 81, the notorious biter, 45 and 46, whom we suspect of having once been a squared couple because of the way they nag each other, and a prime number who's volunteering to be decapped so as to give us tone and cosmic consciousness – in other words a ruddy cerebral nark. Some chain gang! And of course the whole thing is an absolutely flagrant breach of our Decaps' contracts. I wish I'd got into my little bit of trouble a millennium or two earlier, when they still went in for capital punishment. I wonder what's become of my trunk and limbs? What sort of head have they got on my shoulders now? A prime number's, I'll bet. I thought I recognized one of my hands the other day on a visiting delegate. Hope it gets him into trouble.

Thank the Absolute . . . here come Bluey, summoned back from her orgy on account of the crisis in the Lab. She looks a bit dishevelled because they had to dematerialize her and send her home on the beam. Rather a lot of the fireflies seem to have gone out . . . But what's the sense in my making silly cracks like that when in a few days I'm going to be just one great big happy family? This is really ghastly. Still, perhaps the astronomers will go too far, explode the whole cluster of white dwarfs and negate the universe?

I don't know what I've been saying, but you're not to take any notice of it. Bluey has just given me a great big shot of Morpheus Five and I've never felt so good for the last two hundred years. The Lab Super's got a wonderful new experiment planned for us and we're all going to lose our rotten petty little individualities and be all together in a wonderful oneness.

Already I feel wonderfully at one with everyone. Eyes closing now. Good night, Earth dwellers and other poor time slaves. Don't you wish you lived with us in the luminous numinous? Onwards: Forward, Sideways, Backward, Upward, Downward and Outward into the continuum! Progressive March!

The Next Scroll?

This particular Essene community, in so far as it had any fixed base, was in a cave half way up a cliff a few miles outside Jericho. There is now a tiny Greek Orthodox monastery and church on this site which has become associated with the Temptation.

The Essenes lived a strange, remote, unworldly life. They thrived in this low-down plain. They liked the strong climate. The plants, which when you look at them today remind you of sink scrubbers, seemed to them friends. They also liked the Jericho oasis with its delicious green triangle on the umber surround.

There were forty of them. Their discipline was self-imposed. They had succeeded in living a life that managed to obey the Greek principle of Meden Agan; but they took into full account the need for never being immoderately moderate. Their physiological rhythms were peculiar. They fasted often but used the sun for vitamins. They got a high protein diet from locusts, and plenty of other essentials from wild honey. Their sex life was temperate. They loved everybody including themselves. How they avoided clashes with husbands – and wives – we do not know. But whenever anyone had lain with an Essene, he or she always seemed to love everybody else more. Perhaps that is how they avoided unpopularity.

Often they swam in the ludicrously buoyant water of the nearby Dead Sea. This was a sea on which you really could almost walk.

The Prior – let us call him that – of the Community was given to periodical wandering. One day he said to his nearest disciple: 'My feet are restless. I want to walk a long way again. Eastwards, of course. I might be gone two or three years. I am old now' – he was in fact seventy-six – 'and this will probably have to be my last long walk. You are to take care of everybody and do not be too clever, if you please.'

The Deputy Prior had few problems to solve. Then, one morning, he was sitting on a rock watching a black Agamid lizard doing its menacing little exercise – exactly like press-ups – when a shadow crossed his foot. He looked round and saw a young member of the Community. This was a lean athletic looking Judeo-Roman of singular charm. He was much loved.

He told the Deputy Prior that he was feeling troubled in mind. The Deputy Prior listened with sympathy. Presently he remembered a fragment of Taoist wisdom. 'My brother,' he said. 'I do think your trouble is, if not a serious one, at least a real trouble, May I, without offending you, say that you are just a little ill?'

'Yes. That is how I feel.'

'Then you do not need me to tell you the remedy. If you are ill, go out and heal somebody.'

Soon after this conversation, which took place in approximately the year AD 29, the younger member of the Essene Community left. There was nothing uncommon in this. The Essenes came and went.

Two or three years later the Prior returned from his last long walk. He was received with the usual calm yet warm greeting. It was in the Spring. The *khamsin* – that beastly sandstormy electric nervous wind – was blowing. A great black cloud was piled up high to the north. It looked as if it must burst but it didn't. Even the Essenes found this weather trying, despite their equanimity.

The Prior asked his Deputy how everybody was. He looked round. Then he said: 'But isn't there one missing?'

'Oh yes,' said the Deputy. And he told him about the interview with the young man.

The Prior listened. He scratched in the sand with his stick. He said: 'I told you not to be too clever.'

'But, Master, what should I have said to him?'

'What was his trade?'

'He used to be a carpenter.'

'You should have told him to go back to a carpenter's shop. The poor fellow was probably wood-starved. That is one of our troubles here. It is so very dry. Let us see if we can find out what has become of him. I hate hurrying, but I think this may be a rather urgent thing.'

A moderately factual account of the Crucifixion was given to the Essenes by a wandering Bedouin the next morning. The Deputy Prior wept bitterly. His Master comforted him. 'Never mind,' he said. 'These things happen, and it is often impossible to prevent them happening. Naturally we grieve for him. But I am even more unhappy when I think of the chaos which will follow.'

A Prince of Sib-Spreaders

Before proceeding with this brief memoir of Timothy Miskin, whose recent death was such a blow to Public Relations, I had better tell you something about his rather esoteric profession. What is a Sib-Spreader?

A Sib, short for sibilant, is a story or rumour concocted to promote a set purpose, generally the sales of a particular product. A good selling Sib is often oblique with the point in a throwaway line at the end. An example that used to be very popular in the nineteen-thirties, and is still a favourite with professors at advertising colleges, is the following which I reproduce in skeleton form:

> Sib-Spreader's friend is motoring across Salisbury Plain when he is stopped by chauffeur of Rolls-Royce having trouble changing a wheel. He proffers his jack and, in helping chauffeur operate it, experiences a twinge of backache. Occupant of the Rolls-Royce, an elderly professional-looking gentleman, thanks him for his help and says: 'That's a nasty little attack of rheumatism you seem to have contracted. If you take my advice you'll have a rub with ——'s liniment when you get home. It's better than any prescription. I'm supposed to know what I'm talking about. My name is Horder, by the way.'

The qualifications of a Sib-Spreader are various and contradictory. You might think that all that is required is a good mixer, but good mixers are not always reliable. The strain is great. Many an apprentice Sib-Spreader has been found paralysed, long before his day's work was done, suffering from amnesia, aphasia and aphonia. In no branch of the advertising industry is wastage of personnel so high.

Nor is mere persistence enough. For persistence is all too often the prerogative of the bore, whereas it is essential for the Sib-Spreader to establish an instant sympathetic rapport with his public.

Which brings us to Timothy Miskin. There were no indications in his background of the peculiar talent for which he was to become famous, though it has been fancifully suggested that the name Miskin, which is of Slavonic origin, might imply some affinity with the game of Russian Scandal. He was born of respectable subtopian parentage. His father was an accountant for a firm of arithmetic textbook publishers.

As a youth, Timothy Miskin seems to have been an utterly nondescript personality, but a little biographical research reveals a significantly pervasive quality. 'Miskin?' says one who had been at school with him, 'Of course I remember Miskin. Couldn't begin to tell you what he looked like, but he had a funny little soft voice and he was always standing by the radiators in the passage. He usually had something darned interesting to tell you, too. It might be that the moths had eaten all the uniforms in the armoury so there would be no more corps parades, or that the scrum-pox epidemic had got so bad we were all going to be sent home. It was nearly always something too good to be true but it cheered you up no end.'

Obviously, the seeds were already germinating. It was his father's intention to article the boy to a chartered accountant, but Timothy, on leaving school, expressed so strong a preference for a more creative branch of commerce that a post was found for him in an advertising agency – in the Market Research Department.

The agency's Market Research Department was investigating the popularity of a certain brand of cocoa. It transpired that in one of the areas where the researchers were at work the sales of this cocoa had risen to an altogether unprecedented extent. Inquiries were made and the cause was discovered to be Timothy Miskin. Not content with filling in his questionnaire forms, he had embarked on a work of supererogation to swell the sales of the brand. This, according to the story he told, had remarkable aphrodisiac properties, quite benign but perfectly distinct. They were due to the presence in the beverage of the seeds of the Yohimbe tree, which is well known to the natives of

West Africa as the source of a powerful love potion. The site of this particular cocoa company's plantation was liberally dotted about with Yohimbe trees whose seeds, carried by the wind, found their way into the cocoa powder along with the berries.

The agency's Managing Director realized that here was a case of a natural-born Sib-Spreader, a true artist such as only occurs once in several generations.

Henceforward Miskin's career was one long, steady, triumphant procession. His accomplishment was prodigious. Entering a town just before opening time, he would flit from bar to bar like a wraith, leaving no personal impression whatever save for that soft ghostly unforgettable voice which echoed in the ears of landlord and customers for days afterwards:

'Extraordinary story that chap who was in here at lunch time was telling us about his friend and the fortune-teller who told him his life was going to be saved by a bottle with a label with a picture of a fig tree on it!'

'Yes, wasn't it! Shouldn't be surprised if there wasn't something in it, too. Think I'll pop across to the chemist and treat myself to one . . .'

'Arthur, what was the name of the brand of shag the tramp was smoking that Sir Winston Churchill congratulated him on? Bulldog, wasn't it?'

'That's right. You'd better look sharp, though. There are queues at all the tobacconists' . . .'

'According to what he was telling us, and you could tell from the way he spoke that he had it straight from the horse's mouth, there's only one cure for superfluous hair. It's a secret of the Egyptian Royal Family passed down from father to son. Well, this firm has at last persuaded Farouk to let them have it – at a stiff price, of course, to put on the market. But there won't be very much of it, so if I was your missus, old man, I'd shove my order in pdq . . .'

Such was Miskin's strange hypnotic power that no matter how elaborate the Sib, nobody ever forgot a single detail. In order to avoid chaos he used to restrict himself to spreading one Sib at a time. His tours were eagerly followed at the agency's head office. As the sales charts of the product that was being sibbed bounded ceilingwards, the account executives would gleefully raise their glasses of British wine samples and exclaim:

'Good old Miskin! Just look how he's slipping them the Sib. Boy, what a spreader!'

The strain however was tremendous. Not so much the physical strain – Miskin's digestion was a mysterious law unto itself – as the psychological. Miskin, it is now believed, put so much of himself into his Sibs that there were moments when his whole personality disappeared as if drained away.

It is tempting to speculate what would have become of him during the war if he had been old enough to serve in the large department of the Ministry of Information, recruited from the advertising agencies, whose job it was to originate suitable political and military Sibs for spreading in enemy and neutral countries. His inability to speak any foreign language beyond a few words of schoolboy French would certainly not have deterred our Intelligence Authorities from parachuting him into occupied Europe. Would his curious powers of evasion have enabled him to escape the Gestapo? If so, the war would have ended a great deal sooner.

But Timothy Miskin's life was short enough as it was.

The circumstances of his death have given rise to ugly rumours. These can now be categorically denied. Miskin was not nobbled by envious Sib-Spreaders.

His supremacy was unchallenged. To this day publicity men relate with relish the story of how Miskin and his closest rival, a eupeptic extrovert named Charlie Champion, entered, simultaneously, the Long Bar of a celebrated North Midlands hotel and commenced spreading textile Sibs from different ends. Champion's Sib had only travelled a few feet along the bar when it was blocked by Miskin's and, a moment later, Champion had the humiliating experience of listening to his rival's Sib being repeated back to him with that gusto for which the North Midlands are so famous.

With regret it must be recorded that his employers, taking advantage of his preternatural zeal, encouraged Miskin to work himself to extinction. His waking life became a continuous cycle of Sib-Spreading. He was kept in circulation at social functions of all kinds, cocktail parties, dances, weddings and funerals where his *sotto voce* techinique was particularly telling in spreading the Sib from pew to pew.

He was also made a member of every club in London,

including of course the House of Commons, and it was here that the ultimate fatality occurred.

Miskin was sitting for the Party in power, and it was his custom before proceeding to the House to drop in at the advertising agency for his day's briefing. The account executive on this particular morning was either very negligent or very inexperienced. He issued Miskin such contradictory directives that when the House divided he entered first one lobby, where he spread a Sib that persuaded the Government to vote against itself, then the other, where he persuaded the Opposition to vote for the Government. In the small hours of the morning the shrunken corpse of Miskin was discovered in the Strangers' Bar. He had succumbed to the strain – like the chameleon which, so they say, perishes when placed upon a patchwork quilt.

A Great Fireworks Critic

Henry Nimmo: An Interpretative Memoir

The death this week – no less sad because so seasonable – of Henry Nimmo, veteran doyen of British Fireworks Critics, should not pass unnoticed by any who care for pyrotechny. May this brief note serve as a squib to touch off a more fitting memorial, one of those set pieces which Nimmo himself so delighted to evaluate.

Nimmo's career was a triumph of sublimation. He was born in 1854, the son of a fire insurance assessor in Clerkenwell. His early life, it may now be revealed, was a struggle against arsonist tendencies. As a boy Henry was of a markedly literary bent, but his education was perpetually interrupted by conflagrations. School after school which he attended was mysteriously burned to the ground. The crisis came soon after his sixteenth birthday. His father, Samuel, known in fire insurance circles as old 'Guy Fawkes' Nimmo, was entertaining a convivial party when Henry arrived home unexpectedly with the ashes of yet another academy thick upon him. He was introduced, laughingly, to the company as 'My little Firebug'. Coarse professional jests were made: 'A proper spark off the old Roman candle.' 'Bright, says you? Why, the kid looks well alight!'

The effect upon Henry was instantaneously traumatic. Hitherto, as he assures us in his autobiography, *As the Sparks Fly Upward* (privately printed 1907), he had been entirely unaware of his arsonist proclivities, which were prompted of course by a powerful yet unconscious urge to emulate his father. 'I now felt,' he writes, 'as if I had been branded all over . . .'

That night he left Clerkenwell never to return, much to the chagrin of old 'Guy Fawkes' Nimmo. After a brief period of wandering and privation, he obtained honest employment in Fox's Fireworks Factory.

During the night of November 4th, 1875, the Fox Fireworks Factory caught fire. Next day Henry Nimmo applied for the post of Assistant Fireworks Critic to *The Times*. In lieu of qualifications he submitted a notice, thirty-seven pages long, of the conflagration at Fox's Factory. It was entitled 'An Essay in Pyrotechnic Poesy', and remains to this day a masterpiece of style and a model for aspiring fireworks critics. An inimitable feature of it is the delicate irony with which Nimmo treats the impromptu effects, of which there were inevitably very many. It fell into the hands of the paper's Chief Fireworks Critic, the celebrated Joseph Kentish (author of *The Pyrotechnist's Treasury* and biographer of the Brothers Ruggieri), who exclaimed with characteristic generosity, 'More tasteful than Biringoccio!' (Vanucci Biringoccio, author of *Pirotechnia* – Venice, 1540). 'More learned than Websky!' (author, later of *Lustfeuerwerk-kunst* – Leipzig, 1878.)

On Kentish's insistence, Nimmo was appointed Assistant Fireworks Critic at a salary of thirty-five shillings per week. The sublimation process was now complete.

The life of a mid-Victorian fireworks critic was far more strenuous than that of his modern counterpart. Our ancestors, gayer, and perhaps more pacific, were cheerfully addicted to the *feu de joie*. There were fireworks displays on most nights at Vauxhall, Ranelagh, and Marylebone; while in the countryside no landowner's coming-of-age was complete without incandescent effects. There was the Continent, with ever new developments such as the coloured *Globos Iluminados* of Madrid, and the perennial *Girandola* at Rome. Adequate coverage entailed much travelling. Many a timid wayfarer was alarmed by the sight of Henry Nimmo, with singed eyebrows and blackened face, his charred rags flapping in the wind, bounding on board the train to write his dispatch.

Kentish was old and stricken in years. He had never fully recovered from his great effort in reporting, single-handed, in a special supplement, the famous Illuminations at the Crystal Palace in 1865. For some years before his death in 1896, aged ninety-three (the longevity of fireworks critics is a problem for the gerontologist), Henry Nimmo had been doing the lion's share. We can but marvel at his industry:

'This year,' he records in the closing of his diary for 1897, 'I have written some three quarters of a million words of Notices of Displays – many, alas, scarce worthy of the epithet Pyrotechnical – for the Paper. I have completed Volume II, eight hundred and seventy-three manuscript pages, of my *Pyrotechnist's Vade-Mecum*. I have also composed a monograph of sixty-odd pages on "The Garniture of Rockets", and an essay on "Gerbs and Fountains". Tomorrow, greatly daring, I start my biography of Berthold Schwartz, the thirteenth century gunpowder-maker and Father of European Pyrotechny'. Truly a formidable record.

Nimmo's interest in Schwartz did not prevent him from coming down decisively on the side of the Italian school, as opposed to the North European school of Nuremberg, led by Clarmer, when he came to consider – as he did in a classic historical study *The Incandescence of Vulgarity*, the great Pyrotechnical Controversy of the seventeenth century. His preference for the elegant purity of the Italian style flared up, contemporaneously, at the time of Queen Victoria's Diamond Jubilee. So hard-hitting was his notice of the fireworks display, with its condemnation of the set pieces as 'all too apposite masterpieces of the egregious', that *The Times* felt compelled to exercise censorship. Nimmo resigned as a protest and founded his own organ, *The Catherine Wheel*, a voluminous weekly periodical devoted entirely to Fireworks Criticism, but later he yielded to persuasion and returned to Printing House Square.

A similar contretemps occurred in connection with his notice of the National Peace Display in Hyde Park in 1919, perhaps the largest firework display in history. Again the set pieces representing the monarch roused his indignation. He condemned them fiercely in a blistering article headed 'From the Sublime to the Ridiculous.'

When the Second World War broke out Nimmo was living in quasi-retirement near Lewes, ever his favourite English town on account of its elaborate Guy Fawkes day celebration, which he described, tolerantly, in his *Uses and Abuses of the Bonfire*. He hurried at once to London to study effects during air raids, but complained that they were woefully disorganized.

Living, as he did, entirely for fireworks, Nimmo had almost no private life. It was typical of the man that right up to the end he had to be restrained from giving away too much of his scanty substance to children collecting for guys. A certain singularity of appearance, total hairlessness resulting from occupational accidents, lent him a touch of the sinister which was utterly misleading.

Soon after this story was published, I got a letter from an RAF officer in Scotland saying that he was convinced that the critic was a long-lost relative of his.

Fiendish Nuptials

A Horroratorio

Recitative by Edgar Allan Poe:
Lo! As I lay in the grips of my last hangover
With the raven Cirrhosis pecking away at my liver
I had a vision of fiends of fiction
Children all of my sick alcoholic fancy,
Fiends past and
Fiends to come.
And suddenly there was a great unquiet wedding.
Count Dracula's youngest daughter, Lamia,
Affianced to the Son of Frankenstein.
At Castle Dracula on the nuptial eve
A houseparty was assembled
Of every evil printed thing
That ever lulled a bishop off to sleep
Or kept an All Souls Fellow out of mischief.

Chorus:
A feast for vampires
Ghouls gaudy.

Air by Count Dracula:
Awake! The night hag's midnight screech is heard!
Let all Things nameless at our feast make frenzy.

Recitative by Edgar Allan Poe:
In Dracula's great castle hall
Its area thrice exceeding that of Albert's
The floor was already inches deep in tobacco ash.
With every fiend in crime and horror fiction as a house guest
The presents had to be guarded
And what presents!
But let Lamia tell of
Her family friends' generosity.

Recitative by Lamia Dracula:
Friends all and fiends
My heart is swelling at your kindness
So thoughtful too, it is the thought that counts.
A Russell's Viper from Dr Grimesby Roylott,
A Black Widow from Fu Manchu
A werewolf from the Witch of Endor.
The Rokeby Venus from dear Raffles
The Mona Lisa from Arsène Lupin
And from Snow White's stepmother this charming set of
Child-Frightener masks.
From Torquemada, bless his heart,
A new self-regulating rack.
From dear de Sade this nighty of sharpest porcupine quills
And from de Masoch a Self-Crucifying kit.
And look what my dear spouse-to-be has given me:
A dressing table with a built-in
Royal College of Surgeons' Museum,
All complete down to the last afterbirth.
I never thought a Frankenstein could think up such a tasteful
    fancy.

Recitative by Poe:
Were she to tell us all we should be here till dawn.
To guard these presents I've recruited
From Old Poe's Agency for Private Eyes
Every detective you've ever read of and many more.
Holmes, Poirot, Hanaud and Inspector French
And toughs and thugs from California,
Imitations of sad Marlow and cynical Sam Spade.

Chorus by Detectives:
The life of crime
The crime of life
Your guilt is great
But so is ours.
Ask not who did it?
We all know:
You did.
But so did We.

Recitative by Poe:
    The company retired to rest
    Or so they said, for evil never rests.
    Meanwhile a touching scene.
    Took place in Lamia's bedroom.

Air by Lamia Dracula:
    A motherless vampire I
    And wedded to a monster.
    At least I shan't have to sit next to him
    At dinner any more.
    But who shall tell me what I need to know?

Recitative by Count Dracula:
    My daughter vampire
    I hear the call of duty.
    Were your poor mother with us now
    She would herself enlighten you.
    But ever since that dreadful night,
    When I got home on one wing and a curse
    And she was staked out in the churchyard,
    You've been delivered to a father's care.
    The facts of death I'll now unfold.

Air by Count Dracula:
    Infinite greed
    Is the vampire's creed.
    Don't wait for a sigh
    Or the white of an eye
    Show your fangs!

Recitative by Lamia:
    Oh father, dear father,
    You look pale and drawn.
    All this exhausting hospitality
    Must be taking its toll on your blood supply
    Midnight strikes.
    There's a good pull-up for vampires
    In the village.

Recitative by Dracula:
    Oh thoughtful child, I do confess
    The prospect of your marriage to a Frankenstein
    Depresses me.
    Vampire with Zombie!
    It is a union most unnatural.
    But fiction must be served.
    I only hope that from such reckless coupling
    Virtue may not spring. And now
    I must to my peasants.

Air by Lamia:
    He shall feed on his flock like a shepherd.

Recitative by Poe:
    And in the Zombie's guest chamber
    Old mother Frankenstein
    With homely grunts and clockwork creaks
    Endeavoured to brush up her backward boy.

Air by Mrs Frankenstein:
    Stamp on her, tramp on her.
    Don't let her win.
    Remember you marry
    A daughter of sin.
    Keep it mechanical
    Don't spare the spanner.
    Make it satanical.

Recitative by Poe:
    If I were to tell you
    All that went wrong at the wedding
    'T 'ould take from hell to breakfast.
    The ceremony was in a crypt.
    Frankenstein's dam,
    Professing ignorance,
    But in reality to spite the vampires,
    Had hung festoons of garlic all about.
    The Draculas were livid
    But at last they got the pair
    To the altar.
    Pierrepoint himself officiated.

Chorus:
> Let's hang the bride!
> She's dead already
> And she likes it.

Recitative by Poe:
> At the reception it was soon discovered
> That presents were missing right and left.

Air by Count Fosco:
> What fiend has scoffed
> My pet white mice?

Recitative by Poe:
> Fiends and detectives were soon changing
> Their immortal roles:
> Professor Moriarty broke the news to Sherlock Holmes that
> Inspector Lestrade had taken dropsy.
> The Old Man in the Corner, so perverted with his string,
> Had trussed himself up like a chicken.
> Strange cases of weakness afflicted many.
> Inspector Maigret lit his pipe and fainted with a cry.

Solo by Maigret:
> Merde!

Recitative by Poe:
> There were so many patients suffering from acute anaemia
> That the cry went up

Chorus:
> Is there a donor in the house?

Holmes' recitative with violin obbligato:
> Don't touch that transfusion!
> It's the wrong blood group.

Air by Frankenstein Snr.:
> Never introduce your donor to a pal
> Has always been my motto.
> Artificial insemination is
> The curse of our family.

Recitative by Poe:
I, too, came in for much unfavourable comment.
Holmes and Moriarty both attacked me.

Recitative by Holmes and Moriarty:
You have been mixing it as usual.
Fiction and fantasy!
Fiends and Detectives!
You sodden Southern States sot!
We'll need an author to get us out of this.

Recitative by Poe:
I croaked back quickly:
Not yours, I hope.
Sir Arthur Conan Doyle
Believed in spiritualism
And fairies dancing round the night lights.
At least I always got my spirits from the bottle
And never borrowed a horror from no man.
But we were interrupted by a dire procession.
Burke and Hare had chloroformed poor Dr Clubfoot.

Duet by Burke and Hare:
Doctor Knox given a bonus fee
Extra for a little deformity.

Recitative by Poe:
I told them sternly to deposit him
In a place of safety.
But they dropped him in Dr Lakington's acid bath,
In which Bulldog Drummond had just been cleaning
His mashie-niblick.
Phyllis Drummond and Irma Peterson meanwhile
Had been renewing their tender relationship
Which shocked all Surrey in the twenties.

Duet:
Phyllis Drummond and Irma.

Phyllis:
>   Kidnap me again!
>   Marriage is such hell with Hugh!
>   Kidnap me like you used to do,
>   Drag me up the Hog's Back.

Irma:
>   Silly little Phyllis
>   I'm selling you to Stonehenge
>   For a sacrifice.

Recitative by Poe:
>   Just how all this confusion was resolved
>   I naturally cannot be expected to remember.
>   A collective of lady detective story writers
>   Was pressed into service in November
>   And some years later they agreed
>   That wedded bliss must be decreed,
>   Our last scene then is in the crypt nursery
>   Where we see Lamia Dracula suckling her little monster.

Air by Lamia:
>   He's got two heads to his Daddy's one.

Duet by Lamia and Son of Frankenstein:
>   What wouldn't I do
>   To you
>   If I were Dr Fu Manchu
>   And had you in my private zoo?

Profiles

R. M. Dawkins

Some Personal Reminiscences

Professor Richard MacGillivray Dawkins, who died on May 4th of this year (1955), aged eighty-three, was for many years Bywater and Sotheby Professor of Byzantine and Modern Greek at Oxford, and a Fellow of Exeter College and of Emmanuel College, Cambridge. As well as being a distinguished scholar, he was an altogether exceptionally lively and delightful personality, with a very wide range of interests and innumerable friends over several generations. He eschewed all forms of politics and public relations that were outside the orbit of his immediate personal responsibilities; he remains a great twentieth-century university character.

I first met Dawkins in 1924, during the summer term at Oundle, where he was staying for a weekend with his friend, Ted Dickey, a pleasing landscape painter, who was art master at the school. I was finding Oundle rather bleak just then, and Ted and his charming Italianate wife, Eunice, constituted a much-needed oasis for the nomadic adolescent. Round a mirror over the fireplace in their drawing-room, Ted had painted little scenes from *South Wind*. He often spoke to me of Dawkins and I had come to associate him with Mr Keith, who was very much my idea of a mentor. I had been promised that I should be asked to tea on the Sunday of his visit and was eagerly looking forward to meeting him.

I was not in the least disappointed, for, although I had expected somebody rather more worldly and sophisticated, and Dawkins was the very reverse of a boulevardier, I was instantly captivated by his lively interest and sympathy. There was nothing in the faintest degree revolutionary about Dawkins. Indeed, his conservative side, as I later discovered, was strongly developed and he disapproved of many things, including divorce; but he was always on the side of the pupil as opposed to the pedagogue. I immediately found myself chattering away with him as if we were contemporaries. His attitude towards public schools and schoolmasters was one of excited amusement. After a few minutes' conversation, I began to experience a sense of liberation. I think, now, that one of the things that may have stirred his interest in me was the news that I had recently been given the record beating in the history of the school for rebellious activities in my house. Dawkins, though entirely un-sadistic and distinctly radical in his attitude to penal reform, was always rather fascinated, quite frankly and openly, by stories of torture.

Dawkins had the habit of talking very fast, in note form, as it were, while at the same time listening to what you said, carrying on from where you left off, but always handing you the ball back: 'You mean to say he was actually so ignorant as to . . . So in fact this grotesque oaf . . . ? Yes, yes, I see . . .' When it came to a joke, whether one of yours or his own, which he particularly appreciated, he would begin to shake with silent laughter, crouch down, cover his face with both hands, and finally emit a delighted squawk of 'Lord!' Though an intensely nervous, very sensitive, and at times shy man, he was also – in conversation at any rate – utterly unselfconscious.

His appearance, which changed singularly little during the thirty-one years I knew him, was unforgettable and indescribable. He was of middle height and rather slight build; he must have had a very rapid metabolism, for though a big, sometimes cheerfully voracious eater, he never put on an ounce of fat. His movements were all quick and darting, yet somehow slightly sideways or crabwise. He had a fine, large, well-shaped somewhat brachycephalic head, bald on top with the reddish hair growing round the bald patch like a tonsure. He had a moustache of moderate dimensions, a little more luxuriant than a toothbrush, but much less than a soup strainer. His mouth was full, and slightly crooked. Corvo, quoted in A. J. Symons' *The Quest for Corvo*, when in a rage called him in one of his letters 'the blubber-lipped professor of Greek'. The epithet is inaccurate and gives a most misleading impression; in fact, his mouth was what a police description would call firm. He had one of those ugly, characterful, interesting faces which you never tire of looking at. There was something immensely pleasing about him. The precise word to fit this aspect of him eludes me; 'gnomishness' inevitably suggests itself, but has to be vehemently rejected because of its sentimental associations. Dawkins, with his abhorrence of all forms of whimsy or infantilism, would greet it with a squawk of indignation. The first impression he made upon me was one of exhilaration; it remained constant. I always associated him so closely with a mood of mild but sustained euphoria that if I was depressed I would not go to see him or answer his letters. Dawkins and depression simply did not go together; one had no wish to inflict on him the underlying aggression. This was not because he was too frivolous for one to confide in. Certainly he never invited confidences, but he did not lack sympathy; on the contrary, he was so sensitive that he sometimes tended to shrink back in self-protection. Once, I did tell him about a tragedy of which I happened to be a helpless, peripheral spectator; he burst into tears and asked if a tenner or two would help. Unfortunately, it was not a money problem.

One, certainly, of the key-words to his character in middle age and later life, and to what his obituarist in *The Times* called his 'inexhaustible liking for and patience with the Young', was liberation. Dawkins was an escapee, and he never tired of congratulating himself on being one. A favourite dictum of mine when I was an undergraduate, which I was very fond of repeating, was a sentence of Osbert Sitwell's: 'After the average English private and public school the remainder of one's life, however unpleasant, cannot fail to seem something of a holiday'. 'That's it,' Dawkins would say, 'that's the motto. Ought to be prominently displayed everywhere, banks, offices, prisons. Might even bring comfort in the condemned cell. Lord!'

His own schooldays at Marlborough had been miserable. He was bullied and unhappy, hating every moment of it and not getting any consolation from his work. I have the impression, though I cannot be certain of this, that he developed surprisingly late for a person of his intellectual ability. And when he left school he became the victim of one of those enthusiastic parental experiments so often unsuccessful. His father, a retired rear-admiral, RN, had become convinced that electrical engineering was the great industry of the future. His eldest son, Richard, must get in on the ground floor. He therefore arranged for Dawkins to be apprenticed to Crompton's electrical works at Chelmsford and learn how to wind dynamos. So for more than a year Dawkins lived in cheap lodging in Chelmsford and clocked in every morning at eight to wind dynamos. (He probably wound them very well. He was exceedingly deft with his hands and one of his amusements in later life was representational string games, which are played by primitive people and take far more complicated forms than cats'-cradle.) He was lonely and unhappy and frustrated, so much so that he began to take an interest in theosophy. Not being entirely satisfied with the writings of Mmes Blavatsky and Besant, he decided to learn Sanskrit and read the Hindu scriptures in the original. It stimulated his latent linguistic bent and cured him of theosophy as purveyed by Western 'seekers', but I rather think he retained a respect for the purer forms of Oriental mysticism, though he remained very reticent about this.

The captivity in Chelmsford came to an end when Dawkins was left just enough money by a relative to send himself to Cambridge. He got a scholarship to Emmanuel, going up rather older than the average undergraduate. He won a fellowship in 1904, and in 1906 was appointed Director of the British School at Athens. He conducted notable excavations at the temple of Orthia at Sparta, in Crete, on Melos and elsewhere. This, the Greek archaeological, was the first stage in his academic career. The second was the period of his Byzantine and Greek philological and historical studies. I am not sufficiently educated to make any useful comment on Dawkins's scholarship, except to remark that for a man of his massive learning the all-round breadth of his interests was remarkable. And he could turn the full power of his concentration on any subject, however slight. He was, for instance, an enthusiast for the novels of Ronald Firbank; he read them over and over again and had constructed in his mind – he never bothered to put it on paper – a glossary in which various obscure references were tracked down. Firbank's Byzantine shimmer appealed very strongly to Dawkins: 'Extraordinary chap. Bit silly, oh, very silly at times, touch of the nineties, you know, but quite unlike anyone else, and wonderfully funny. Lord! Remember the Abbess, Mme Marie du Coeur Brisé!' Dawkins was particularly fond of jokes about pious Catholics.

Soon after his appointment to Athens, a second big chance
came in Dawkins's circumstances. He inherited, I think from
an aunt by marriage, an estate in Wales. It included three
houses, two of them very large, and a pack of beagles. The
second house he let; it became a preparatory school and Evelyn
Waugh taught there for a term or so, after leaving Oxford, and
before writing *Decline and Fall*. The third house, Plas Dulas,
built on two levels on a steep hillside by an amateur architect
in the eighteen-fifties or thereabouts, he lived in himself, during
vacations, with his sister, Annie, to housekeep for him. Life was
now very pleasant for Dawkins. Though not madly rich, he was
certainly comfortably off (he left some fifty thousand pounds),
able to travel where he pleased and pursue all his interests.

About this time came his encounters with Corvo. They met
with the Pirie Gordons in Wales. Dawkins, with his penchant
for the odd and the grotesque, especially when it was accompanied by intelligence and talent, was instantly fascinated. The
circumstances of his offer to stand Corvo-Rolfe a holiday in
Italy, and of the inevitable quarrel when the eccentric paranoid
author of *Hadrian VII* flew into a rage because Dawkins refused
to provide entertainment on the lavish scale which Corvo
expected as his right, are told in detail in A. J. Symons's *The
Quest for Corvo*. I often heard Dawkins refer, sometimes almost
wistfully, to Corvo; but I do not remember his adding anything much to Symons's account, except the text of Corvo's
final communication. This was a postcard containing two
words: 'Bitterest execrations'.

Dawkins's activities in the First World War consisted of
doing intelligence work in Greece and the Aegean with Compton Mackenzie's celebrated circus. This entailed a commis-
sion as a lieutenant in the RNVR, which led to the temporary
removal of Dawkins's moustache; it was celebrated, so Hope
Johnstone, another member of the circus, told me, by Compton
Mackenzie with an ode beginning: 'The Royal Naval Volunteer
Reserve.' I mentioned this once to Dawkins and he was not at
all pleased. He was inclined to be vigilant where his personal
dignity was concerned. (He was furious, I remember, when an
Exeter man who had taken to journalism wrote a fanciful
paragraph about him and the pack of beagles.) I think he felt
that someone had been trying to make a monkey out of him; in

any case, I have the impression that the bouquet of Compton Mackenzie's personality – very strong, very agreeable, but undeniably theatrical – was not quite to Dawkins's taste. This, I think, accounts for a hint to two which Dawkins let fly, now and again, of a performance which he, Dawkins, could put on, were he so minded, of Mackenzie, impressing the peculiar intensity of his sufferings during an attack of sciatica on some disciples. Dawkins's friends used often to amuse ourselves with private speculations and fantasies about the Professor's exploits as a cloak-and-dagger man in the Aegean. A delightful and true if all too brief account was given, not long after Dawkins's death, in a note to *The Times* by Admiral Stevenson, who commanded the trawler in which Dawkins spent many uncomfortable days and nights off the coast of Crete.

I find myself impressed at this point in trying to review the course of Dawkins's life, by the way certain vital threads recur in a pleasing manner; thus, his interest in Crete was always intense, and during his last years he got great pleasure from his friendship and correspondence with those two adventurous Cretophiles, Paddy Leigh Fermor and Xan Fielding.

In 1920 Dawkins became Professor of Byzantine and Modern Greek at Oxford and took up residence in white-panelled rooms in the front quad of Exeter College. It was there that I went to call upon him, and his great friend Nevill Coghill, who had recently been made a Fellow, as soon as I came up to New College in the autumn of 1925. Among dons who became social centres of undergraduate life, two main types may be distinguished. There is the austere mentor, or *éminence grise*, with an eye always on the future careers of his pupils; of him in the early twenties the late Sligger Urquhart of Balliol was the leading example. Then there is the urbane, witty sociophile who acts as a liaison between Oxford and the world and dispenses most useful object-lessons in the gospel of enlightened self-interest and capacity for enjoyment. Dawkins did not fit into either category, and the comparative remoteness of his subject isolated him from, or, better to say insulated him against, the stresses of the academic rat-race. He was so opposed to all forms of pretentiousness and humbug that he regarded careerism as almost obscene. He was, however, immensely sociable. And the kind of undergraduates whom he liked best and who

were drawn towards him were the gay ones among the intellectuals, the temporarily anarchistic hedonists. I can think of
scores of names, but one, whom I met first in Dawkins's rooms,
during the first week of my first term, still somehow epitomizes
for me the qualities of unique contradictoriness accompanied
by all-round intellectual curiosity that so appealed to Dawkins.
He is Archie Lyall, A. L. Lyall, author of *Lyall's Languages*, that
indispensable, international phrase book, and some excellent
travel writing. The fact that Archie had been to Winchester
used to give Dawkins special pleasure. 'Lord!' he would
squawk, 'was there ever anyone less like the typical Wykeham-
ist than Archie! I wonder what some of those New College dons
make of him! Lord!'

Dawkins's rooms expressed his personality most accurately.
The Near Eastern sojourns and the Byzantine element was
present in hangings, rugs, candlesticks and icons, also some
amusing pictures of Biblical scenes painted on wood by
nineteenth-century pilgrims to Jerusalem. In one of them
David is looking down on Bath-sheba through a telescope. The
Victorian academic, essentially unsmart, quasi-subfusc strain
in Dawkins came out in a certain bareness and dilapidation at
floor level. The walls expressed his contemporary interests. He
was fond of modern painting of the more decorative sort; his
pictures included a Paul Nash, a Roger Fry ('It's not quite as
good as a Cézanne, but a fraction of the price'), a Henry Lamb,
a posterish Ethelbert White and an Ernest Procter of a Burmese
river scene with brightly dressed Burmans in the forecourt.

He was very hospitable. He gave lunch parties most Sundays
during the term and was always delighted to see anyone at tea
or between tea and dinner. The conversation ranged all over
the place; it was apt to be a bit jerky, owing to his own nervous
mannerisms, the silent laughter, the covering of the head with
the hands and the sudden delighted squawks. Among a few of
his favourite lighter topics were crime, criminals and the
underworld; the absurdities of schoolmasters, and Roman
Catholic ideologists and certain Oxford heads of houses; Victorian and Edwardian scandals; Cambridge humbugs, with
special reference to Oscar Browning. The personalities of some
of his colleagues used both to fascinate and exasperate him. He
made a special study of R. R. Marrett, the genial anthropolo-

gist, who was Rector of Exeter, and whose hobbies were golf
and the island of Jersey.

He was always ready to talk about books, and kept up well
with modern literature. His favourites, apart from Norman
Douglas, included Proust, Firbank, Osbert Sitwell, and later
William Plomer. He had, always, an interest in oddity, and was
one of the first to spot the novels of E. H. W. Meyerstein, who,
later, became one of his personal friends. His enthusiasm for
Norman Douglas, as a repository of the living Greek spirit, was
so great that he expanded an essay, which he wrote for a college
literary society, into a short book. It was perceptive but
perhaps over-inclined to treat Mr Keith in *South Wind* as a
self-portrait, and identify Douglas with his character. Dawkins
met Douglas in Italy during the late twenties, and saw something of him when he came to England during the war. I got the
impression, then, that he found the personality of his idol
almost too strong, too gamey, but they corresponded amiably
until Douglas's death.

In general, Dawkins's attitude towards modern literature
was rather like his attitude towards his friends. He kept his
disputatious, aggressive side – and he had plenty of aggression
– for his scholarship; outside of that he was an appreciator, on
the look-out for positive qualities. He was always delighted at
any success of his friends, and never failed to squawk with joy at
a new Betjeman poem or Lancaster cartoon. His letters were
full of other people's doings. He was a tremendous correspondent, typing very fast and with quite incredible inaccuracy,
with two fingers, cursing cheerfully as he typed. His letter-
writing style was delightfully fluent and colloquial.

One particularly exhilarating Dawkins episode I remember
was our Irish expedition in the summer of 1927, in Michael
Shawe-Taylor's car, starting from Queenstown, where my parents were then living. We drove through Cork and Kerry round
the Dingle peninsula and on to Galway. Michael had been most
optimistic, before we started, about how many people he knew,
en route, with whom we should be able to stay for as long as we
liked. But on the morning we set out there arrived a sheaf of
letters and telegrams, all making excuses. 'You seem to be
about as popular in this country as Cromwell, Michael', said
Dawkins. More of these put-offs followed us en route. 'Sorry,

house shut up,' telgraphed Lady Dunraven, with whom Michael had been proposing to lodge us at Adare, 'but our former butler keeps excellent hotel in village.'

There were only two rooms available: one an attic with two truckle beds, the other a tapestried chamber with a four-poster. I suggested to Michael that we should take the attic. 'Nonsense,' he snorted, 'there is no reason why Dawkins should be pampered. We'll toss for it.' We tossed and I won the tapestried chamber. In the night there was a storm. Next morning, when I went up to the attic, I was startled to see a pair of feet on Dawkins's pillow, and his head sticking out at the foot of the bed. Rain was pouring into the room through a broken windowpane. Michael Shawe-Taylor was in a black sulk. From then on a spirit of farce seemed to take possession. Dawkins, on the way to the bath, collided, squawking, with a female form in a peignoir. She turned out to be the Queen of Boar's Hill, Lady Keeble, formerly Lillah MacCarthy, wife of the Professor of Botany. The next stop was Coole. 'Now, here,' said Michael, who was a great-nephew of Lady Gregory, 'I can promise you a little hospitality at last. We really can stay with Great Aunt Augusta as long as we like.' But at dinner Great Aunt Augusta asked, very pointedly: 'And where is it you and your friends are going to the day after tomorrow, Michael?' The spirit of farce persisted. Dressing for dinner the second night, in the half darkness, Dawkins got his dinner-jacket covered with candle grease and came pattering along the corridor for help. Michael and I melted it off with a candle flame, all three of us laughing hysterically. At dinner Mary Ann, Lady Gregory's aged parlour-maid, let out a thunderous belch and detected me in the act of hiding my laughter with my hand. She had her revenge by filling my glass so full with claret that it spilt as soon as I touched it; meanwhile she stood behind making loud 'tck-tck-s' of disapproval to draw everybody's attention to my clumsiness. Dawkins was immensely delighted. I have heard him tell the story several times since.

Great Aunt Augusta was graciously pleased with Dawkins, at first. She established proprietorial rights. 'My Professor', she called him. Talking about Middle Irish, in the drawing-room sacred to Yeats, among the statuary they got on like a house on fire. Then Dawkins rather blotted his copybook by pointing out the essential inferiority of Irish folklore as compared with Greek. She was a very regal old party. Before we left we were summoned, one by one, to her presence for little audiences, admonitory chats. I like to think she told Dawkins that he should try to cultivate more respect for the Celtic spirit. His most cherished memory of that Irish trip, however, concerned an aged sportsman named Sir Harry Greer, with whom he and Michael stayed on their way back to Dublin. After dinner Sir Harry used to drum very solemnly for hours on a jazz drum to the accompaniment of his grand-daughter's governess on the piano. The recollection of this twenty years afterwards still amused Dawkins so much that he would cry with laughter.

Another euphoric occasion, but belonging to a much later period, was his eightieth birthday. This was after he had broken his thigh, as a result of which he had to have his right leg in irons, could only hobble about on sticks, and suffered a good deal of pain as well as disability and frustration, all of which he bore with stoical fortitude. He was on one of his very rare visits to London and I asked him to have dinner with myself and my wife at a restaurant. I wanted to provide some sort of surprise in the form of an unexpected guest, and I suddenly thought of Wilfred Macartney, who had been a member of Compton Mackenzie's outfit in Greece, and of whom I had heard Dawkins speak with his own special brand of amused interest, though they had not met for more than thirty years. I knew that Macartney's decidedly unusual experiences gave him a special curiosity value in Dawkins's eyes, and that Dawkins, though a Tory of Tories, would always put personal relations above politics. The result was a distinct success. I do not know whether it was due to Dawkins's powers as a *dompteur*, but Macartney behaved beautifully and made one or two nicely timed references to the years between which made Dawkins chortle; the two of them maintained a nice balance between the present and their wartime Levantine reminiscences.

The last time I saw Dawkins was in early March of this year, a few weeks before he died. I went to Oxford to spend the day with him and stay the night. (He had been elected a life Fellow of Exeter and kept on rooms in the college.) It was very cold and there was still snow on the ground. At luncheon I thought, for the first time, that he was beginning to show his age, looking, as the old do look, just a size smaller than his ordinary self. He complained, rather alarmingly, I thought, of having fallen down three times in the snow, but he cursed about it quite cheerfully. By teatime he had perked up consideraby; he is quite ageless, after all, I thought; there is no reason why he should not notch ninety. He was leading as active a mental life as ever. The second volume of his translations of folk tales from the Dodecanese had just been published. He took immense pains over these, and both they, and his earlier translation of the *Cypriot Chronicle of Makhairias*, which was his principal professorial task, read exceedingly well, in English. I pointed out a distinctly Freudian motif running through one of the stories. 'Now surely, Dawkins, you must admit . . .' 'I'll admit nothing. What's Freud got to do with it? Freud didn't invent incest, did he?' He had also just finished a paper for some historical society on Harold Hardrada and the Varangians. And, which delighted him enormously, he had acquired a post-graduate pupil, a most promising young philologist. The pupil came in after dinner. Dawkins treated him with his usual egalitarian courtesy. Presently they were chattering away about some knotty point on the borderline of modern Greek philology and mural scatology. Suddenly Dawkins ducked down, covered his face with his hands, and shook with laughter. Then looking up at me, and pointing at the postgraduate pupil, he squawked: 'Lord! Best pupil I've ever had! I've learnt more modern Greek smut from him than I'd have believed possible.'

Coming from an eighty-three-year-old scholar of international reputation, this remark seems to me a most endearing display of zestful humanism.

Portrait of a Yorkshire Yogi

Dr Alexander Cannon, MD, DPM, Ph.D, MA, FRGS, Kushog Yogi of Northern Thibet, etc., psychiatrist and occultist, of Douglas, Isle of Man, has such an overwhelming presence that for a moment you are inclined to doubt whether he is really there.

Square and stout with a very large head, entirely bald except for patches of greying hair above the ears, he reminds you a little of an outsize Pickwick. His round clean-shaven face is pink but a trifle blotchy; his mouth pursed. He wears an enormous, but literally enormous, wing collar and a vast, but vast, bow tie – the combined effect of which is distinctly hypnotic. Black coat, striped trousers, spats, and the scarlet ribbon of one of the foreign orders of which he is a member – he prefers to be known as 'His Excellency Doctor Sir Alexander Cannon' – complete one of the most striking ensembles in medicine.

Dr Cannon is reticent about his age. 'We Yogis never tell,' he says. 'It is is a cardinal principle that a Yogi is as young as he feels.' He looks as if he were a bit on the wrong side of fifty, which squares with the known facts. Like most middle-aged men of sedentary occupation, he carries rather too much weight. He is a teetotaller, non smoker, and practically a vegetarian, with a hearty appetite for farinaceous foods.

His manner is affable and courteous. He waves you to a heavy carved chair in his long dining-room which, like the rest of his house, is crammed with oriental ornaments, Buddhas, masks, screens, carvings and brasses and little figures innumerable. His mood is one of elation. His voice is powerful in proportion to his physique. He speaks rapidly with a touch of Yorkshire accent, so rapidly that he sometimes mispronounces a word – incredulous for incredible, irreverent for irrelevant.

His talk flows but you could not call him a subtle conver-
sationalist. If it were not for the oriental furniture and the
occultism and that Brobdingnagian collar and tie you might
take him for a Yorkshire business man.

Dr Cannon has been resident in the Isle of Man since 1940,
and has become a well-known figure. His sharpest impact,
however, on the lay public of the entire British Archipelago was
made fifteen years ago, on the morning of Sunday, December
10th, 1933, when readers of the *Sunday Express* found him the
subject of the lead story splashed across three columns on the
front page. Under the headlines:

BLACK MAGIC STORIES
SPELL THAT KILLED
MR JUSTICE
MACARDIE
YOGI MYSTERIES
Man Who Floated Over A Ravine

they read that Dr Cannon had been asked to resign from his
post as a medical officer on the staff of Colney Hatch Mental
Hospital (since rechristened Friern MH), the 'reason given
being the publication of his book *The Invisible Influence*.'

Nobody would deny that *The Invisible Influence* was a strange
book for anyone to have written, as even the most cursory
perusal will demonstrate. The preface claims to bear testimony
to the existence of 'Black Magic ... the real levitation
phenomena . . . with historical evidence of the transportation of
the body from one place to another over incredible distances in
the twinkling of an eye'. In the first chapter the author
describes how on a journey in China 'my usual baggage was
thirty-five large trunks . . . fearing not bandits or robbers . . . as
I had been taught how to cast a spell, and to form an opinion at
a glance; also space was of no consequence to me'. Then comes
a journey to Thibet where the author is greeted by a messenger
of the Lama Convent ... 'the Knight Commander who
brought me the great tidings that I was to be soon honoured
with that highest of titles, Knight Commander of Asia, which is
equal to an earl in this country' – and who had only one arm, his
left arm having been removed by 'a means that could not be
accounted for, humanly speaking', though it is hinted that he

lost it in a struggle with a satanic practitioner of the Left Hand
Path. And finally the trip back starts, in the course of which 'we
should, once more, by the transportation phenomenon, cross
the gulf'.

Dr Cannon immediately appealed to the LCC Staff
Appointments Committee. A Dr David McLeod, described by
The Times as 'a medical specialist', testified to his character and
sincerity and the Roman Catholic priest at Colney Hatch gave
evidence as to the doctor's good work at the hospital. The
appeal was successful. The LCC authorities transferred Dr
Cannon to an equivalent post at Bexley Heath Mental Hospital. Dr David McLeod's wife was reported to have declared to a
press representative that the whole affair had been foretold by a
medium.

The Sunday Dispatch, which had taken over the running of the
story from its rival, triumphantly declared that 'Dr Cannon
had himself talked to the Committee for two hours on magic.
He held them enthralled and convinced them all'. Mr John
Macadam, better known today as a sports writer, wrote a full
page review of *The Invisible Influence* that began: 'Wonders are
simmering in the mind of man, wonders that almost any day
now may flood over and invest the world as we know it with a
new meaning and a new majesty.'

Information about the early life of Alexander Cannon is not
easy to obtain. When questioned, the doctor displays his customary Yoga reticence and takes rapid evasive action in a
good-humoured flow of conversation about hypnotism and
telepathy. He considers personalities to be 'trivial, irreverent, I
mean irrelevant, only of interest to trivial minds'. It is established that he was born in Leeds of Yorkshire middle-class
parentage, that he was educated at a local secondary school
and that his favourite game was cricket. He admits to having
done work of national importance during World War I, and
gives you to understand it was of a scientific nature not uncon-
nected with the invention of the gas mask. He took his medical
degree – MB, Ch.B, – at Leeds in 1924, and his MD, also Leeds,
in 1928. In some editions of the *Medical Directory* he is described
as MA Cant. – an abbreviation of Canton. He is unmarried.

China played a vital part in Alexander Cannon's life. He
went there in the middle twenties to a public appointment in

Hong Kong and stayed several years. He lectured at Hong Kong University and was, according to the *Medical Directory*, 'Alienist and Medical Jurist – High Court of Justice and Government Pathological and Medical Officer in charge of Prisons Hong Kong.'

On returning to England he obtained the post of Medical Officer in the LCC Mental Hospital Service, was appointed to Colney Hatch, and passed the examination for the Diploma in Psychological Medicine. His colleagues in the medical officers' mess at the Hatch often twitted him about his occultist ideas. Cannon remained imperturbably cheerful and self-controlled. He was immensely energetic, spent a lot more time in the wards than most medical officers, and took his duties very seriously.

Part of his immense energy was employed in compiling a textbook entitled *The Principles and Practice of Psychiatry*, for which he had the collaboration of Dr E. D. T. Hayes, MD. Its reception from the medical press was scarcely encouraging.

Cannon, however, was undaunted, his energy undiminished. He was busier than ever – in the wards and with an apparatus of his own invention called the Cannon psychograph, a simple manometer arrangement for indicating respiratory movements on a graph. Inevitably it was hailed by the press as a 'lie detector'. He tried it out on a very different type of occultist, the late Aleister Crowley, who claimed to have the secrets of Yoga breathing. Crowley, an exotic bon viveur with an incurable taste for ether cocktails, had broken training and gave a deplorable performance.

Cannon did not stay long at Bexley Heath. Inside the hospital he was as punctilious as he had been at Colney Hatch. Outside he embarked on more occultist activities. In June 1934 the press published a letter by him to Lord Ampthill, chairman of the Magicians' Circle, in connection with a challenge to perform the Indian Rope Trick. Cannon wrote that he had only offered to perform the Rope Trick in London under certain conditions: 'with the assistance of my Yogi colleagues, provided you are willing to lay down a sufficient sum to enable me to bring over to England and keep there those adepts, and also to bring to England a shipload of special sand, heat the Albert Hall to tropical heat and produce my own lighting.' He also gave a series of tea-time lectures at the Mayfair Hotel. At one of them he put Miss Kira Nijinsky, daughter of the dancer, into a hypnotic state in the hope that she would produce a feat of levitation. Miss Nijinsky executed some noteworthy muscular contractions. Dr Cannon afterwards recorded cheerfully: 'Although levitation did not take place, the body of the girl became raised to a pitch quite unattainable by any gymnastic means.' At another lecture there was a sudden interruption by Mr Aleister Crowley who leapt to his feet to volunteer a correction. The two occultists eyed each other severely for several seconds.

His resignation from Bexley Heath came exactly two years after the Colney Hatch affair. After resigning he set up immediately in practice and soon the *Medical Directory* was listing him as of both 53, Welbeck Street, and 152, Harley Street. He was assisted by two ladies, sisters, Miss Rhonda de Rhonda and Miss Joyce de Rhonda, whose telepathic faculties were employed as an aid to diagnosis. He used hypnotic and suggestion therapy assisted by coloured lighting and music, and static electricity to his heart's content. He took part in further occult demonstrations, one of the most striking being at the Queen's Hall when an Egyptian named Tahra Bey gave a notable performance.

The exodus to the Isle of Man took place in the late summer of 1940. In this massive operation the doctor was assisted by the faithful de Rhonda sisters. How often, as he wrestled with Buddhas, carvings, vases, and figures innumerable must he have longed for the 'transportation phenomenon'. For a time he installed himself in Ballamoar Castle, near Ramsey, but it was commandeered and he found it a tight squeeze to fit all the oriental objects into the new house.

The Isle of Man was a safe area and life was fairly tranquil for the doctor and his entourage. The house could accommodate a few patients – mostly nervous subjects – living in. The electrical equipment – revolving coloured lights, giant Whimshurst machines that produce static, blue sparks, and a strong hygienic smell of ozone, short-wave equipment – was installed in a set of rooms at the back of the house to which the doctor gives the name of 'the Isle of Man Clinic'. 'We split the atom here every day,' he says with a huge chuckle.

A minor worry was the defection – the word is used in a

purely playful sense – of Miss Joyce de Rhonda, who left the doctor's employment to marry an officer in a Scots regiment. Her sister, Miss Rhonda de Rhonda, a plump, handsome, dark-haired girl, carries on and her powers are sometimes displayed at evening demonstrations in the doctor's drawing-room.

The performances at these demonstrations are the subject of typed memos signed by those present. One of them, perhaps the most remarkable, dated December 17th, 1944, includes the following account of a 'materialisation experiment': 'Rhonda's hands were tied tightly with a white handkerchief. After about twenty-five minutes, the lights were turned on and the hand-kerchief, Rhonda's hands, blouse, and part of Mr Kearley's coat were covered with black matter that resembled soot. When her hands were untied, three small figures were found. Later it transpired that one of these figures had come from a shop in South London which had been destroyed by a V2, and it was the only thing in the shop that had not been destroyed. Doctor then woke Rhonda and said we should leave the room within fifteen minutes as all the ether had been used up.' The signatory adds: 'I left more firmly convinced than ever that truth is far, far stranger than fiction.'

And there the matter rests. To visitors, the doctor presents his courteous, benign, self-assured, larger-than-life presence. He is at pains to make it clear that he must, in accordance with the dictates of the General Medical Council, eschew any dis-cussion of his medical work, and confine himself to his work as a scientist and traveller. He proceeds to give what he calls an occult demonstration but what the sceptic would term a display of masterly conjuring tricks.

These include going through a well-shuffled pack of cards and telling the spectator what each card is; telling the numbers of dice placed into the box held behind his back; and blindfold readings. For these last the doctor insists on being enveloped in a large quantity of cotton wool and white towelling. His read-ings are almost invariably correct.

The only times his benign sang-froid becomes at all ruffled is during his demonstrations of hypnotism. He invites you to sit in a chair with your legs extended, rests his thumb on your forehead and attempts to persuade you that you are unable to get up. If you say: 'Oh, but I can!' he exerts considerable pressure and reiterates: 'Oh, no you can't!' But at least on one occasion he was wrong.

Virginia Bath

At home with her animals and spaghetti spoons in Wiltshire, or outstripping the men on an East End pub crawl, Lady Bath still embodies the enigmatic spirit of the Trees.

The Tree family, as I once remarked to Virginia's Aunt Iris, have been lucky in the chromosomal lottery. They inherit brains, beauty, talent, wit and charm. They have what psychiatrists call 'therapeutic personalities', and can tame animals and even men. All these qualities they share with their relations, the trees of the woods. You remember in the New Testament the blind man whom Jesus cured, how he said, 'I see men as trees, walking.' An admirer of the Tree family, especially its distaff side, would adapt this to: 'I see Trees as trees walking.' And indeed they do have a certain slouching, rocking gait that suggests a tree in the wind. Virginia herself sometimes gives you the impression that she is swaying in a gale.

I suppose one has to say that the Marchioness of Bath, wife of Henry, Sixth Marquess of Longleat, in Wiltshire, has a public role, although in her case there is no difference between the public and the private face. What she does is a quite important part of the general stately homes operation that opens Longleat to the public so as to make sure that its upkeep (reckoned to cost around one hundred and twenty-five thousands pounds a year) is maintained. Major attractions like the lions, initiated by Henry Bath and his partner, Jimmy Chipperfield, in 1966, which put Longleat at the head of the Stately Homes' League and turned Ian Bedford temporarily green with envy, are all very well but they need to be flanked by a variety of sideshows. Two of these are Virginia's own contributions. One of them is helping to run Pets' Corner, where there are at present three gibbons, goats, a family of otters who have bred twice, and various exotic birds. Their conditions are excellent. It's no exaggeration to say that making animals happy is one of the things Virginia lives for. She has that veneration for all forms of life which Hindu and Buddhist sages teach, though there is nothing in the least cranky about her, and she is no vegetarian or teetotaller. She refuses to swat wasps and disperses them with a non-toxic spray.

At Job's Mill, where she and Henry live, the pets include Leo, a Rhodesian lion-dog with a fur ridge along his back, said to denote kinship with the hyenas; Bobby, a temperamental white cat, who, although of farm origin, gives himself the airs of a fairy prince; and flocks of doves, bantams and guinea-pigs.

Virginia's other contribution is the Kitchen Shop, which sells an exciting selection of kitchen articles, from spaghetti spoons to miniature cutlery sets.

Virginia is the daughter of Alan Parsons and Viola Tree. Alan was the son of a country clergyman and grandson of an Italian lady. A classical scholar, he went to Eton and Magdalen and became drama critic of the *Daily Mail*. He was also for a time private secretary to Montagu, the Secretary of State for India. Viola Tree was the eldest daughter of Sir Herbert Beerbohm Tree, the famous Edwardian actor-manager whose performances as Svengali and Fagin used to delight our grandfathers. Lady Tree, née Maud Holt, was an actress and a wit. One of her most quoted sayings was: 'I've just seen poor so-and-so' (referring to a notoriously bibulous lady) 'making her way along Piccadilly with all Vine Street in her hair.' As a mother, her guiding principle was that children must be happy at all costs; as a grandmother, she passed it on to her daughters, Viola, Felicity and Iris.

Viola was an actress and a not unsuccessful one, though Virginia thinks she was really a better writer than actress. Her principal book was *Can I Help You?* published by the Hogarth Press in 1937, and based on a column she did for the *Daily Dispatch*. It was certainly very unlike the average column of the time. Here is one entry taken at random from a chapter called 'Manners To Children':

'I keep a mental black book against myself. I take it down and read it in moments of deep night or gloom; the entries on not being fair to children or dogs are perhaps the most flaming and the most tragical.'

It is illustrated with drawings, including a really fine drawing of hyacinths and cyclamens, by the author's daughter, Virginia.

Virginia had private lessons with, first, Duncan Grant, and then William Coldstream. When she was sixteen she went to the Slade. Her life had been peripatetic, subject to the earnings of her parents. One of the best times was when Viola collaborated with Gerald du Maurier to write a play called *The Dancers*, in which Tallulah Bankhead made her West End début. The de Mauriers were great friends of the Parsons. Virginia went to school at Frognal with Jeanne du Maurier. The famous charm of Gerald du Maurier, which some said was put on, was, she says, entirely natural. And the same went for Ivor Novello.

She loved drawing and had a distinct talent. This is borne out by her work and also by what people say of it. I was talking about her to William Coldstream the other day:

'Remember her?' he said. 'I should think I do. Most exquisite creature. All long legs and soft hair behind which she used to hide. She was very shy, you know. Quite unlike her mother in that respect. I went out to a house at Broxbourne they had, and there was Virginia in a swing with those marvellous long legs of hers reaching right up into the sky. I wish she'd gone on with her drawing. Perhaps she'll come back to it.'

Yet more than anything, she loved, and still loves dancing.

When she was seventeen she paid a visit to her uncle, Max Beerbohm, in Rapallo. Max Beerbohm and Sir Herbert Beerbohm Tree were half-brothers, but the relationship was closer than between two ordinary half-brothers because their mothers were sisters.

Virginia stayed three weeks with Max and found him delightful, as witty as she had expected, ageless and full of marvellous stories of the Edwardian stage scene. Max gave her a cartoon which he drew for her, specially captioned, 'The Dandy of 1895 and The Dandy of 1935'.

Virginia's first marriage to David Tennant was sparked off by a party at Augustus John's house at Fordingbridge in the

New Forest. She can't remember who was there precisely, except for Cecil Beaton and some of the Gathorne-Hardy family. David came in late, looking very romantic in a black leather coat. He was at the time married to the actress Hermione Baddeley, but when the break-up finally came the atmosphere was friendly, and relations between Virginia and her step-daughter, Pauline, have become increasingly affectionate over the years.

David Tennant, second son of Lord Glenconner, was a curious fellow. Dark, very good-looking, witty and, in some ways intensely practical – he was an excellent engineer – he had some self-destructive strain. He called himself 'the Crystal Man' as if he was in search of truth and prepared to be seen through himself on the road to it. It was with David that I first met Virginia, in a night-club famous among the pre-war generation, Frisco's, in Frith Street. Frisco was a Negro from Panama, of ageless vitality, who oscillated between London and Paris. My wife and I were very friendly with his trumpeter, Cyril Blake from Trinidad. It was very dark and very hot; Cyril Connolly wrote in Frisco's Visitors' Book: 'The only mixed hammam [Turkish bath] in London'. I teased Virginia about her hair which she then had done in a kind of Yorkshire terrier fringe. It was a part of that shyness which will probably be with her to the end of her days, but it is the shyness of the strong.

After their marriage. David and Virginia lived below the Gargoyle in Dean Street, Soho. Among David's friends were Robin Mount, the gentleman rider, married to Julia Pakenham; and Dick Wyndham, the delightfully eccentric owner of Tickeridge Mill, who was killed reporting the first Arab-Israeli war for, of all papers, the *News of the World*. There was also Ivan Moffat, Virginia's dearly loved cousin, son of her Aunt Iris, Philip Toynbee and the unpredictable John Davenport, who was felled by a bar stool wielded by an unknown hand and carried to the Charing Cross Hospital, where, on coming to, he nearly strangled the night staff.

David's own unpredictability was due to drink. He didn't look like a drunk but he did drink far too much, especially brandy, most dangerous drink of all. Its effect on him was to make him say wounding but often all too true things to people. Sometimes there were repercussions. To the painter, C. W. R.

Nevinson, admittedly a somewhat aggressive person, he said, quite loudly enough for half the Gargoyle to hear: 'The trouble with you, Nevinson, is you're the greatest failure in the history of painting.' Nevinson jumped up and punched him on the nose. It was a fine aquiline nose and the punch made it as crooked as King Valoroso's after Betsinda had crowned him with the warming-pan in *The Rose and the Ring*. Virginia begged him to get a doctor to set it. David shook his head. 'I shall attend to this personally,' he said. He went upstairs, took his nose between his finger and thumb and straightened it.

During the war David was a gunnery instructor for a time, and a very successful one. It was about this time that his friendship with Dylan Thomas began. With Dylan, he could lose whatever self-consciousness he might have possessed and rave and pun to his heart's content in a way that might have embarrassed the more rarefied type of intellectual. I remember one ecstatic evening in about 1943 which began in the Swiss in Old Compton Street with extracts from translations. My own contribution was this, from a mid-Victorian version of Lermontov: 'Oh! Oh! Oh! Ejaculated his interlocutor.'

Virginia loved Dylan, She says he had such lovely manners and was so endearing. She has this poem which he wrote for her in the fly-leaf of one of his books:

'When I was old enough to learn
To kill the flesh and make it burn
I was stern to the skin and I hurt the bone
I would not leave my shame alone.'

Another friend was Anthony Carson, alias Peter Brook, Freiherr von Bork, that delightful and original travel writer and picaresque character whose death came far too soon.

Tennant wasn't the easiest of husbands, yet it was a happy marriage. There are two daughters: Georgia, tall, dark, sensitive and a little wistful, with a very sharp critical sense; and Sabrina, so pretty that she looks as if her rightful habitat was 'under the glassy, cool, translucent wave', like her namesake in *Comus*. Both get on excellently with their stepfather.

The Virginia-Henry marriage was the result of love at second sight. Virginia admits this as far as she was concerned, and I know Henry would admit it too, though I dare say he played his hand with cunning. One of Henry's specialities is pretending to be less bright than he is, which is in fact very bright indeed. In this he reminds of me of the greatest boxer of all time, the Dixie Kid, who used to sham groggy on the ropes and then come back like a stone from catapult. In fact, they took some time before finally deciding to take the plunge. They were married at Warminster Registry Office in July 1953, the witnesses being Henry's sister, Emma, and Virginia's Aunt Felicity, her brother David, and Prudence and Harry Weatherall (one time tennis correspondent of *The Observer*). Relations between Henry's first wife Daphne (née Vivian) now married to Xan Fielding, and Virginia are most friendly. Virginia helped Daphne write her book, *The Rainbow Picnic*, about Virginia's aunt, Iris Tree. Virginia is on excellent terms with her stepsons, Alexander Weymouth and Christopher and Valentine Thynne. Virginia and Henry have one daughter, Silvy, a tall, beautiful girl of fifteen. One of her names is Cerne, in honour of the Giant of Cerne Abbas, that weird hillside monument cut out in the chalk, whose legendary powers of fertility were succesfully tried by her parents.

One of Virginia's favourite amusements on her periodic visits to London is an East End pub crawl, generally conducted by myself. Last time we all set off from the Ritz, with the blessing of the head waiter, Michael Twomey; first stop The Prospect of Whitby in Wapping Wall. At the last moment we were joined by an old friend whom I will call Irish Fox. I had grave doubts as to his stamina but Virginia wouldn't hear of his being discouraged. At The Prospect he stood swaying on the riverside balcony reciting Eliot: 'The barges drift on the turning tide, past Greenwich Reach and the Isle of Dogs.' My suggestion that we should each throw a silver coin as an offering to the river god dismayed the prudent Henry. 'Do you realise that's money you're chucking away? No good can come of that, you know.' 'You can always come back at low tide and pick it up,' Virginia said.

Inside, a three-piece band was playing a very fast arrangement of *Yellow River*. Virginia, with her gift for appreciating the details of people's performances, pointed out the skill of the double bass's fingering:

'What's he got that I haven't got?' said Henry.

'Well, for one thing he's got a double bass.'

At The Grapes in Narrow Street (The Six Jolly Fellowship Porters in *Our Mutual Friend*), where you get a better view of the river, Irish Fox was still in full quote. He tripped up over one line: 'My people, humble people, who expect something for nothing.' He apologized tearfully for the unintentional insult to the proletariat. It should, of course, be 'nothing for nothing'.

On to the Rose and Crown in Pennyfields, kept by Slim Watts and his wife, Queenie, the singer. Slim's barman, Dave, is a staunch Labour supporter. Here we formed a fantasy cabinet in which Count Dracula was Minister for Foreign and Home Affairs, and, of course, Minister of Health.

There was just time for a quick whirl round the Isle of Dogs. My friend Norman left his wife at the dartboard to drive us, because the topography can be very confusing. In one pub a little man was jumping up and down over by the TV set. 'What's he doing?' said Henry. 'He can't be still celebrating the Election. That was weeks ago.'

Norman shook his head. 'That's just his usual way of getting from A to B. His name is James Havehard, commonly known as Jumping Jimmy.'

Back at the Rose and Crown Henry chatted up the Alsatians. He muttered to himself: 'I mustn't show off'. This referred to an earlier expedition, when at the Iron Bridge in Canning Town he had staged a three-cornered tug-of-war, with a dog at each end of his red-spotted handkerchief and himself on all fours. Presently he said he was feeling tired and it was time for a minicab. I suggested Irish Fox should go with him, but was met by a mutinous glare. Leaving the Fox under the care of the experienced Slim, we went to eat in the Chinese restaurant next door. Just before closing time, we opened the door of the saloon bar to see Slim and Dave carrying Irish Fox, about to lay him on a bench. His mouth was wide open and there was blood on his forehead. For a moment I thought he was dead. The compassionate Virginia rushed over to him. 'Not to worry, Virginia,' Slim said. 'He'll be alright. It was my fault, really. I oughtn't to have let him stay on his stool. I didn't serve him any more drink, of course. But when my back was turned he fell off and hit his nut on the brass rail. He's snoring nicely. Give him a half an hour longer and we'll get him a minicab.'

Half an hour later we dropped Irish Fox at his flat and went on to dance at Los Andaluces in Tottenham Court Road. At a quarter to four I dropped Virginia at their hotel and reflected, once again, on the stamina of the Trees. And I remembered that the first time Henry took me round Longleat and drove me about the surrounding countryside, he confessed that he was an ardent tree-lover and liked to put his head against their trunks.

The Burglar as an Old Man

James Ferguson is aged ninety-three and has spent thirty-one of those years in prison. He is England's oldest burglar, or rather ex-burglar, for he insists that he finally retired from his profession last autumn when he was bound over on condition he went to live in a Church Army Hostel.

He is a tiny, little, monkeyish old man, scarcely five feet tall. He had a curly grey beard in which there are still a good many ginger-brown hairs, a large, rather flattish nose, and little deep-set blue eyes. His wrinkled cranium is beautifully domed; if you put a skull-cap on him and tidied him up, he would look like Anatole France.

He has a very high degree of objectivity, one quality which is said to be an attribute of greatness. He talks about himself, the deficiencies of his memory and his legs, this present destitute situation, his long and lawless life, with detachment and no trace of self-pity. This, you feel, is the way an aged and honoured philosopher, on his sheepskin-covered seat on the city wall, might have discoursed to youth of life. It is how James Ferguson discourses from his seat on a bench beside a popping gas fire in the Church Army Hostel in Brighton.

It is impossible for even the most austere to deny that Ferguson has both dignity and charm. Even prison governors have testified to this. Captain Hitch, the officer in charge of the Church Army Hostel, had taken a fancy to him. 'You can't help liking the old fellow,' he says, 'he's got a real way with him. And he's a good mixer too. Gets along well with the others. Never out of temper. Some of these very old 'uns can give you a rare lot of trouble. They're downright nasty to each other at times. But not old James. He's a real good boy, he is. Aren't you, James?'

'That's me,' says Ferguson piously.

James Ferguson was born in 1855 on a farm near Southwick,

in Hampshire. His parents were poor yeomen farmers. Ferguson, a tiny, mischievous, ape-like boy, was village school truant Number One – not so much from a distaste for learning as from a romantic passion for horses. He yearned to be the jockey for which nature seemed to have designed him. At fourteen he ran away from home and was taken on at the Hambledon stables. He worked there for three years as stable-boy. Soon after he was seventeen a licence was taken out for him and he became a professional steeplechase jockey.

Presently he found himself skipping about like some little whiskered marmoset in the golden glowing world of Victorian sport; 'hobnobbing,' as he puts it, 'with the nobbiest of the nobs.' He rode winners for Lord Poulett and General Talbot, and Colonel Fox, the famous boxing referee. He went into horse-coping partnership with a character named George Gale, who kept the Queen's Hotel at Aldershot.

He remembers many details of this glowing period of his life with lingering affection, and talks about it with the sense of values of a gossip writer:

''Nother gent I rode for was a Captain Middleton. Society man he was. You must excuse me mumblin' a bit cos I an't got no teeth, see. They was pinched in a casual ward. This Captain Middleton, he was paid ten thousand pound by Hooley, the financier, to launch him in society. Rare one for society, Hooley was. Middleton was just the chap for him. He used to pilot the Empress of Austria out huntin'.' He paused. 'Friend of old Teddy's, he was,' he said, referring to King Edward VII. 'Rare sport, old Teddy, and not a bit proud. Very good to jockeys he was too. "Put not your trust in princes," they tell you, but a jock could always trust Teddy.'

It takes time to stop Ferguson once he is embarked on his court period. He is abetted in this by Captain Hitch, who takes a personal pride in his charge's exalted connections, and likes to divert his attention from crime.

It was shortly after riding for Captain Middleton that the débâcle came. The exact date is difficult to determine, but it seems to have been in the late eighteen-eighties, because Ferguson is positive that the sharp prison sentence he received in 1899 was not his first.

Ferguson was now married and had four children. He was

doing well in an irregular way. He was due to ride a horse called Harkaway in a steeplechase at Cheltenham. Harkaway, a fine, big jumping Irish horse, was owned by two stockbrokers and started a heavy odds-on favourite. Just before the race the stockbrokers gave Ferguson instructions that Harkaway was on no account to win. 'Fine horse he was, too. It seemed a shame.'

He was such a fine horse that Ferguson had a job to stop him winning. He pulled him so hard at the water jump that he brought half the field crashing down on top of him. There was an inquiry and James Ferguson's licence was taken away. He went to Ireland and rode for the officers at the Curragh; but there wasn't much money in it. When he came back to England he was definitely on the crook.

At this point Ferguson extends a long-fingered apish paw, cocks a thumb at the ceiling and chuckles:

'Seein' as how I was light o' foot and light o' finger,' he says, 'I went where many an ex-jock has been afore me – "up the pipe".'

After that his life was to be a rhythmical series of burglaries and sentences, with a few months' fun, racing and horse-coping in between.

He is not certain now which was his first large-scale burglary, but he thinks it was a 'nice cosy little crib' near Epsom, always a favourite resort of his. He got away with it that time and popped the swag with a fence in Aldershot. Soon afterwards he got what he calls his first real sentence – quite a sharp little touch-up of three years' hard, caught red-handed breaking into a house near Taplow. 'Trouble was I was a bit boozed, see, or I'd never have made such a ruddy noise.'

It is surprising to learn that Ferguson is a bottle-man at all. His skin is smooth, his little blue eyes are bright and clear, and his hands steady. The flesh of his ninety-three-year-old nose is firm and there are no broken veins, like the red ink rivers on a schoolboy's map, on its sides. He doesn't look as if he'd ever touched a drop.

'Lor' bless you,' he says, 'I was one of the biggest boozers for me size in Britain. Still am, if I get the chance. Took to it extra special when I notched me seventieth birthday. That was when I stopped going up the pipe. I could drink anyone under the

table. I'd sit up in the boozer, straight as a poker, tossing back
first beer then whisky and not blink an eyelid. I wouldn't feel
any effects until I was half a mile on the way home. Then all of a
sudden the earth would up and cop me one. Oh yes, many's the
lagging I got through booze.'

He attributes the worst lagging he ever got partly to booze
and partly to the late Mr Justice Grantham – ' 'e was mustard,
a real perisher' – who sentenced him to ten years for burgling a
house at Box Hill in 1905. Ferguson was caught in Aldershot
disposing of the swag. 'I was so boozed I took it to the wrong
jeweller's shop. Bit o' bad that was.'

Another misfortune which Ferguson declares was responsible for several years of his prison life was his adoption of the
nom de guerre of Gray. 'If it hadn't have been for that, the
coppers'd never pinned half what they did on me.'

He took all the obvious 'security' precautions, burgled alone,
distrusting 'a mate who may either nark on yer or hold back
some of the stuff'; but sentences fell thick and fast. It was not
until many years after that he discovered that there were two
other burglars named Gray, brothers, and he swears that he
served at least ten years that ought in equity to have been
theirs.

He dated his most successful burglary shortly after the turn
of the century. Ferguson had been out of prison for some weeks
and was sunning himself on the turf – in the silver ring at
Newmarket – when he was approached by one of his racing
friends who offered to put him in the way of a real bit of good. It
appeared that an eccentric swell, a colonel according to Ferguson, was in deep with the book-makers, and his father refused
to give him another penny. The swell's idea was that one
of the boys, briefed by him, should burgle his father's house.
Ferguson agreed to do the job. The evening was a brilliant
success. He got away with thousands of pounds worth of jewel-
lery and a valuable collection of coins which the colonel sold to
America.

'You don't,' says Ferguson wistfully, 'get jobs like that nowadays.' But one of his chief criticisms of the electronic age is
levelled against the austerity of its interior decoration, and the
decline in the vogue for small solid silver or gold ornaments,
easily portable, easily melted down and disposed of. 'I've been

in drawing-rooms what had half-a-dozen glass cases packed with the stuff. Don't get that nowadays, I can tell you.'

The Scrubs, Pentonville, Maidstone, Dartmoor, Parkhurst, Chelmsford, Oxford, Bedford . . . Ferguson knows these and several more prisons like the palm of his hand. The only convict prison he has never visited is The Bill, which is reserved for men in A1 physical condition. He did not measure up to this on account of his ribs which have been broken so often steeplechasing. His favourite prison governor was Marriott of Chelmsford. 'To show you what a sport he was, once I was with a bundle of lags being transferred from the Moor to Parkhurst, and Marriott, quite by chance, got into the same train at Exeter. "Hullo," he says, "convicts, eh?" You'd have thought he'd have had enough of convicts, but not he. He pokes his head round our carriage door. "Any of my boys here?" he says. "Any Chelmsford boys?" Right pleased to see me he was. Gave me a cigar.'

He nurses a long-standing grudge against the governor of Bedford Gaol, the circumstances of which throw a certain amount of light on Ferguson's eighth decade.

He had just finally relinquished the joys of going up the pipe, and was in Bedford on the look-out for a nice, cosy, ground floor crib to crack. He found it on the Sunday the papers carried the story of the Dartmoor Mutiny, and spent a happy evening in a boozer, making caustic remarks to local crooks about the namby pamby habits of the modern lag as compared with the much tougher generation before 1914.

But the crib proved less cosy than it looked, and on Monday morning Jimmy awoke in Bedford Gaol. His Sunday newspaper, containing a full account of the Mutiny, had been taken away from him, and no amount of appealing to the governor could get it back. The librarian's offer of a work by an illustrious former occupant of Bedford Gaol, named Bunyan, was met with contempt. 'Must have been soft', is Jimmy's comment on the author of *The Holy War* and *Pilgrim's Progress*; 'why 'e went and got lagged without even being on the crook.'

Time in. Time out. Time flies. Ferguson was in Parkhurst for the Boer War and on the Moor for most of World War 1. He was back again in Parkhurst for some of World War 2. His wife was dead long ago. Two of his children were dead for certain. A third he has lost touch with. The fourth he thinks emigrated to Australia. And still he went on cracking cosy little cribs and bragging to the younger generation in flash kens and boozers, and still the treacherous earth would rise up and hit him over the head as he shuffled home. One night in 1939 he was bragging to anyone who would listen to him in a pub near King's Cross, a haunt of one of the racecourse gangs. Ferguson never did like racecourse gangs. 'Nasty low lot. They'll try and do you even when they know you. Stick at nothing, they don't.' He was not only bragging; he was flashing his money about. Some of the boys followed him out of the boozer and 'blow me if they didn't try and do me in the public convenience.'

To be attacked at the age of eighty-four by half-a-dozen members of a racecourse gang late at night in a public lava-tory. . . The predicament is perhaps worth relating. 'A tougher spot than any Dick Barton was ever in,' says Ferguson. He lashed out with his stick and hollered blue murder; the racecourse gang took to its heels.

The Church Army Hostel, where he had fetched up by arrangement with the governor of Oxford Prison, is a cheerful place, not in the least institutional, and he likes it. He shares a dormitory with four other men and can come in and go out as he pleases. At first he was a little embarrassed by the newspaper publicity he'd had, and he was upset when people recognised him in the street, but he's got over that. He goes to the cinema in the afternoon, but his greatest excitement is to come when Brighton Races are held. He chose the Church Army Home at Brighton specially on account of the races. He talks gaily of expeditions farther afield, to race meetings all over Sussex.

Ferguson is now drawing his full old-age pension, for which he was been eligible for over twenty years. But up till now he has never claimed it; just as he has never claimed his ration card or his identity card. In addition to being the oldest bur-glar, he is also the oldest butterfly in Britain.

The Church Army takes 27s 6d a week, for which they house, clothe and feed him. His only complaints: that he can't get a pair of shoes to fit his very small feet, and he wants stronger spectacles for reading. Otherwise he is reasonably contented. He says, 'I don't suppose I ever robbed anyone who wasn't insured, and I never used no violence. I don't hold with that and 'twouldn't have been much use, me being such a little 'un, anyway, Yes, I done thirty-one years' time, but I've had some fun, and I'm ninety-three and still livin', though I don't think me legs is going to carry me much longer. But I ain't grumblin'. What's the use?'

To which there does not really seem to be much to add.

Pseudologia Fantastica – Munchausen Syndrome

Some of the oddest freaks in the museum of literature come from that tenuous borderland where satire and fantasy merge with nonsense. Among the oddest of all is the Munchausen cycle. Everything about it is odd; its origins, its affinities which range in every direction from Lucian to surrealism, its amazing popularity. How a booklet of forty-five pages, written in English by a fugitive German savant who used as sources medieval and Renaissance *facetiae* and the after-dinner stories of a live eighteenth-century sportsman, was added to by publishers' hacks until it became a kind of intellectual folk-myth – how it was translated into many languages and reprinted in edition after edition – makes almost as unlikely a story as any told by the Baron himself.

Munchausen's adventures, as Mr Carswell points out in his valuable introduction to this, the first definitive edition,* have rather more merit as satire and social commentary than is generally attributed to them. The secret of their popularity, however, is to be sought in the domain of nonsense. Successful nonsense communicates to the reader a peculiar sense of release and exhilaration, as if a spark had flashed painlessly across a gap in the brain. Sparks are plentiful in the Munchausen ambit. The mood is one of exuberant megalomania. The Baron triumphs over the impossible by a crackling flight of ideas. The short circuit of wish-fulfilment on which he relies is as crudely ingenious as a schoolboy's 'wheeze'. It derives from a primitive part of the mind where ideas are indistinguishable from actions, and to which all kinds of tall stories and absurdities appeal, from the grotesque, Rabelaisian corporeal fantasy, to the specialized lie of aggrandisement by which loyal Texans

* R. E. Raspe and Others: *Singular Travels, Campaigns and Adventures of Baron Munchausen*. With an Introduction by John Carswell (Cresset Press).

used to express their local patriotism, and which has a department to itself in American folk-lore.

The original Baron, Hieronymus Karl Friedrich von Munchausen, with whom Rudolf Erich Raspe, the creator of the Munchausen cycle, seems to have had at any rate a slight acquaintance, had served in Russia and taken part in the cavalry charge which captured Oczakov. In 1750 he retired to his estates on the Weser, where he hunted and entertained and became locally renowned for keeping the table in a roar by telling, with a dead straight face, the most fantastically impossible stories. In 1785, when the first edition of Raspe's booklet *Marvellous Travels and Campaigns in Russia* appeared, he was sixty-five. The experience of becoming internationally famous in his own lifetime as a fabulous figure, with sightseers who had read about him in Burger's German translation peering through his park gates, had a most distressing effect on the genial old gentleman. He became touchy and morose, like some crusted club character, who enjoys being regarded as a buffoon by his own intimate circle but bridles indignantly at the laughter of strangers. He never recovered from his fame, and the rest of his life was spent trying to live down the legend.

In the Baron as he appears in Raspe's original version there is a perceptible strain of sadism, which has become rather more apparent now that Mr Carswell has purged the text. He flogs a fox out of its skin, explodes a bear, and generally behaves like a surrealist on the rampage. His fur coat, after an encounter with a mad dog, catches the infection and begins to assault the rest of his wardrobe. This vein of 'light-hearted malevolence', as Mr Carswell calls it, which reminds us of the chattering antics of a gifted ape, is the personal contribution of Raspe himself, the brilliant failure who chose for his hero in fantasy Munchausen, 'the fabulously successful man of action'. It is to him, then, as the creator of the saga and the source of its mood, that we must turn for the other half of the Baron's basis in reality. Mr Carswell provides us with much the most careful account of him that has yet appeared in English.

Like so many writers, Raspe had a remarkable intellect. That is perhaps the first thing to be said about him. But for an unfortunate taint of apish delinquency, and the feckless, overweening conceit that was its counterpart, he might easily have acquired a solid European reputation and have died a much respected scientist and man of letters, a bright luminary in the academic constellation. Born in Hanover in 1737, the son of an accountant in the Department of Mines, he went to Göttingen University. A scientist and antiquarian, his reading was very wide, his versatility quite formidable. The subjects of his published works include Volcanic Geology, Leibniz as a Mathematician, an Introduction to *Percy's Reliques* and a study of Ossian that turned out to be one of the pioneer works of the Gothic Revival in Germany. Raspe could not complain that his talents were neglected by authority; he had only himself to blame for the catastrophe that was to ruin his academic career. He became Secretary of the Hanover State Library; then, in 1767, he was appointed Councillor, Professor of Antiquity and Keeper of the Collections to Frederick II, Landgrave of Hesse Cassel, and was made a Fellow of the Royal Society of London. The position at Cassel and the salary it carried may not have been dazzling, but it was a sinecure from which a man of talent could work as, and at what, he pleased, and could safely plan the next step in his career. Instead of regarding it as a niche, Raspe proceeded to behave as if he had attained the pinnacle of fame. His projects and energy were frantic, grandiose. Even so, if only he could have kept out of debt, or at least kept his debts within reasonable bounds, all might yet have been well, and the darts of the many enemies whom he made by his sharp wit and strident vanity, and who banded together against him under the motto of 'Brekekekex,' would have rebounded harmlessly from his leathery ego. But as creditors kept on pressing, Raspe took to embezzlement as the only way of settling with them. In 1774 it was discovered that for the past four years he had been selling *objets d'art* from Cassel Museum. A servile appeal for mercy to the Landgrave had no effect. Presently a police notice was circulated throughout northern Germany requesting the apprehension of 'Councillor Raspe, born of Hanover, of middle height, face long rather than round, small eyes, nose somewhat large, beaky and pointed, red hair under a short stumpy periwig, wearing a red coat with gold facings . . . walks in general rather hastily.'

From Holland, where he first fled, Raspe crossed to England. He arrived in the autumn of 1775, penniless and bedraggled, like some dilapidated jackdaw who has just managed to stagger through the pattern of the farmer's gunshot. News of his depredations soon followed, and he was expelled from The Royal Society, in whose patronage he had placed great hopes. He made a partial recovery as an academic hack and, owing to the influence of the Bishop of Peterborough and others, including Dr Lort, Mrs Thrale's Cambridge friend, he was 'given the entrée to Trinity College Combination Room'. No doubt, as Mr Carswell opines, his Cambridge visits were among the happiest times of his stay in England. But there were some unpleasant incidents. Once 'an angry professor had him turned out of his favourite coffee house; and the university librarian watched him narrowly as he experimented with the pigments of the mummy cases and transcribed manuscripts'.

Horace Walpole tentatively extended a little patronage, but withdrew it again when Raspe, sinking deeper into difficulties, was arrested by a tailor. He struggled on as a hack for two years more. Then, when he seemed to be reaching the end of his tether, he was taken up by Matthew Boulton, the Birmingham iron magnate, partner of James Watt and one of the founders of the Birmingham Lunar Society. Boulton installed him as master of an assay office at Entral, near Camborne, and kept him more or less regularly employed for the rest of his life. It was in Cornwall, during a few idle summer evenings, that he wrote *Munchausen*, which was first issued from Oxford in 1785. He wrote it in English, of which language he had become almost a master. As evidence of the Cornish background, Mr Carswell draws attention to some interesting little points in the text. There is the 'evening hymn' played by the frozen post-horn when it is thawed by the fire, 'which may have originally come to the exile from the miners' chapel close to his lodgings'. (The story of the horn itself first appears in Castiglione's *Courtier*.) And there are the references to the 'otherwise incomprehensible slopes', or stopes, by which Munchausen, after falling from the moon, digs himself out of the hole 'nine fathoms under grass', the latter being a term peculiar to Cornish miners.

Soon after writing *Munchausen* Raspe left Cornwall for London, where, from lodgings in Air Street, he acted as 'scout and industrial counterspy' for Boulton. He compiled an immense catalogue of jewels for James Tassie, the modeller, a task that must have had some painful associations. He also made a mineralogical tour of Western Scotland, where one of his projects was an Argyll Marble Company and where, Mr Carswell suggests, his curious personality may have left an impression which Scott made use of for the character of Herman Dousterwivel in *The Antiquary*. An aura of mystery and uncertainty surrounds all his doings at this period, but there appears to be no truth in the rumours that he acted as a kind of mineralogical confidence-trickster. He died in 1793, aged only fifty-six, from scarlet fever caught at Muckross, in Donegal where he had gone, with his usual maniacal optimism, to prospect for coal. We leave him, in Mr Carswell's words, 'a stumbling, lonely but talented figure, fawning still, but with a jauntiness which had its roots in a profound consciousness of his intelligence and abilities'.

The text of *Munchausen's Travels*, as usually reprinted, is, as Mr Carswell shows, 'the product of a long tradition of revision and improvisation'. Its history is a bibliographical maze. Raspe himself was the author of less than a sixth-part of what is printed in this edition, which takes the canon up to the end of the eighteenth century. He had some hand in the authorship of the second instalment, *The Sea Adventures*, produced by a London publisher named Smith. In these the Baron begins by embarking at Portsmouth for North America, is stranded on a whale's back and, later, a tree, then returns to his Turkish experiences, and eventually takes off, significantly from Cornwall, in a balloon. Another Baron, De Trott, founded on a well-known French Hussar adventurer, is introduced, partly as a foil to Munchausen, partly as a vehicle for an attack on the Pope and the Catholic Church. In 1786 Kearsley, formerly the publisher of Wilkes, took over from Smith and set his hacks to produce a new instalment. This appeared tacked on to the next edition, entitled *Gulliver Revived*, and contained topical episodes ridiculing Lord Mulgrave, the Polar explorer, and the balloonists Blanchard and Lunardi. Later editions from the same firm made use of Brydone's *Travels in Sicily* and the *Travels of Captain Hamilton*, and finally lapsed into outright plagiarism from Lucian and Sindbad. At this time all traces of Raspe's original characterization had long since disappeared in a pother of flowery Augustan journalese; and, not content with their inventions, the hacks had revised and somewhat devitalized the staccato style of Raspe's original fragment.

Meanwhile another publishing house, Symonds, had made use of Munchausen in order to ridicule Bruce, the remarkable and perfectly genuine Abyssinian explorer, by producing *A Sequel To The Adventures of Baron Munchausen*. This instalment, which Mr Carswell prints at the end of his edition, was the work of a single author with a sophisticated taste for the rococo and literary pastiche. He introduces characters such as the Lady Fragrantia and a courtier, the noble Hilaro Frosticos. Don Quixote appears and is persecuted by frogs in a passage that burlesques the Miltonic organ. There is also an amusing skit on Sterne.

Mr Carswell's purpose as editor has been to arrange the text so as to 'preserve the continuity of the narrative while using the earliest text available for each portion of it'. One of the results of his scholarship is that the first and second sections, Raspe's original text and the Raspe-Smith second instalment, *The Sea Adventures*, now appear uncorrupted for the first time in English since their original publication.

Any selection from the additions to the adventures, made by the various translators, into other languages would involve incalculable labour, though it would almost certainly yield some entertaining results. Munchausen, as has been remarked, has affinities in every direction. When Raspe's original authorship was still undisclosed, Southey, in his *Omniana*, suggested a Portuguese origin for the saga. One additional anecdote, which appeared in a German version that was used as a first reader for schools, may be recalled. The Baron, in Poland, dines at an officers' mess, and is challenged to a drinking bout by a veteran Prussian major, unbelievably battle-scarred. He accepts, thinking it will be easy to drink the poor crock under the table in no time. But the major quaffs flagon after flagon of brandy and Munchausen's head begins to sing ominously. He notices that the major pauses between drinks to raise his hat slightly. Suspecting a ruse, he stumbles and knocks off the veteran's hat and wig. He discovers that the major, as the result of one of his innumerable wounds, has been trephined and wears a silver plate on his skull. Every time he raises his hat he lifts his wig and with it the plate, thus allowing the brandy fumes to escape from his brain. There is something very Teutonic about this rather ponderous little absurdity, but what distinguishes it from an original Raspe anecdote is the fact that it is the Baron who is put at a disadvantage. That Raspe would never have allowed. The distinction between a genuine Raspe story and an imitation is plain enough even when he himself is borrowing wholesale. Take, for instance, his use of the familiar Beanstalk, which he prefaces by a typically nonsensical incongruity about two bears chasing a bee for its honey.

It remains to say something about the illustrations. The Baron has been depicted by various hands, including, it is said, that of Raspe himself; by Rowlandson, the brothers Cruikshank, and – in a French version 'liberally expanded' by Théophile Gautier – by Doré. In an English edition of the nineties he even appeared in Bearsleyish guise. It is a pity that Mr Wood's woodcuts to this admirable edition, though attractive pieces of decoration, should so completely miss the malevolent, sparkish element which is essential to the whole conception and should present us with an insipid little puppet suitable only for a Christmas card.

Luncheon with Beast 666

I have never been able to understand how anyone in his right mind could begin to take Aleister Crowley seriously. I had seen him several times over the years; and had heard his strange, rather cockneyfied nasal voice in bars, intoning, 'Triple absinthe, please', when asked what he would have to drink; and once, at the Eiffel Tower, saying to Stulik, the proprietor, 'I trust Lady Dean Paul hasn't been putting cocaine into your soup today'. But I did not meet him until 1939.

I had written a review of some Soho rapscallion's autobiography, Ironfoot Jack, I think, he was called, and ended it by saying: 'He reminds one of a more agreeable Aleister Crowley in a minor way of business.' Crowley wrote on his phallic-headed writing paper to protest: 'Perhaps in future before you pass animadversions on my character you will take the trouble to make my acquaintance.' I thought this was fair enough and telephoned him. He seemed pleased, and asked me to luncheon. 'I shall not be too hard on you, Mr Richardson.'

He was living in a furnished flat high up in a house on the borderland between Pimlico and Belgravia. He opened the door himself. He was wearing a suit of green plus-fours and an enormous tartan bow tie. It was an ensemble that suggested the music-hall stage rather than the golf course, but I made the appropriate comment. 'I used to be plus 4 at Hoylake', he said. It was typical of him to overdo it. If he had said his handicap was 4, I might have believed it, knowing that he had his sporting side, and I would have been impressed. But plus 4 at Hoylake was altogether too much.

Crowley was sixty-four. His once athletic physique had become blurred by fat. He was bald as a stone, and his huge expanse of naked hairless yellowish face was faintly suggestive of an enormous penis, which is no doubt why the adjective 'obscene' has often been applied to it. His eyes protruded like gooseberries. The only comparable eyes I have seen were those of J. L. Garvin, the formidable editor of *The Observer*. It was difficult not to keep staring at them, though the hypnotic effect clashed with the tartan bow tie.

He poured me out a large glass of vodka and turned on the gas fire, one of those self-lighting ones. 'Magick', he said, as it popped into flame. 'Is not that magick, Mr Richardson?' He pronounced 'magick' with the 'k' at the end. He made little jokes about magick all through lunch. I think he had taken my measure as a rationalist sceptic, not to be conned by mumbo-jumbo, but capable of being charmed by jocular eccentricity.

Luncheon was brought in after several more glasses of vodka by his housekeeper, a Scots lady so indeterminate as to age, status, and nubility that she seemed like one of those anthropological reconstructions with 'conjectural parts in black.'

'Kathy, say Will with me', said Crowley. He began to recite his well-known slogan, 'Do What Thou Wilt Shall Be The Whole Of The Law. Love Is The Law, Love Under Will.' I joined in politely. 'Hurry up, Aleister,' said Kathy, 'the potatoes will be burnt.'

The first course was a lobster bisque. Pointing to the scarlet tip of a crustacean appendage sticking up out of the beige soup, Crowley said: 'Looks like a devil roasting in hell, does it not, Mr Richardson?'

The diabolical bisque was followed by roast duck, then a deliquescent brie. We drank several litres of tolerable white chianti. Kathy brought coffee, Jamaica Blue Mountain, which Crowley made in a Cona with much muttering and incantation for my benefit, a bottle of Cyprus brandy that would take the shell off an egg, and strong black Mexican cigars.

I can't recall the conversation in any detail. Crowley spoke slowly with long pauses in between sentences, words, even syllables. I distinctly remember him saying that D. H. Lawrence knew nothing about women because he was homosexual and that Freud knew even less. Getting back to magick, he said it was his duty to protect the gullible, the oh so gullible public, from the depredations of rival occultists like Major Yeats Brown and Dr Alexander Cannon. I wanted to clap. At some time or other I know I started on a diatribe about fear being the root of all evil.

It was five o'clock and we had drunk a great deal of brandy. Crowley for me was now just a benevolent old freak. I said how much I had enjoyed myself and I was sorry to have animadverted on his character. There was just one thing, said Crowley: could I, would I, do him a great personal favour and write him a little note of apology? He handed me a writing-block and his fountain pen, which was inscribed 'Baphomet' in gilt lettering. I found I was too drunk to write. 'Mr Crowley', I said, 'your hospitality has overwhelmed me.'

In that case, said Crowley, since it had been such a happy encounter could we repeat it in a week's time? I said I should be delighted and made my way unsteadily down the stairs.

I had every intention of writing Crowley some sort of apology but a knowledgeable friend forewarned me. 'For heaven's sake,' he said, 'how can you be such a mug? If you write any apology for what you said in print, that's admitting liability. He'll take it to a solicitor and he'll bung in a writ. They won't get much, of course, probably settle out of court for a couple of hundred, but it won't do you any good with your paper. That's what the lunch was all about.'

At the next lunch there was another guest, Gerald Hamilton, famous as the original Isherwood's Mr Norris. He and Crowley were old friends. They had lived in the same house in Berlin. Hamilton told me later that they had each been paid some very small sum by British Intelligence for reporting on each other's activities. This was the first time I had met Hamilton, though I had heard about him and knew him by sight. His appearance, with another bald head and naked face of quite exceptional ugliness, was as unforgettable as Crowley's. I suppose he was there in the role of consultant con man.

Vodka, food, wine and brandy were as profuse as before. Hamilton paid elaborate compliments to Kathy and her cooking. Crowley brought up the subject of Berlin and *Mr Norris Changes Trains*. He assured me that 'the real Mr Norris, my dear Mr Richardson, is a far more vicious person. Now, if I were a real magician, I would be able to produce him for you at this table, would I not?' Hamilton muttered nervously. I did not let on that I knew.

We went on drinking brandy until late in the afternoon. Again I was asked to write a note of apology, and Baphomet and the writing-block were produced. Again I pleaded intoxication. I saw Hamilton shaking his head. 'But next time, Mr Crowley', I said, 'you must have lunch with me.'

I had arranged to meet Crowley at the York Minster in Dean Street. He arrived, preceded by an overpowering smell as of an old-fashioned operating theatre. This, he told me, was his daily eye-opener, half a pint of ether. He was dressed like a duke in a musical comedy in swallow-tail coat and sponge-bag trousers. Asked what he would drink, he answered automatically: 'Triple absinthe, please.'

It was summer and war was getting very near. Various dug-outs from the Kaiser's war were starting to appear unexpectedly. One of these, a genial naval captain in uniform, greeted Crowley: 'Aleister, old top! I haven't seen you since the days of the Ragged Ragtime Girls!' These, I learnt, were a troupe of English violinists and dancers, whom Crowley had managed on a tour of Tsarist Russia in 1914. They opened up vistas of an improbable swinging Crowley phase.

Two more triple absinthes followed the first. At luncheon in the Escargot he ate three dozen snails, wild duck pie, and camembert, drank a bottle of burgundy and several brandies. The cigars weren't strong enough and a waiter had to be sent out for his favourite black Mexicans. We parted on the friendliest terms, and that was the last I saw of him. Once by way of a Christmas card he sent me a book entitled *Little Essays Towards Truth* by 'Baphomet'. I found it incomprehensible. I did not know then that Crowley had been a heroin addict for some time and was on the Home Office list. He was to survive on his customary diet of rich food, large quantities of the strongest possible drink and tobacco, and dangerous drugs galore, to the age of seventy-three. His physique must have been exceptional. And here, I am convinced, lies an important part of the explanation of the Crowley phenomenon, that curious combination of manic paranoid charlatan and mystic mountebank. Crowley was a perfect example of what the American typologist William Sheldon calls over-endowment, both physical and temperamental. He was carrying too heavy a load. As for his blood stream . . .

Another aspect of Crowley, which people are apt to overlook, is that when you got used to his eccentricities, and so long as you were not impressed by his mystical pretensions, he was apt to become a fearful bore. He had no capacity for selection, no notion of when to stop. How sinister was he? Obviously he would con a mug, pluck a pigeon. He treated those unfortunate consorts of his, the Scarlet Women, abominably. He is said to have had a nasty streak of cruelty. Isherwood told me a story of Crowley in a Berlin night club gratuitously raking a boy's chest with his talons. I can only say I found him quite amiable. I have never believed in his magical powers, even though I did once hear Nina Hamnett, a fairly hard-headed person in most respects, warn a young man: 'You be very careful if you have anything to do with AC, my dear. He once made fire come out of my studio floor, my dear.'

Somerset Maugham met Crowley, as he explains in his introduction to later editions of *The Magician*,* which was first published in 1908, in Paris in 1897. Crowley was then twenty-five. He was introduced to him at a restaurant in Montparnasse by Gerald Kelly, whose unfortunate sister, Rose, Crowley later married. Maugham took an immediate dislike to him, but gave him credit for being a man of parts: first-class mountaineer, champion chess and whist player. 'He was a fake but not entirely a fake.' He dismisses his poetry, quite rightly, as inferior imitation Swinburne. He does not mention Crowley's short stories. Some of these had merit. One in particular about the daughter of a puritan evangelical bank clerk who brought home from her art class a statuette of the Venus de Milo with appalling consequences, is extremely funny.

After their Paris meetings Maugham saw no more of Crowley, though years later he got a telegram from him: 'Mother of God and I starving. Aleister Crowley.' When *The Magician*, in which Crowley figures under the name of Oliver Haddo, appeared, Crowley reviewed it in *Vanity Fair* and signed his review 'Oliver Haddo.'

The style of *The Magician* is apt to be, as Maugham himself says, 'lush and turgid with many more adjectives and adverbs than I should use today'. You can detect the influence of his

* W. Somerset Maugham: *The Magician* (Heinemann, *hardback*; Pan Books, *paperback*).

master, Maupassant, of course, but there is a profuse inlay of ninetyish romanticism. What does surprise one, is that he should have given his chief character supernatural powers, so that what might have been an interesting case history turns into an occult shocker, and a crude one at that.

Oliver Haddo is very closely modelled on Crowley; almost the only physical difference is that he is much taller. Otherwise he is Crowley to the life, though viewed sensationally. His clean-shaven face has 'a disconcerting nudity', also 'the look of a very wicked sensual priest'. His glance is 'uncanny' and 'looks straight through you'.

Another strange thing about him was the impossibility of telling whether he was serious. There was a mockery in that queer glance, a sardonic smile upon the mouth which made you hesitate how to take his outrageous utterances. It was irritating to be uncertain whether, while you were laughing at him, he was not really enjoying a joke at your expense.

At the beginning of the book, Haddo is an entertaining grotesque. He insists on ordering his dinner backwards, tells a preposterous and typically Crowleyan story about his lion-shooting exploits. Soon, however, his magical powers assert themselves. At a fair, he is bitten by a snake-charmer's viper; he mutters an incantation over his wrist and comes to no harm. A foil to Haddo is Dr Porhoet, a benign student of magic and the occult who acts as a kind of chorus. Maugham must have done a lot of reading, for he covers the whole field very thoroughly from Paracelsus to Eliphas Levi.

The plot turns on Oliver Haddo's revenge on Arthur Burdon, a young surgeon engaged to Margaret, an English art student who finds Haddo infinitely repulsive. When her dog bites Haddo, instead of muttering incantations, he kicks it savagely. Arthur knocks him down. Haddo gives him a look of 'inhuman malignancy, satanic hatred', but he apologizes for kicking the dog and slinks away.

Next day Haddo pretends to have a fainting fit outside Margaret's flat. She takes him in and he proceeds to put a spell on her, beginning with a recitation from Pater. She becomes his slave and starts using strong acrid oriental scent. 'It was as though fiends of hell were taking revenge on her loveliness by inspring in her a passion for this monstrous creature. She trembled with the intensity of her desire.' A few days later she elopes with Haddo.

After this the story starts to collapse. Margaret tries to break away from Haddo, and is helped by the faithful Arthur, but Haddo lures her back. She dies mysteriously. Finally, Arthur, Dr Porhoet and Margaret's friend Susie break into Haddo's country house in England, taking various occultist precautions. They find Oliver Haddo strangled, and several bottles full of homunculi in various stages of atrocious liveliness. 'Was it for these vile monstrosities that Margaret was sacrificed in all her loveliness?', asks Arthur, before setting fire to the house. I suppose you could say that the last laugh was with Crowley for inspiring Maugham to write such rubbish.

Incidentally, I wonder what has become of little Aleister Akhnaton Crowley? I remember, now, that Crowley showed me with paternal pride a photograph of this infant at our first luncheon. He was sitting on a rock at Mousehole. He should be thirty-nine today, an age of significant mystical potency, I believe.

Portrait of the Wrestler as a Philosopher

At seventy-two, George Hackenschmidt looks a very solid fifty. But for the lumbago which has curtailed his morning jump, standing, over two chairs, and which, from time to time, contorts his large, russety slavonic face with twinges of pain, he would probably look much younger.

Today, Hackenschmidt is five feet, nine and a half inches tall, and weighs sixteen stone; but there is very little fat on him. The hands with which the Russian Lion tied into knots such giants as Paul Pons and Ahmed Madrali are still like a pair of machine tools. A natural born ascetic, Hackenschmidt has lived almost the whole of his life in training. He is a teetotaller and a non-smoker. The only cigarette he ever smoked put him flat on his back after a few puffs. At the height of his wrestling career he was a considerable meat eater, his idea of a light snack before dinner was a steak and half a dozen eggs. But he always eschewed tinned foods. For many years now he has been a strict vegetarian. At present his staple diet is the apple. He munches about fifty a day. And as he munches he discourses to you of his philosophy, of how the apple changes into Hackenschmidt and Hackenschmidt changes into the apple, and a man can become one with his environment.

His expression is gentle and benign. From underneath a huge and imposingly domed skull, which rises to a sudden point in the middle, his clear grey eyes look at you mildly, but fixedly, through gold-rimmed spectacles. His ears are very large, but beautifully shaped, a cross between the faun's and the elephant's. His voice, coming from so solid a man, is surprisingly high. His manner, as he pleads for a general acceptance of the principles of Hackenschmidtism, which, he is convinced, can solve all the problems of the human race, is almost wistful. 'If only there was some way of getting Bevin and

Attlee to understand,' he says, 'they would have no difficulty in settling all this bother with Stalin in a moment.'

The clear and comprehensible exposition of Hackenschmidt-ism, an all-in system of physiology, psychology and philosophy, which makes existentialism seem like *Reading Without Tears*, has always been a problem. Hackenschmidt remembers how, when he came back to England after being interned in a German prison camp during World War I, he went to see a friend of his on the *Daily Mail* and expounded to him the first outlines of his cogitations. 'Stop it, Hackers, you're driving me crackers,' said his friend, after listening for half an hour. Hackenschmidt went out and stood for several hours on the embankment, by Cleopatra's Needle. Suddenly the revelation came to him: 'All experience is unsound. You must consult your own bodily system.' It was one of the simpler elements of Hackenschmidtism. Further complications were to follow.

George Hackenschmidt was born in the town of Dorpad in Esthonia, then part of the Tsarist Empire, in 1876. His father was a dyer of Swedish extraction. Hackenschmidt was a strong, very sturdy boy. At the age of sixteen his great strength began to stir inside him and he started weight-lifting. On leaving school he went to an engineering works in St Petersburg, where his perfect physique and weight-lifting performances attracted the attention of Dr Karajevsky, one of the court physicians who was a patron of the St Petersburg Athletic Club. 'You can become the strongest man in the world,' said Karajevsky, 'if you will only train, train, train.'

Hackenschmidt began training in earnest, and wrestling in front of Athletic Club patrons, such as the Grand Duke Vladimir. His weight-lifting feats included a Right Arm Press – eight times with 180 lbs. and four times with 217 lbs. He took naturally to wrestling and, at eighteen, was the amateur champion of St Petersburg – Graeco-Roman style, in which the holds are above the waist only – and Catch-as-Catch-Can. He lived quietly and cautiously, eating great steaks like planks at Dominic's restaurant, which was a haunt of wrestlers, strongmen and circus people, such as Samson, the strong man, whose weightlifting challenge he accepted, and Durov, the famous circus proprietor, and the greatest animal trainer of all time.

'Before a bout,' he says, 'I was as carefully chaperoned as a young girl!'

Outside the ring his disposition was as gentle as ever. Sometimes he would amble about the city streets during the long white nights of the Petersburg summer. If he saw one of his more volatile acquaintances becoming involved in a brawl, he would seize hold on him and carry him off bodily out of the danger zone.

Inside the ring he was a terror. He developed a turn of speed which was quite new in wrestling. He used to spring at his opponents, often men several stone heavier than himself, and literally pull them apart. His confidence in himself was almost phenomenal. He never boasted.

Hackenschmidt became a professional wrestler soon after he was eighteen, when he was due for military service with the Tsar's Life Guards. He gave up engineering and started travelling round Europe wrestling in the capitals. For a time he teamed up with Samson, the strong man whom he had met over a weight-lifting challenge in a Petersburg music hall. But he soon found that Samson's way of living was too furious altogether for his quiet ascetic tastes, and they separated. His greatest fight of this period was in Vienna, when he threw the famous Paul Pons, a gigantic Frenchman, who was the acknowledged champion of Europe. Hackenschmidt threw him with almost ludicrous ease.

Hackenschmidt's first appearance in England was in 1902. His reputation had preceded him, and when he climbed on to the stage of the Alhambra to accept the challenge issued to all and sundry by one Jack Carkeek, a wrestler of the familiar showman type, a hush of awe rippled over the sporting fans. It rippled also over Mr Jack Carkeek, who announced hurriedly that he would have added: 'all comers excepting, of course, Hackenschmidt', had he realized that the Russian Lion was in the house. Hackenschmidt's physique was a sensation. The late Harry Preston declared he had the finest body he had ever seen.

English wrestling at the time was in a rather curious condition. There was a keen public for it, but the only really first-class wrestlers were all too light to stand up for long to Hackenschmidt. He was given a contract at seventy pounds a week, but he threw all his opponents one after the other and the evenings became rather monotonous.

A little later he was taken up by Cochran. Hackenschmidt was featuring on a programme at Collins' Musical Hall, Islington, before a gay and very lively audience, with champagne corks popping from the box where that celebrated and effervescent lady of the theatre, Kate Cutler, was giving a party. The time came for Hackenschmidt, having wiped the floor with his opponents, and done his weight-lifting performace, to issue his challenge. And lo and behold, an enormous man, weighing sixteen stone six pounds, strode on to the stage, stripped off his fur dressing-gown, drummed on his chest, and announced that he was ready to wrestle with Hackenschmidt as soon as a match could be promoted. This was Ahmed Madrali, known as the Terrible Turk, an ex-stevedore, who had been very skilfully publicized.

The match, promoted by Cochran, took place at Olympia. It caught on and attracted an enormous amount of attention. By the time the great day came, Madrali had been built up into an ogre of terrifying legend. It was even rumoured that in one of his early bouts, in some barbarous, near eastern fastness, he had pulled the head off one of his opponents. Several sporting commentators and half the Stock Exchange intoned the old saying, 'A good big 'un 'll beat a good little 'un any day', and tipped him to win.

The wrestlers faced each other. The Terrible Turk bared his teeth as he had been taught. The Russian Lion fixed him with a stare of concentrated Hackenschmidtism. As Madrali circled for a hold, Hackenschmidt sprang at him, seized him in a terrible grip and began to lift him off his feet. Madrali shot out his right hand and tried to push Hackenschmidt's head back. Hackenschmidt lifted him higher, got his shoulder under him and threw him halfway across the ring. The Terrible Turk lay stunned. There was no need to pin him. He had broken three ribs. The bout had lasted forty-four seconds.

It was the most publicized fight of Hackenschmidt's career and one of the shortest and easiest. The hardest bout of his English tour was against a Polish wrestler named Zybsko, who gave him quite a tussle. It was Zybsko whose defensive tactics in a later match helped to kill Catch-as-Catch-Can wrestling in

England as a box-office attraction. Shortly before the outbreak of World War I, long after Hackenschmidt had left England, Zybsko was matched with a very skilful Indian wrestler named Gama Bux, one of three brothers, sons of a phenomenal father who used to wrestle against all three of them. Bux was a good deal lighter than Zybsko. He threw him by sheer skill but couldn't pin him, and Zybsko stayed down on the mat on all fours, grunting and groaning, but stubbornly resisting all Bux's attempts to turn him over for two hours, by which time the White City had emptied.

Hackenschmidt, meanwhile, had set off on a triumphant world tour, throwing all his opponents with the same monotonous ease. The enthusiasm which his prowess evoked was so fervent that on his arrival in Australia a Sydney newspaper broke into verse and greeted him with these lines:

'Hail, modern Samson! Living Hercules!

New Milo, hail! Thine advent here will please!'

Hackenschmidt's only defeats were both at the hands of the American wrestler, Gutch. Their first match was in April, 1908, and the return in September, 1911. In both, Hackenschmidt withdrew with a knee injury caused by an attempt to free himself from a toe-hold which he claims was illegitimate. He retired; he had lost his world championship but he had never been thrown.

The outbreak of World War I caught him in Germany. He had a nasty four years in an internment camp. It was there that the seeds of Hackenschmidtism began to germinate. Apart from the consolations of philosophy, it was a particularly disastrous war for Hackenschmidt, for he lost a large part of his savings in being unable to look after his investments.

After the war he oscillated between England and France, where he had bought a farm in the hills behind Nice. He never revisited Russia, but once in Berlin he had a brief reunion with his old friend, Durov, the animal trainer. Hackenschmidt had gone behind the scenes of the circus to chat to the strong man when he saw a familiar bearded figure, festooned in performing mice. 'Vladimir!' 'Georgi!' The two Russians embraced in a bear-like hug. Durov took him to see the Soviet consul in Berlin, and Hackenschmidt expounded to him the principles of Hackenschmidtism. The consul listened politely and said he was sure the Soviet authorities would offer a warm welcome to the Slavonic Hercules should he care to revisit Leningrad. But Hackenschmidt declined the invitation and went back to England.

He ran a school of physical culture and continued to take a keen interest in wrestling, which he has always maintained is a splendid exercise for the intelligence. and gave any amount of help and advice, gratis, to young amateurs. Meanwhile, he continued to work on the principles of Hackenschmidtism and developed a peculiar and peculiarly obscure theory about memory. 'Instinct,' he says, 'never tends towards the acquiring of memories; it cannot, and never does direct the human being to rely on them . . . the constant flow of his lifepower is always towards the breaking down and erasing of memories.'

An instance of the Hackenschmidtian logic in action, when he entered on a controversy with Shaw, is more direct and intelligible. Shaw had protested against the absurdity of a heavyweight champion boxer earning more in a few minutes than the Archbishop of Canterbury could earn in a lifetime.

'Highly fallacious,' commented Hackenschmidt. 'Mr Tunney, for instance, is a most intelligent man, but it would be difficult to train him to perform the functions of an Archbishop. It would, however, be extremely difficult, nay, impossible for the Archbishop to win the World's Heavyweight Championship.'

Hackenschmidt spent World War II at his farm in Nice, where he was staying in 1939 with his wife, a charming, very petite French woman. The Germans didn't interfere with him, but he felt their presence as 'something very unwholesome in the environment'. After the war he came back to England. He now has a small flat in Hampstead but spends much of his time in the country.

There are only two subjects about which this quiet, gentle, benevolent creature displays any irritation. One is his fight with Gutch, which he is very reluctant to discuss. The other is all-in wrestling.

'Disgusting buffoonery,' he snorts. 'All faked. Aesthetically revolting. Degenerate fooling about with human beings. Almost worse than murder; because murder, however horrible, is at least sincere.'

Richard Ingrams's Idols

The Authors Club in Whitehall Court was a snug, if faintly fusty little enclave with a pleasing Edwardian atmosphere. On the walls were William Morris tiles and framed letters from Shaw, Wells, Kipling, Barrie, Rider Haggard, Quiller-Couch, Maurice Hewlett, Anthony Hope. Here, as late as the autumn of 1947, you might find the three friends who form the subject of this triptych: Hesketh Pearson, Hugh Kingsmill and Malcolm Muggeridge.

Kingsmill would be reclining on a small battered black leather sofa with his white hair floating out over a brass ash-tray, his crimson face beaming with benevolence. Pearson sat at his head; Muggeridge at his feet. Kingsmill did most of the talking.

His voice was exactly like a corncrake's but much amplified. It was a Georgian literary man's voice, well adapted for animadverting on human folly in the teeth of a Cotswold gale but apt, in a confined space, to trephine the unaccustomed skull, like that West Indian reggae music which can make elderly white parents beg for mercy. Whenever he paused for breath, his friends burst into roars of totally unforced laughter.

Young clergymen, who had been recommended the club as 'exceptionally good value and so nice and quiet if you want to think things over or do some writing', crumpled up their sermon notes in despair. The late Mr Midgley, known as the poor man's J. B. Priestley, abandoned his leading article 'A Bookman in Bradford' for *John O'London's Weekly*, of which he was the editor, and stumped off home to Clapham Common. Yet, such was the current of bonhomie engendered, it was difficult for even the most etiolated of sensitives to feel menaced by agents from Philistia. Kingsmill, in particular, had that rash but indisputably Christian habit of treating complete strangers as old friends. You would not have guessed that he was tormented by gastric ulcers and had little more than a year to live.

All three of these ebullient literary journalists, nature's Thespians, with markedly cyclothymic temperaments, have, or had – for Muggeridge alone survives – much in common. There might have been some danger of their fusing under the biographer's hand into one composite figure, like the three poets in Osbert Sitwell's fantasy, *Triple Fugue*, especially as Richard Ingrams stresses the triune aspect. In *God's Apology** he has, however, been careful to preserve their very different identities. He never met Kingsmill or Pearson but Muggeridge, always the most generous of friends, has primed him with detail, and he seems to have fallen in love, by some necrophilous proxy, with them both. The result is a very readable and on the whole successful experiment.

Of the three rather complex case histories, that of Hesketh Pearson (1887–1964) is perhaps the simplest. An unusually intelligent and well-educated actor, he turned biographer and used his natural gift for empathy to identify with characters as diverse as Oscar Wilde, Conan Doyle, Shaw, General 'Jan' Nicholson, hero of Delhi in the Mutiny, and Gilbert and Sullivan. He went through several bad patches, emotional and circumstantial, but became deservedly a best-seller and can be labelled a distinct success. His literary vicissitudes included writing a joke book of diplomatic memoirs, attributed to Sir Rennell Rodd, which, owing to the pusillanimous spite of Allen Lane, landed him in court; also a surprisingly naïve admiration for Frank Harris. A natural establishment baiter, he was vital and humorous, physically the tall good-looking clown type. It is easy to see why Ingrams finds him so sympathetic.

Hugh Kingsmill (b. 1890, son of Sir Henry Lunn of Lunn's tours, but he used his Irish mother's surname) was chronically unsuccessful, so much so that he became at moments a tiny bit paranoid. He too had experienced the Harris phenomenon (as Shaw said of Harris, 'He is neither first rate nor third rate nor tenth rate; he is simply his unique abominable self') and put Frankie unadorned into his first novel which he wrote in 1918 when a prisoner of war.

* Richard Ingrams: *God's Apology: A Chronicle of Three Friends* (André Deutsch).

Some of Kingsmill's fans, among them William Gerhardie, carried away by his personality, would maintain that he was unfairly treated as a writer. Yet he does not re-read well. Even Ingrams found *The Poisoned Crown*, his biographical study of power corruption, heavy going. He was an excellent talker, full of ideas; he had a deep feeling for literature and at times remarkable psychological flair; but I suspect that when it came to arranging words on paper with white spaces in between, he suffered from some congenital awkwardness and lacked the necessary insight, or inhibition, to make a style. A humanist with a strong strain of mysticism, he is the centrepiece of the triptych, grappling the others together, Pearson by his zest, Muggeridge, who admits to having found him a powerful civilizing influence, by his emphasis on the transcendental. Both were captivated by the glow of his infectious euphoria, like a textbook case of hypomania, which he never ceased to emit even under the bleakest circumstances. Richard Ingrams has vivified him skilfully, though I wish he had told us more about his last wife, a Jungian lady practitioner, I believe. One wonders how she and Muggeridge got on.

Malcolm Muggeridge's later phases, the electronic apotheosis and consequent religious enthusiasm, are outside the scope of the book. He features mainly and very agreeably in relation to his friends. One or two warts are carefully and faithfully painted in, possibly on his own instructions. There are also some interesting pages about *The Earnest Atheist* (1936), his savaging of Samuel Butler, of which E. M. Forster said: 'an attack so disgruntled and so persistent that it may well be the result of a guilt complex'.

Some of the younger generation may think it strange that a professional iconoclast and perpetual student like Richard Ingrams should elect to venerate three such old-fashioned, albeit lovable, Georgian josses. If so, it would be a superficial judgment. Such short cuts between points of adjacent curves of history's spiral are not uncommon. For the sworn debunker, avowedly anti-intellectual, anti-Bloomsbury, anti-avant-garde, anti-scientist, non-political yet brimming over with crypto-HSP (High Serious Purpose), the choice of idol is extremely limited. And Ingrams's fervour is really rather endearing; it does less than no harm to the book, except once or

twice when, in a mood of middlebrow militancy brought on by
some slight to one of his darlings, he consigns to limbo good
critics: the genial Desmond MacCarthy, the perspicacious and
generally most unpretentious Edmund Wilson.

Rich and Strange

We had some interesting millionaire undergraduates at Oxford in the nineteen-twenties. The richest of them all was Jock Whitney at New College. He wasn't up for long because his father dropped dead playing golf on Long Island and he had to go home to rule the Standard Oil dynasty. This was in the early days of transatlantic telephone calls. Mrs Whitney spoke to Churchill, the porter, a venerable figure of immense distinction, often mistaken for John Sparrow's father, and said she would hold the line. Her son could not be found, but, said Churchill reassuringly, he would be bound to be in by midnight because all the young gentlemen had to be in by then, and he was not on the list of those who had leave to stay out. So Mrs Whitney went on holding the line while Churchill administered tactful consolation. She went on holding it until breakfast time and beyond because, of course, Jock Whitney had gone to play polo at Hurlingham and had stayed out on the tiles. The cost of that call was several thousand pounds.

Bill Astor was another New College millionaire but he was a gentle, modest little person, very strictly brought up and told to avoid any hint of extravagance or flamboyance. At Brasenose College there was Teddy Hulton, who had his own man-servant, a sort of Jesuit Jeeves, whom he consulted about everything. It was even suggested – without the slightest foundation – that he would go into the examination schools and write Master Teddy's papers for him. At Balliol there was Villiers David, of whom it was said, 'It's not possible to look like that without being a millionaire.' Jobbing back now, I can discern a faint aura of Groucho Marx about him; if you can imagine Groucho educated at Harrow and heavily tranquil-lized. He claimed to have read every word of Gertrude Stein's *The Making of Americans*. There was also at Balliol the riproaring

Alf Duggan, eloquently described by Peter Quennell in *The Marble Foot*:

> 'Alfred was the heavy Edwardian swell. At Oxford he kept a string of hunters, and every night, wearing full evening dress, he would journey in a hired motor-car to a London night club, the nefarious 43, and spend the next few hours drinking and talking and "having a woman" – an essential part of the ceremony – before he travelled back again. Once he returned, he was obliged to scale the façade of the college and struggle through his first-floor window. The bribes he paid his scout, he told me, ran into several hundred pounds a year. . .'

At Christ Church, especially in Peck – Peckwater Quad – you could hardly throw a stone without hitting a millionaire. There was the Duke of Norfolk, a slow developer, at one time erroneously thought to be educationally subnormal. His success in passing Responsions had led to gossip about a frame-up in the academic equivalent of the weighing-room. What happened was that Norfolk's crammer, one of the astutest men in the business, realized that some extra inducement was needed to arouse his pupil's interest in Latin; so he hit on the device of pornographic texts:

'Now, Duke, see if you can construe this.'

'*Lasciva puella* . . . the lascivious girl.'

'Well done. Splendid. Now carry on; use your dictionary and find out what the lascivious girl gets up to.'

Then there was William Acton, Harold's manic younger brother, the painter, who, if not precisely a millionaire, behaved madly like one, combining the worlds of the ballet and the Bullingdon, riding in point-to-points and giving immensely lavish parties at which the servants would stagger in with hip baths full of lobsters. His end nearly came when he fell wildly in love with a millionaire banker's son and, finding his passion unrequited, jumped out of a second-floor window in Canterbury Quad. He landed on grass and made a sizeable crater.

Another millionaire who belonged to an earlier generation but used to haunt Oxford at weekends, giving fancy-dress parties at the Randolph, his own favourite disguise being Rosita Forbes, the explorer, was Evan Morgan (Lord Tredegar).

Nobody has done a full treatment of this fantastic figure who was a favourite model for novelists. Ivor in *Crome Yellow* is a rather insipid, heterosexual version of him. He was a strange mixture of naïvety and sophistication. One moment he could be extremely funny; the next you wondered if he had any sense of humour at all. Once, after a party, he remarked solemnly: 'Any undergraduate with an allowance of three hundred and fifty pounds a year is far better off than I am with all my responsibilities.' Evan's greatest gift was for handling birds. He could do anything with them. I remember him buying a seemingly witless, thoroughly educationally subnormal, Australian parakeet at Thame market. He taught it, heaven knows how, to creep up his trouser leg and poke its head out through his fly buttons. The effect on old ladies can be imagined. In London he had an enormous blue macaw with the terrifying habit of seizing your ear in its beak. If you shrank away, it nipped. There must have been some inexplicable rapport here. Evan's features were strikingly avian and his mother, old Lady Tredegar, made kingfishers' nests as a hobby. I was reminded of Evan's gift by one of the later photographs of Edward James in Mexico. He is smiling up at a macaw and the macaw looks exactly as if it were smiling down at him.

At Oxford, Edward James – of whom Philip Purser has written a delightfully sympathetic, elongated profile* – was one of the literary-artistic, by no means altogether unathletic millionaires; far quieter than William Acton, not so quiet as Bryan Guinness (Moyne). In those days he was slight, slender and very pink. When I looked at the photograph of him on the jacket I thought for a moment that some unexpected metamorphosis had taken place: Edward James into Ernest Hemingway. The illusion of bulk is due to the folds of his Mexican blanket. In fact, the aspect of the grizzled, bearded head is more commanding and more serene than that of poor old Hem in his sad state of alcoholic degeneration.

Philip Purser disposes once and for all of the rumour that Edward's mother, Mrs Willie James, was Edward VII's mistress. The truth is more interesting. She was his daughter, begotten, it is thought, in the heather near Balmoral c.1870.

* Philip Purser: *Where is He Now? The Extraordinary Worlds of Edward James* (Quartet Books).

She was certainly an Edwardian to her fingertips. There is a splendidly Firbankian story of her sending to the nursery for a child to take to church:

'Which child, madam?'

'How should I know? Whichever one goes with my blue dress.'

Edward's American father, Willie Dodge James, died when he was quite small. His childhood at the house in West Sussex was very rich but wholesomely rural. At Eton he found Harold Acton, just hotting up for his role of neo-ninetyish aesthete and General Manager, Sitwells', Oxford Branch, a trifle tedious and cloying. Oxford was quite different, with his rooms at Christ Church surrealistically decorated and friends ranging from Randolph Churchill and Ava to the ubiquitous, mercurial Betjeman, whose first book of poems, *Mount Zion: or In Touch With The Infinite*, James published.

After Oxford there was a short interlude as Honorary Attaché in Rome, which ended when he made a ludicrous gaffe over a piece of decoding. Then back in London came the fatal marriage to the exquisitely pretty but stonehearted Tilly Losch, and the brawling divorce. The surrealist involvement and friendship with Dali followed. The high spot of this was the visit to the aged Freud, a refugee in Hampstead, and Dali's drawing of Freud's head, modelled on a snail's shell.

Munich more or less coincided with James's own setback over the reception of his poems *The Bones of My Hand*; Stephen Spender then at the peak – never very lofty – of his communist phase, was a bit rough with James in the *New Statesman*, though it must be admitted that as a poet James had only amateur status. His novel *The Gardener Who Saw God*, a Firbankian satirical allegory, is far more considerable; it has real charm and a quite strong feeling for mystical experience.

The James ego was too sensitive to be cushioned by money and he suffered quite sharply, He lit out for California and lived among the mystics, admiring Aldous Huxley but finding Maria snobbish. He found it difficult to maintain an equilibrium. In his most recent phase at his 'ranch' in the Mexican jungle near Xilitla, treasuring moments of ecstasy produced by clouds of butterflies, and building – he has always been interested in crafts – he seems to have attained tranquillity. You can feel him radiating good will. Philip Purser has made a careful study of him, though he still finds his personality elusive. There are one or two minor errors. Auden was up at Christ Church for three years, 1925–1928, not just one as is suggested. Lady Cunard never 'boomed'; she piped. As for the Mexican animal that 'locals call *el scorpion* which in fact is not a scorpion at all, it's a kind of slimy scaleless brown lizard and just to touch it is enough', this is obviously a myth.

Crime

The Moors Murders

'If those two were sane they'd have gone mad long ago.'

I was rather impressed by this comment – by a local hall porter – on the psychology of Ian Brady and Myra Hindley. Behaviour so atrocious can only be described in terms of Irish or Hegelian logic, the logic of contradictions. How does one begin to explain it?

It is all very well to say that we were all once polymorph-perverse infants, and that Mr Everyman's unconscious teems with sado-masochistic impulses. True, of course. But there is nothing impulsive about their dreadful calculated performances and the elaborate decoying that must have preceded them. I find it less difficult to empathise with Jack the Ripper than with these two. Odd how one always calls them Brady and Myra.

The other peculiar feature here is the dual element. *Folie à deux* in which two people go mad together is not unknown. An hysteric who falls in love with a psychotic will share the psychotic's delusions so long as they are together. Separate them, and the hysteric recovers while the psychotic remains insane. And, according to Freud, hysterical women may share the perversions of their lovers.

This looks very much like such a case. Indeed I am convinced it is one. Myra is an hysteric. Brady is a psychopathic sadistic pervert: it is conceivable that his perversion may mask a germinating psychosis. His passion for the Nazis (which the prosecution decided to play down so as not to appear to be overloading their case with politics) is no accident; he was looking for some sort of social sanction for his violent impulses. In a Nazi regime he might have flourished, become a Belsen guard, and Myra with him, or perhaps have risen to a higher post. He is a remarkable specimen of a lumpen-proletarian intellectual. Strange to think that he was only eight when Hitler died. His enthusiasm for the Nazis started when he was a schoolboy.

Their backgrounds: what would have happened if they had never met? You can't tell about Myra, but I think Brady would have got into bad trouble anyway. He had a hopeless start and probably drew something sinister in the chromosomal lottery.

Brady was born on January 2nd, 1938, in the notorious Gorbals in Glasgow. Nobody knows who his real father was. His mother was a teashop waitress, who registered his birth in her maiden name, Steward. He was brought up by a good foster mother and took her name, Sloan. He was quite bright at school, but a persistent thief, and he showed a cruel streak. He was put on probation on condition he went to live with his mother, who had married and moved to Manchester.

He stole again, was sent to Borstal (Hull and Hatfield), then settled down for a bit. His first job was working with his stepfather in the Manchester meat market. He had a spot of bother over pinching some lead, but no further convictions apart from a drunkenness charge. At Millwards, the chemical works, where he started as a stock clerk in February, 1959, he had the reputation of being a meticulous worker; unsociable, yet not particularly difficult to get on with, though given to fits of violent temper if crossed or if he had lost at betting.

Myra's people are fairly solid working class, from Manchester and the industrial fringe of Cheshire. We saw her mother in court; she had a long, sad, rather distinguished face and wore a thin, black scarf over her head. Myra was brought up by her gran. Her sister Maureen, who married David Smith, stayed with her parents; but they all in fact lived within a stone's throw of one another in Gorton, a pretty tough working-class quarter of Manchester.

Myra went to a secondary modern school, and stayed on and took a commercial course. At the age of thirteen, she saw a boy drown in a canal; this had a profound effect on her. She became religious, thought of becoming a Roman Catholic and received instruction. Later she became a bit flighty and unstable. She was said to be a good baby-sitter. There was an engagement that bust up. She had several secretarial jobs before she fetched up at Millwards in 1960.

Myra fell in love with Brady immediately and set her cap at him. For months he wouldn't take the slightest notice of her. She kept a diary with entries such as: 'He wouldn't look at me . . . I almost got a smile out of him today . . . Ian wore a black shirt and looked smashing . . . He's a crude uncouth pig . . .' Then the tone changes: 'Took Ian home; he was ever so gentle.'

As their association developed, Myra became tougher; 'posher', more flamboyant, going in for multi-coloured hair-dos, also more secretive. Asked why they didn't marry she said Ian didn't hold with marriage, it was meaningless.

It is difficult to get their relationship straight. We know she was obsessed by him. ('I loved him . . . I still . . . I love him,' she said in the box.) He must have had quite strong affection for her. His attitude now is not unchivalrous.

One is inclined now to picture them as spending all their time in abnormal or criminal activities; taking pornographic photographs (he took many of the pair of them), planning crimes, visiting victims' graves on the moors – that strange Gothic obsession of theirs. In fact, for much of the time they must have led a quite ordinary domestic life. Their family photograph album, the respectable one in a tartan cover, is full of the usual banal snapshots: there is one of Myra in a black evening dress with a cocktail glass in her hand; one of Brady picnicking on the moors, looking jovial, brandishing a bottle; several of them playing with the dogs.

Both were very fond of these dogs. Brady spent hours combing them. He still believes, you could tell from his evidence, that the police destroyed Puppet to punish him. Puppet died under an anaesthetic being X-rayed. Myra, when told of Puppet's death, said to the policewoman: 'You're a lot of f-----g murderers.'

I wonder what a quiet evening was like at 16 Wardle Brook Avenue – on the Hattersley over-spill estate, an abysmally under-planned housing expedient with its skyscraper-flat blocks, and rows and rows of little, grey, brick boxes?

Brady would be playing records of Hitler's speeches; or reading aloud from *Mein Kampf*, or one of his favourite paperbacks: a history of torture or a book of Nazi atrocities. Myra might be learning German, which she did with Brady's encouragement, dyeing her hair a still brighter shade of Nordic blonde, or cleaning her revolvers. (We heard in evidence during the committal proceedings how she always hankered for a Luger.)

It is too easy to make them sound like a family out of a horror comic. I am afraid that doesn't help one to distinguish between the precise shades of criminality and psychopathy.

In the box, we heard Brady speak for the first time on Tuesday afternoon (April 26th), but it was during a legal submission and couldn't be reported because the jury were out. He has a strong Scots accent and a schoolmasterly manner. Pedantry and perversion, photography and pornography join hands in this case. He is fond of words like 'approximately' and 'phraseology'.

He had a little spat with the Attorney-General, who was testing him out like a matador indulging in some preliminary cloak-play, about taking the oath. The Attorney-General suggested, after Brady had said he didn't believe in it, that it was just a symbol he could have affirmed. 'I suppose there are more theatrical ways of getting round it,' Brady said with heavy sarcasm. You could sense adolescent aggression and scorn coming off him like steam. Having heard him I could now believe that David Smith was really frightened of him.

On the Friday, April 29th, during his examination in chief by his own counsel, his manner was more subdued. At his day-long cross-examination by the Attorney-General on Monday, May 2nd, he was a bit more fiery, but for long periods he was merely answering 'No', or 'I wouldn't know' – which he tended to pronounce 'noo.'

The cross-examination of the accused in a murder trial is always the obvious high-spot, like Act IV in a Shakespearean tragedy. This cross-examination was perfectly successful. It compelled Brady to tell lie after lie. It went a long way towards corroborating Smith's evidence about the murder of Evans. It made hay of Brady's 'explanation' that the tape recording of Lesley Ann Downey was made as a kind of insurance in case anyone else interfered with the child, of his attempts to incriminate Smith and exculpate Myra.

Nonetheless, for some of us it was a bit of an anticlimax in that it never managed – how could it? – to get right inside Brady's mind. He knew he was done for and didn't hide it: 'My train of thought now is that I will be convicted anyway.' Yet he went on keeping up some sort of front and using a form of quibbling ingenuity that must be characteristic.

Perhaps one of his most revealing answers came when the Attorney-General asked him about his collection of pornographic books: 'Better collections than that in Lords' manors all over the country,' said Brady. This made one wonder if he mightn't be seeing himself as a latterday de Sade. Obviously his head is stuffed with romantic compensatory fantasies.

Myra was in the box for nearly as long as Brady. She spoke in a low, rather husky voice in that flat, north-midland accent, with an occasional hint of a Scots intonation. She complained of a sore throat and for a moment I thought she might be going to crack. Then, when they asked her to speak up, she snapped at them. You realized she was in control of herself. Very articulate, she had Brady's barrack-room-lawyer's facility for raising sudden quibbles.

Of the two, I think she is possibly the more intelligent. Brady is the pseudo-intellectual, a mood-man. She has a down-to-earth quality. If you were to give an IQ test to the two accused and the two principal witnesses, I suspect the order might be first Myra, then David Smith, then Brady, with Maureen Smith (Myra's sister) last.

Her account of her role during the Lesley Ann Downey tape-recording was preposterous. And when she was contrite, admitting to having been cruel, she seemed to go just so far and no further. And, whenever possible, she revived the fiction that Smith had brought the child to the house and taken her away. She, too, showed remarkable stubbornness in maintaining her front; I felt there was something specifically north country here. She hated being made to read aloud one passage from the tape transcript; when she said to the child, 'don't dally'. It seemed to me that the word 'dally' was too unsophisticated for her liking.

The Attorney-General was scrupulously polite, always calling her Miss Hindley: 'Your shame is a counterfeit shame, Miss Hindley . . . oh, Miss Hindley . . .' She stayed self-possessed. When the Attorney-General asked her why they had kept one photograph of her standing by the grave of John Kilbride – because it was 'hardly the most attractive picture of you, Miss Hindley?' – she came back instantly: 'There are a lot of unattractive pictures of me.'

I got the impression of a distinctly powerful personality, whatever she may have been like before she took up with Brady.

In the dock, Brady is thin, bony, rather gangling. Lean face with straight nose jutting out under his rather flat forehead. His dark brown hair is neat and tidy, yet looks faintly dusty. His clothes – grey suit, pale blue shirt, ultramarine, mildly artistic tie – are dateless, not like those of David Smith, who goes in for the gear. One of the first things you notice about him is his bad colour: pale mud. He really does look terribly sick.

Myra by contrast is blooming. Her hair, naturally brown, has been changing colour from week to week. First silver-lilac, then bright canary blonde. She is a big girl with a striking face: fine straight nose, thinnish curved lips, rather hefty chin, blue eyes. Full face she is almost a beauty. The Victorians would have admired her.

She wears a black and white speckled coat and skirt, and a pale blue shirt open at the neck: it matches Brady's. I suspect she imitates everything he does, even to always keeping her handkerchief neatly folded. At a glance she looks as smartly turned out as a duchess, but when you look closer you see at once that this is mass-produced supermarket chic; there is an ambience of bubble-gum and candyfloss.

Both take copious notes and lean over the front of the dock to prod their solicitor, the eupeptic Mr Fitzpatrick, with a pencil. Occasionally they offer each other a packet of mints. Once, during David Smith's evidence, Myra flashes Brady a quick bright smile. When he goes into the witness box she gazes at him. When it is her turn, he draws faces on his scribbling pad.

Tea – yes – with some of the hosts of detectives working on this case. We talked about modern youth, violence, censorship, permissiveness and all that. One of them, who is a bit of a sociologist and has a highly specialized knowledge of swinging Manchester, thought there was a dangerous current of perversion in the air. Kinky had become a household word. He'd seen a shop advertising: NEW LINE IN KINKY RAINCOATS. Why, he said, don't they label them raincoats for sexual perverts and be done with it? He said it twice over. This may be an unduly puritan reaction; it is quite a common one. We shall encounter it more often as a result of this case.

Fantasies: crime reporters are friendly fellows. They go in a good deal for professional cynicism and make use of the whimsicalization of horror as a defence. The Charles Addams drawings and the TV 'Munster' series are much to their liking.

I asked one of them if he ever dreamed about this case. He said no, but he'd had one rather nightmarish experience when his routine method of sending himself to sleep had failed him. This, which he adapted from Hemingway, consisted in playing an imaginary round of golf on his favourite suburban course, which he knew backwards. Ordinarily, he would drop off after a few holes. This time it was no use. As soon as he drove into a bunker his ball turned into a child's hand.

I haven't myself dreamed about the case at all, but occasionally in court towards the end of an afternoon I've caught myself lapsing into fantasies. These have taken the form of carrying out vengeance on the accused, which shows how careful you have to be. Once, I said to myself: If I were to put on Batman's gear, swoop down on the dock, which I could easily do from the gallery, what would the *News of the World* pay for my life story?

I lie awake at 2am because some race-going son of Belial – there are night clubs now, even in Chester – has jammed the horn of his car. I try to find a suitable text in Sartre's *Saint Genet*, which a kind local friend has lent me; he thinks that Brady might conceivably turn into his opposite. I'm afraid he has a long way to go, and he lacks Genet's talent. How about this?

> 'Thus the evil doer is the Other. Evil – fleeting, artful, marginal evil – can be seen only out of the corner of one's eye and in others . . . The Enemy is our twin brother, our image in the mirror . . . For peace-time, Society has in its wisdom created what might be called professional evil doers.'

> These evil men are as necessary to good men as whores are to decent women. They are fixation abscesses. For a single sadist there is any number of appeased, clarified, relaxed consciousnesses. They are therefore very carefully recruited. They must be bad by birth and without hope of change.

*　　　*　　　*

H'm. I think I know what Mr Justice Fenton Atkinson would say to that. And I rather think I agree with him. We've had rather a surfeit of evil up here. Evil is horrible; it is also banal. I incline at this moment to agree with my favourite crime reporter, who likes to pretend that all murders are fish-and-chips cases – something to wrap the supper in.

And if this sounds unduly philistine, let me put it another way. Quote from the schoolmaster Wagner, a celebrated German mass murderer, a paranoiac who went mad in 1913, killed his wife and four children, burned down some houses and a school and shot nine men. Recovering some sanity, he declared:

> 'The feeling of impotence brings forth the strong words. The bold calls to battle are emitted by the trumpet called persecution-insanity . . . The signs of the truly strong however are repose and good will.'

A big murder trial when capital punishment has been abolished is like a Portuguese bullfight. I'm an abolitionist myself, but naturally I can't help wondering how differently those two would behave if they were facing the death penalty. I also wonder if there may not be something in the idea that we, the public, feel that an execution acts like a symbolic scapegoat ceremony.

Waiting for the verdict you feel like a privileged spectator at the Apocalypse. The time factor, however, raises acute mundane problems. Back in court the sense of dramatic symbolism becomes very strong. The prisoners are brought up from the pit to which they will return. The body of the court is the world. The judge re-enters at his own detached prophetic level.

But now, perhaps for the first time, you realize that the jury, as they troop down into their box, have become invested with superior power. Their foreman, who looks like, and, I think, is, an intelligent grocer, has acquired charisma.

Mr Justice Fenton Atkinson has made a great impression here. Always utterly in control, he has been exquisitely civil to everybody. His personality, unlike that of some judges, has a therapeutic quality; it has done a lot to desensationalize the atmosphere. He pronounces sentence in the same quiet tone he has used throughout, and refrains from any additional execration. He has already said all he needs to say in two words of his brilliant summing-up: 'utmost depravity.'

As far as I could see, and I was standing quite near, neither Myra nor Brady showed any emotion. They were whisked away one after the other, in a trice. Brady made a wonderfully characteristic last public utterance when asked – between verdict and sentence – if he had anything to say: 'Only that the revolver was bought in July, 1964.' (This referred to a question which the jury had returned, briefly, to ask.) Myra said nothing. She may have swayed slightly.

Raining hard. The crowd outside, which includes a few small children, forms a lane by the door out of which they think They will emerge – though this looks to me like a police diversion. An old white-haired woman, with her leg in an iron brace, is brandishing an enormously thick stick. A Welshman is muttering: 'Ghouls, all bloody ghouls the lot of you! Who's taken my car keys?'

An English Murder Trial

Cool, grey Monday morning in Lewes, and few signs of excitement. At 8.30 am there is only one photographer outside the gaol. This, with hollyhocks lolling against castellated flint walls, and fresh terraced lawn, must be one of the prettier English prisons.

At breakfast in the White Hart, knowing crime reporters forecast a very short trial: 'And don't expect too much drama, old boy. They're not going to put him in the box.' The manageress is cross. 'I've got five empty rooms simply because for the past week you press people have been telling the world the town's full up.'

Across the street, the Sussex constable, watching the short queue outside the white stone Regency County Hall and Assize Court, pretends to be blasé:

'We're used to big murder trials here. Mahon. Field and Grey Mancini . . .' he ticks them off on huge white-gloved fingers. 'If you want to see life in Lewes, you should come on Guy Fawkes night. Biggest celebrations in the country. They have bonfires on the Downs; torchlight procession, and burn an effigy of the Pope, regular.'

Some of the charm of this delightful museum town has filtered into the stuffy, pitchpine-panelled little courtroom. The atmosphere is very English, informal, rather social. On either side of the Judge's bench sit guests of the Sheriff, whose daughter wears a high-pointed straw hat like a little Sussex steeple; for some time I cannot take my eyes off it. Robert Montgomery. On the Judge's right, looking fiercely stern throughout, sits the High Sheriff of Sussex, Sir Stephen Dimitriadi, in black velvet with lace ruffles. Next to him is the Judge's Chaplain, Bishop Crotty (retired colonial) of Hove, his pectoral cross hanging low over ample amethyst soutane.

'Put up John George Haigh.' The eighty-two-year-old Judge's voice is beautifully clear, with a slight crackle. He treats the jury as friends and equals, is exquisitely polite to counsel. He seldom interrupts, and then only to simplify matters. But when Mr Howard, assisting for the prosecution, asks some very leading questions, he raises a finger: 'I can understand your evidence perfectly, Mr Howard, but I am not quite so clear about that of the witness.'

Once he becomes the least bit testy: when the acid-drum, rumbling ominously, is trundled into court for the second time. 'There's no need to drag that great thing in again. Take it away.'

The morning passes with a procession of witnesses for the prosecution. The nearest approach to a sensation is Haigh's nonchalance in the dock. After carefully adjusting the trouser creases of his smart single-breasted fawn suit, with which he wears a cream shirt and red and blue check tie, he puts on gold-rimmed spectacles, unfolds a newspaper and, as I can see plainly from the gallery, proceeds to do a crossword puzzle. Meanwhile, his statements confessing to nine murders are read out.

One of the strangest features of the case is the preponderance of Kensingtonians. The background to this ghoulishness is a snug world of private hotel lounges and Tudor tearooms. Haigh himself continues to match it perfectly from the dock, so that it is easy to understand how, until his arrest, he was known as 'ever such a naice man'. One of the Kensington witnesses is so meticulously refined that, when asked by counsel where she lives, she answers primly: 'I reside . . .'

Leading counsel contrast strongly. Sir Hartley Shawcross looks remarkably pink and fresh and young. His address is urbane, conversational; his tone towards witnesses positively caressing. Wig and gown emphasize the Roman cast of Sir David Maxwell Fyfe's large pale face, and grave manner. His opening speech, in which he outlines his theory of Haigh's insanity, and relates the dream of the forest of crucifixes that turn into bleeding trees, is a valiant attempt at applied psychiatry. The jury look glum. At repeated references to the 'paranoid constitution' and 'pure paranoia', the Judge taps his teeth with one of his six pencils. Sir Theo Matthew, the

Director of Public Prosecutions, who sits in front of counsel, frowns until his bushy brown eyebrows form a solid bar.

The town is very quiet this evening. In a pub in the Cliff district, the far side of the River Ouse, a soldier says to the landlord: 'I wonder if he finished his crossword?'

Back at the White Hart, I learn from 'an unimpeachable official source' that Haigh fills in the last square over dinner in the prison hospital. Before going to bed, he demonstrates his needle-threading inventions to the doctor.

The tempo of the closing stages of the trial is uneven. The Attorney-General's raking cross-examination of Dr Yellowlees, sole witness for the defence, provides moments of conflict and drama. After that there is no more suspense, though the tension remains.

At luncheon the prison doctors – from Brixton and Lewes – are a little disappointed not to be called to rebuttal, but cheerful – quite good-naturedly – over the discomfiture of their natural enemy, the psychiatrist for the defence. (I use the word enemy metaphorically, and in a purely professional sense.)

A very close afternoon. Haigh looks up once as a jet-plane whistles through the sky above the court. He has abandoned his crossword and sits sideways, eyes closed, with his head against the back of the dock.

The homely reminiscential, but scrupulously detailed summing-up is rather longer than we expect. It demonstrates, amongst other things, that even while the Judge was reading – during Sir Maxwell Fyfe's address to the jury – the disputed textbook of psychiatry, he missed nothing that was said in court. You wonder how notes that have been written so slowly can cover as much.

The jury are out for fifteen minutes. The white-haired foreman's voice quavers as he pronounces the verdict, which has never been in doubt. The only woman member, an imposing matronly lady in a large hat, has been crying. That tiny elderly juryman, who sits on the extreme right in the back row, looks frailer and gentler than ever.

Haigh's enigmatic calm is unshaken. Asked if he has anything to say, he answers in a high mincing voice with a sardonic lilt: 'None at all.' He might have been answering a hotel manageress's domestic query: 'Oh, Mr Haigh, would you have any objection if we moved you to the annexe?'

He listens to the sentence, bows ever so slightly to the Judge, turns to smile at a friend in the gallery, and walks briskly down the steps from the dock to the cell below, as natty and dapper as when he came into Court.

Meeting A Multiple Murderer

I was having a drink with a man who is supposed to know a lot about the underworld. I asked him if he could suggest any interesting characters who might be persuaded to sit for their profiles.

He thought for a bit. Then he said: 'What about a triple murderer who escaped from Devil's Island? You'd have to go to Paris to meet him but that wouldn't be any great hardship.'

It sounded promising, and as soon as I had one or two more stories lined up in Paris I gave him a reminder. Cross-examined, he admitted that he'd only met the triple murderer once and didn't know his name even, much less his address, but what he really could do was to give me a note to a friend of his named Raoul who was the boss of an Algerian mob on the left bank. Raoul knew the triple murderer like a brother.

The day after I arrived in Paris I presented myself at Raoul's address, which turned out to be a small bar called The Sanctuary in a furtive little side street in the Latin quarter. It had been decorated rather half-heartedly in log cabin style and painted dark brown. There was not a soul in the place except for the girl behind the bar, a redhead with rather coarse chubby features. She had no idea – shrug – when M Raoul would be back. Yes, I could wait, if I liked. Why not?

The problem of what to drink while waiting for people in Paris bars at odd hours without contracting alcoholic poisoning can generally be solved by a sparing use of mineral water, coffee, and syrups. But in Raoul's bar the choice was limited to Cinzano or brandy. I waited for an hour, drinking three Cinzanos that tasted like distilled hiccoughs. Then I went for a walk and looked at the books in the galleries round the Odeon. Raoul was still absent when I returned.

The same thing happened the next day, but on the third day Raoul was actually there. And a remarkably handsome young man he was too, tall with black wavy hair and an air of brooding authority.

He read my note of introduction, muttered something about journalists being too talkative, put out his tongue and made snipping motions with his fingers.

The bar began to fill up with other Algerians a good deal less handsome than Raoul. My conversation with him was constantly interrupted by his disappearing into his back room with them for private conferences. The Cinzano ran out, but I felt it would be rude to stop drinking and switched to brandy. The door on to the street was wide open and there was a chilly draught. I went over to shut it but Raoul called me back. He liked it left open because that told the world that The Sanctuary had nothing to hide.

By seven o'clock, I judged that the atmosphere had thawed enough for me to mention the object of my errand. I discovered that the triple murderer's prowess had been underestimated.

'Mais sans doute,' said Raoul, 'il a tué quatre hommes au moins, peut-être beaucoup plus.'

Yes, he could effect an introduction. Why not?

When? Ah, that was the difficulty. Raoul much regretted that he had to leave Paris that very night on urgent family business. His brother in Marseilles was the victim of a gross miscarriage of justice. Attacked by a dirty toad of a Corsican, he had defended himself gallantly with a knife and was now charged, if you please, with murder. His lawyer hoped to prove that the seven stabs in the Coriscan's torso and abdomen were but pinpricks and that the toad had really died of heart failure. Meanwhile, fraternal support was urgently needed. However, if I would present myself at the bar at midday in a week's time, he would effect the introduction without fail.

The chill I contracted that evening in The Sanctuary was slow in maturing. At one time I thought I had it whipped with grog and Veganin, but it counter-attacked strongly. When, a week later, I re-presented myself at the bar, I was feeling so miserable that I hoped Raoul was still in Marseilles and I could creep back to bed.

But Raoul was standing at the bar with a bottle of Cinzano at the ready. He recognized me with an effort and tried politely to hide his irritation. I croaked an enquiry after the health of his brother. He had been found guilty and given one of those fluid French sentences of from five to ten years. No doubt if Raoul could find the money he would be out in eighteen months.

It seemed a matter for congratulation. *'Pas mal,'* I croaked, *'pas mal du tout.'*

Raoul gave me an outraged glare and vanished into his back room.

When he re-emerged twenty minutes later conversation was sticky, but we arranged to meet again at six that evening. This time he really would effect the introduction to the quadruple murderer.

I waited three hours in vain for Raoul that evening. There were moments when I felt so ill that I had to grip the bar with both hands.

Next morning I felt slightly better and soon after twelve noon I trapped Raoul in The Sanctuary. He was surprisingly amicable. He apologized for having let me down the evening before, but he had been seized with grippe.

I said it was all for the best. I too, had been ill, and in consequence deaf, deaf as an adder. *Sourde comme une vipère.* I was pleased with that but it proved to be yet another *faux pas*, for in Tunisia, where Raoul came from, they held vipers to be so unlucky that even to mention the name of one in conversation ruined the entire day. Nevertheless, we arranged to meet again at six-fifteen.

With the same unconquerable determination that had distinguished my entire conduct of the case of the Triple Murderer, I arrived at The Sanctuary at six-fifteen that evening. Time passed, some two and a half hours of it. At first, full of optimism, I engaged the redheaded girl behind the bar, but as the quarters dragged by I relapsed into the dark brown, Cinzano-flavoured gloom that was the prevailing mood of the establishment. Then, just as I had decided that I had had enough, that an end had been reached, a car grunted up the narrow cobbled street and stopped outside. The next moment Raoul was ushering the quadruple murderer into the bar.

I leap from my stool and held out my hand: *'Enchanté, Monsieur,'* I cried. *'Enchanté de faire votre connaissance.'*

He, the murderer, was of medium height with a nutcracker chin and a big curved nose, hollow cheeks and periwinkle blue eyes. A three day growth of white stubble contrasted with his pink bald head. He was dressed in roughish working clothes and wore no tie. He looked to me to be about seventy.

His manners were perfect. With a murmur of *'Enchanté, Mme Raoul'* – his voice was sonorous and bell-like – he bowed low to the girl behind the bar and printed a light kiss on her chubby freckled paw. Madame Raoul! Good heavens, and I had been calling her Mam'selle all the time.

And still his prowess had been underestimated. He had murdered five men, not four. His name was Pascal Bonsignore. He had been born in Bizerta, where his father was a barér of mixed French, Italian, Tunisian, and Maltese parentage. He was, he said, delighted always to meet an Englishman. English friends had come to his aid when he was in a very bad situation indeed, the worst, in fact, that a man could be in. He sketched with finger and thumb the outline of a noose in the air.

This, I said to myself, is it: journalistically perfect, well worth all the agony, the dark brown hours, the perpetual taste of hiccoughs. I got out my notebook: *'Alors,'* I said, *'ça sera plus convenable, je crois, si nous pouvons commencer avec un bref histoire de votre vie, Monsieur.'*

The quintuple murderer gulped down his Cinzano, sprang to his feet and said he had much regretted it but he must be going. He had only looked in to make my acquaintance. Tomorrow evening, early, he would return and place himself entirely at my disposal.

'And I,' said Raoul, who was standing over us, 'will make a cous-cous which we shall eat after you and our friend have finished your conversation.'

The next evening, I arrived at The Sanctuary at five-thirty. It was empty, of course, but I was now so confidently optimistic that when a particularly wizened and apelike Algerian came in I stood him a Cinzano and started to talk to him. He was one of the touts who stand outside the Madeleine and offer to change money for tourists at black market rates. On the strength of a vocabulary of 'changey dollars, changey pounds', he fancied himself as an English speaker. He had a terrible stutter and I got the impression that parts of his brain were not connected up right.

At seven-thirty-five they arrived. Pascal Bonsignore was transformed. He wore a smart blue suit, spotless white shirt and an American saleman's tie like a fire in a paint factory. He was freshly shaven and smelt strongly of scent. I put his age down as sixty. He seemed to be as delighted to see me as I was to see him. At first we avoided the subject of murder and chatted politely of how the blue evening mist that had set in compared with the famous London fogs. Presently I suggested we might sit at a quiet table in a corner and get down to business.

I was just beginning to translate the sum which I was prepared to pay for his life story into francs, when Pascal Bonsignore stood up.

He was very sorry, he said, but he could not stay. His wife was ill and alone and he must go back to her. She had waited for him, utterly faithful, during his twenty years in various prisons and on Devil's Island. He had written to her from Cayenne telling her that he was done for, that it was better for her to commit bigamy than die a widow; still she had waited. Such a woman must be given the utmost consideration. But if I would come to Paris again, in a few weeks' time, when his domestic affairs were settled, and spend a day with him to go through his press cuttings . . . I tried to persuade him to stay, but his mind seemed to be made up. After so many anticlimaxes one more didn't seem to make much difference to me. I just felt flat and bored, not even particularly disappointed. But Pascal Bonsignore had reckoned without Armand. Armand had gone off somewhere in his car, and until he returned Pascal Bonsignore was marooned. He didn't like to make use of any public means of transport because he wasn't really supposed to be in Paris at all. His police *permis de séjour* forbade him to enter any large town. He was not even allowed to visit his mother's grave.

I said we might as well fill in the time by getting the facts about him. Reluctantly, with an eye on his watch, Pascal Bonsignore began to talk, and his voice resounded like a bell. His real age, I discovered, was only forty-eight. Ten years in Cayenne did not make one look one's best. He was lucky to have kept sane, but – shrug – he had always had a certain spiritual force. He also had a flow of calendar philosophy. '*Que voulez-vous, monsieur*,' he kept intoning at the end of each fresh misfortune, 'that's the way of the wheel.'

He admitted, cheerfully, to having killed five men. Was that the total? He winked. Possibly not, but that was the official score. Of course, I understood that they were all dirty types,

police informers and various species of twister. That, too, was
the way of the wheel: '*Ou on est né un voyou, ou non.*' Either one is
born a cad or one isn't.

He ticked them off on his rather rheumaticky fingers.
Number one was done in Marseilles, when he was only seventeen, soon after he had run away from his father's bakery in
Bizerta. He – the victim – was one of the local boys in the Ditch
(the red light quarter of Marseilles). They had fought over a
girl 'whose protection was in dispute'. Bonsignore knifed the
other boy in the liver.

The second affair happened in Brussels, almost exactly a
year later, and under precisely similar circumstances. This
time he had launched a frontal attack and punctured the aorta.
Not to be recommended; far too messy. His lawyer had pleaded
self-defence, but they had given him eighteen months. However, the Belgian prisons were the best in Europe, so refined.

The third was the one for which they sent him to Devil's
Island. For the first and last time in his life he had used a pistol,
beastly noisy thing like a silly firework. He had lain in wait for
his man in an alley in Montmartre and plugged him in the guts
as he walked past. Why? Because he was an informer, wasn't
that a sufficient reason? Cayenne had been absolute hell.
Nothing that was ever said about it could be bad enough.

The fourth? Well, as a matter of fact, now that he came to
think of it, that had happened on Devil's Island, right inside the
penal settlement. The 'subject' was a trusty, a real 'saligaud'
who was running a filthy extortion racket and swindling
everyone. He had done him in the night with a hook-file,
pinched from the governor's office and straightened and shar-
pened. Next morning half the settlement had drunk his, Bonsignore's, health in palm toddy. There had never been a more
popular assassination; no, not since the doing of Nero.

The fifth? Ah, that was indeed a curious affair. In the middle
of the war he had managed to escape from Devil's Island in an
open boat. After drifting for days, he had been picked up by a
British destroyer and interned, if you please, in a concentration
camp in Trinidad. There he had found an old enemy and
ripped him up with a six-inch nail.

Further confessions were cut short by the return of Raoul,
who was cursing and spitting like an angry cat. A black market

petrol spiv had filled his tank with three thousand francs' worth of water, and vanished into the blue evening mist. The car had stalled and Raoul had had to borrow another. There would be no time to make a cous-cous, but I must stay and dine *en famille* with him and Madame. Meanwhile, Pascal Bonsignore must be returned to the suburb of Clignancourt where he resided. They dashed out into the night leaving me sitting with another glass of Cinzano.

Raoul was still in a vile temper when he came back. He cursed Mme Raoul for not emptying the ashtrays and raised his hand as if to clock her. I wondered what I should do if he did, and rehearsed a French sentence in my mind: *'Mais non, mais non, M Raoul, il ne faut pas frapper votre femme. Notre ami, Pascal Bonsignore, serait très fâché.'*

Instead, he dragged me out to buy a steak. On the way he read me a lecture about my conduct towards Pascal Bonsignore. Did I realize that I had gravely affronted the sensitivity of that noble spirit? Either I should not have mentioned money at all, or I should have suggested a reasonable sum. Fifty thousand francs was an insult. After all, he had killed five men *au moins* and escaped from Devil's Island . . .

Buying the steak entailed visiting several bars in the quarter, drinking more Cinzano and standing by while Raoul instructed some of his compatriots how to play that not particularly inspiring card game, belote.

It was past midnight when we got back to The Sanctuary. We drank more Cinzano while the steak was cooking; it was twelve-forty-five before we sat down to eat it in the back room. The atmosphere was strained. Mme Raoul, red-eyed, made a plucky attempt to brighten us all up by arranging the fruit in a suggestive pattern, but Raoul raised his hand and slanged her for being *grosse*.

I slouched back to my hotel ruminating on Pascal Bonsignore, the quintuple-murderer plus, with his strange naked pointed face and bell-like voice, and of all that I had endured in my quest for his life story. That, I said to myself as I climbed into bed, is the way of the wheel; *ou on est né un voyou ou non*. But it took me a long time to get to sleep. Whenever I shut my eyes I was back again in The Sanctuary, counting the black nails in the dark brown woodwork.

Travel

Easter in Jerusalem

April 5th 1947. A very hot Easter. Hotter than usual for the time of year, hotter by English standards than the crest of the fiercest freak August heatwave.

You see the heads of large black lizards silhouetted against a copper-sulphate blue sky, peering over rocks and housetops. After periods of motionless basking they make menacing movements as if exercising for some outburst of reptilian terrorism.

It is difficult at the moment for even the keenest of sun worshippers to enjoy the heat because it is accompanied by the hateful Khamsin – a sultry east wind that causes depression and fits of violent irritation. The Khamsin (it means 'fifty') is supposed to blow for fifty days in the year; this year it has been having its innings early. It is a recognized excuse for rudeness and bad temper among all communities.

The Khamsin makes life additionally hard for the four infantry battalions (of a total of sixty-three thousand British troops in Palestine, eighty per cent under canvas) standing by in Jerusalem. Their average age is under twenty and, what with twenty-four hours' guard duty and forty-eight hours' 'ordinary' duty, including screening and searching, some of them do not get more than one night's sleep in four. Their scanty amenities have been further restricted by the new security orders on account of the present tension, and Easter will not be much of a holiday for them, though some have been taking part in religious processions.

Easter, with its multitude of ceremonies, seems to add to the confusion which is an integral part of the atmosphere here. Jerusalem, with its two entirely distinct towns, the old and the new (in the latter's Mamilla-road – the Arab Bond Street – photographs of Kings Farouk and Ibn Saud, and the inevitable

Mufti, confront Rita Hayworth and the latest Egyptian cabaret star) is subdivided further by the zoning system and the proliferation of barbed wire.

Zone passes have been granted to only a few taxis, and the general atmosphere of constraint, combined with Khamsin-induced indolence, tends to reduce people's movements to a minimum. In these circumstances, despite the lifting of the twelve hour dusk-to-dawn curfew, the Christian Easter cere-monies, which mainly take place in the Old City – whose ancient wall encloses the religious shrines – or on the slopes of the Mount of Olives, inevitably assume a faintly remote character.

They began with the mile-long Palm Sunday procession, from the Latin Church of Bethphage past the Garden of Geth-semane at the foot of the Mount of Olives (sadly disfigured by the pink pseudo-Byzantine church completed in 1925), into the Old City through St Stephen's Gate. This was headed by Polish troops. Following them, soldiers of Irish regiments each carried a palm branch in one hand, rifle in the other.

Thursday's principal ceremony was the Washing of the Feet. For the Latin Church this formed part of a three-hour service, during which the huge doors of the Church of the Holy Sepul-chre were kept locked, in contrast to other occasions, when worshippers stroll in and out at will for coffee and cigarettes.

The Washing was performed over a large silver bowl by the Franciscan custodian, the Right Rev. Alberto Goni, who exchanged his gold and purple robes for a purple-backed white lace apron, and washed, dried and kissed the feet of eight Franciscans and four seminarists while clouds of incense drifted up to the dome.

Yesterday morning I watched the Catholic procession of the Stations of the Cross wind its way up the narrow-arched and shadowy Via Dolorosa. At each Station the procession, about five hundred strong and mainly Polish, knelt and prayed, rose and went on its way. It was a simple, unostentatious affair, but its spiritual appeal was slightly swamped by the large numbers of police who handled the crowd as if they were at a Cup Final.

This year the Jewish Passover coincides with the Christian Easter – an event which occurs once in four years. In addition, there is the Moslem festival of Nebi Musa (the tomb of Moses).

This was instituted traditionally by Saladin as a counter-attraction to the Christian Easter.

Saladin announced that he had dreamt that the tomb of Moses, venerated by Moslems as a forerunner of Mahomed, had been moved from Mount Nebo to a site near Jericho. Pilgrimages to its alleged site, accompanied by dervish sword dance and volleys of shots fired into the air, set out from the Dome of the Rock.

Throughout the week Arab pilgrims have been plodding up the hillsides to take up their lodgings in the Old City, already enlarged by several thousand Christian pilgrims including four thousand Copts from Egypt. The lucky ones had heavily laden donkeys, almost invisible except for legs and ears, under piles of bundles and webbing suitcases. The less fortunate, sweating profusely, pushed handcarts stacked high with bedding, cooking utensils, provisions, and sacks of vegetables, as well as boxes of eggs which they hope to sell to the inhabitants during the festival, competing with vendors of Christian Easter-eggs, dyed vermilion.

The Nebi Musa Festival culminated yesterday afternoon with the 'unfurling of the banner', in the airy, stone-flagged precincts of the Mosque of Omar. In the morning, lorry loads of cheering members of the two Arab paramilitary organizations, the Najjada and the Futuwa, were driving through the town to attend it.

Only Moslems may attend the ceremony, but from a perch on the city wall I watched the procession emerge into the dusty open space between the Mosque precincts and St Stephen's Gate.

The vanguard consisted of members of the Najjada bearing an immense coloured photograph of the Mufti. Then came the Supreme Moslem Council, grave and venerable in black, with the white wrappings denoting Islamic sanctity round their tarbooshes. Behind came the band, and all around surged the crowd of enthusiasts who saw them off as they climbed into their taxis outside the Gate for the downhill pilgrimage to the site near Jericho.

The atmosphere was Bank-holidayish, quite friendly and extremely cheerful. There were swingboats for the Arab children and dervish dancing in circles to flute and drum, rather like Highland reels infinitely prolonged, and a wonderful dwarf strong-man-cum-fakir who rested from feats of weight-lifting on a bed of nails.

A young Arab told me, rather sadly, that before 1936 Arabs, Jews and Christians used all to dance together outside the Gate.

Despite All Woes

Irish Notebook, April, 1957

The peculiar social obliquity of Ireland is so marked, the tricks
which its aquatinted light and soft dreamlike atmosphere play
upon the senses so confusing that the visitor is apt to find
himself seriously disoriented.

'I must', he says, 'make an effort to find out what Ireland is
really all about – apart from race meetings and salmon fishing,
house parties, nylons, and steaks, and beautiful chestnut horses
against insanely green grass, under a low ragged sky with dark
blue mountains all round.' But there are no certain authorities
to consult. Even the iron Marxists seem to suspect that the
infallibility of their doctrine breaks down when applied to the
strange mixture of conquered and conquerors inhabiting the
western island.

Who wrote this?

> 'Ireland still remains the Holy Isle whose aspira-
> tions must on no account be mixed with the profane
> class struggles of the rest of the sinful world. This is
> no doubt partly honest madness on the part of the
> people, but it is equally certain that it is also partly a
> calculation on the side of the leaders in order to
> maintain their domination over the peasant.'

Engels, in a letter to Marx dated 1869. With a little more
emphasis on the honest madness, in which there is often a good
deal of method, and a little less on the calculations of the
leaders, which have the human habit of going astray, it can
stand as a useful definition today, when the Holy Isle has
become a Roman Catholic republic of small farmers (average
holding; thirty acres) and shopkeepers (population three million, 94.4 per cent of them Catholics, with the Protestants

dwindling steadily) more prosperous, if not more stable – some say stagnant – than ever before in her history.

But not even a whole choir of Engels could tell you just exactly how Ireland stands with regard to the international situation.

'There's a far greater sense of urgency and emergency here today than ever there was in 1939,' said a younger Senator with whom I lunched. In the next breath he went on to tell me that, despite the universal detestation of communism, there were some tricky cross currents of opinion.

There were those who would countenance a military alliance which included Britain, only after Partition had been abolished. There were those who would have nothing to do with Britain at all and preferred a unilateral pact with America. There were those who, because of Ireland's remoteness – and past sufferings – thought she should remain neutral in all future wars no matter whom they were between. And there were those, among them many devout Catholics and fervent anti-Communists, who vowed that they could never fight on the same side as England in any future war, not even one against Russia.

The Young Senator went on to reassure me that supposing a protective military occupation of Ireland was ever considered necessary, I could be quite sure that the Irish nation would infinitely rather be occupied by British than by Americans. I reminded him that I had been told that the only place in Ireland where it was safe to sing 'God Save the King' was Castlepark – a well-known Anglo-Irish private school.

That might be, he said. Nevertheless, the English were extremely popular in Ireland. Didn't I know that on the occasions of Princess Elizabeth's marriage, nobody in Dublin could be got to attend to business for a week? Hadn't I heard the way they'd cheered the winning English team at the horse show? Now, if only Partition . . .

Meanwhile, I gather that Fianna Fáil are a little concerned lest Partition should be abolished before they are back in office, but that the innate philosophical dignity of its leader, Mr de Valera, has triumphed over the difficult situation of having had his political clothes stolen while bathing and watching the thieves parade them in front of him. He keeps a restraining hand on his bright young men who urge him to cut loose, and continues to support the present administration in most respects, though he differs from it in advocating some urgent specialized rearmament.

And, although the slogan 'Abolish Partition!' is on every lip and front page, actual discussions of the subject seem curiously abstract. A stock joke is this: 'They'll not do away with the border now that smuggling's become a major industry.'

In general, the domestic political air feels free from tension. The militant forces lie low. Apart from an occasional mutter of 'that cursed opportunist traitor MacBride is next on our list!', the IRA show no signs of emerging from the wholesome decline into which they sank after the wartime arrests. Peadar Cowan's Private Army, a body whose expressed aim is to recapture the Six Counties, still drills in a desultory fashion in Phoenix Park, but nobody takes it very seriously. A recent parade was dismissed by mutual consent when it was discovered that all the volunteers that evening were informers.

More interesting, perhaps, is the movement on the other side of the border, where some of Ulster landowners are casting envious eyes on lower Irish taxation and wages.

One gets the impression that Eire is jogging along fairly comfortably. In the towns, the new middle class, and the visible process of suburbanization which accompanies them, are making themselves increasingly felt. Already intellectuals are saying: 'Soon, except for the mountains, the whole island'll be a nest of villas.' Unless the present decline in population, slight but distinct – due to continued emigration – is reversed, this is, to put it mildly, improbable.

Tourists continue to provide a huge slice of the national revenue (said to exceed that derived from the sale of cattle), but the boom is past its peak, and this season's figures are the lowest since the war. Even so, Dublin ran out of nylons before the end of Horseshow Week.

The English residential invasion (representing a capital of ten million pounds, according to Sir Stafford Cripps), known as The Retreat from Moscow, has been checked by legislation. Since 1949, only thirty English – or Irish who had not been resident in Eire for three years – have been allowed to buy property. Among those who are installed, a perpetual secret war is waged. Object? The luring away of trained domestic servants.

The Anglo-Irish culture and the nationalist literary revival have vanished utterly, and there is nothing and nobody to take their place, though at this moment rehearsals are about to start on the annual Christmas pantomime in Gaelic.

Meanwhile, as the priest remarked in the tote payout queue at Tramore races in the rain, after Martin Molony had ridden a hole right through the card: 'Despite all woes, there is still this and that to be thankful for.'

The Quest for Lantos Eva

In May, 1961, I was rung up at the *New Statesman,* where I was writing the 'London Diary' under the pseudonym of Charon, by the press secretary of the Hungarian Embassy. 'I wish to invite you to my country . . .' They were opening a new airline, London–Budapest, and were inviting a party of British journalists, representatives of culture, and two Members of Parliament.

Fortunately, I was in the journalists' group. We were treated as convivial, cerebral lightweights. The culture vultures got heavier academic handling and kept being marched in and out of museums and the British Council. The last I saw of the Members of Parliament was at Brussels.

Journalists on a junket generate a current of euphoria. Free travel is a wave of the wand from the Fairy Wishfulfilment. I don't know why the cunning Magyars had chosen us, but it certainly wasn't for our left-wing politics. Most of us didn't seem to have any politics at all, and I was quite prepared to keep mine under my hat for the sake of pleasure.

There was Peter Earle, the surprisingly civilized crime reporter of the *News of the World*; George Atkinson of *The Birmingham Post* – now dead, alas; the Foreign Editor of the *Evening News*; and Raymond Fletcher, then of the *Tribune*, now a Labour Member of Parliament. He became known as Engelbrecht because of his resemblance – according to Peter Earle – to James Boswell's illustrations of my dwarf surrealist boxer.

It was only five years after 1956 and first impressions of Budapest were that everything was more relaxed than might have been expected. The Hotel Gelert, where we stayed, was in Buda on the right bank of the Danube. It was built in 1912, in Ritz style, but had been redecorated, after getting a bashing during the fighting for Budapest in 1944, in Swedish modern

with a lot of wood and black glass. It was exceedingly comfortable. The waiters were slow as tortoises and no one tried to
hurry them. In the garden at the back was a superb swimming
bath – Budapest has the best in the world. For the last five
minutes of every hour, there were artificial waves. A few steps
above the pool was a little thermal spring, bubbling at blood
heat. You could lie in it on a slab of rock and look up at the iron
gates of the villas and imagine you were back in 1914, the lover,
perhaps, of the Queen of Romania.

We had three bear-leaders. The senior was André Polgar,
aged about thirty-six, obviously a dedicated party member, but
far more sophisticated than the Russian equivalent. He enjoyed
being teased by the journalists:

'André, you've got night clubs in Hungary?'

'Of course. Some stay open till four-thirty.'

'All nationalized?'

'Naturally.'

'But you haven't got striptease. They've got it in Poland. I've
seen it.'

'Ah, but Poland is a Catholic country.'

And when he took us to the Matthias Church to hear the
Mozart Mass, he said:

'You see, ours is the only communist country that subsidizes
religion.'

'How do you make that out?'

'We lend them our state orchestra free to play at their Mass.'

I was also the *Observer*'s TV critic and I'd arranged with
Terry Kilmartin, then Entertainments Editor, now Literary
Editor, to write a piece about Hungarian television. André
deputed Paul, a rather pretty young man, to organise a television set. Paul explained that reception was very bad because
the hills of Buda stood right in between the Gelert and the
transmitting station. He fiddled about with the set for a long
time and got nothing but Hungarian vermicelli, and an occasional roar in incomprehensible Magyar. Clearly I should have
to use my imagination. I asked Paul to tell me about Hungarian
TV. He got rather flustered, and almost the only fact I got out
of him was that the Hungarians had one day of abstinence per
week – no television at all. But André Polgar rose to the
occasion (as he always did) and gave me a long account, with

mime, of a Roman Catholic priest, Father Pescos, who was an ace at popular scientific lecturing. He captured the audience's imagination so deftly, what did it matter if he occasionally popped in a little God-propaganda among the nuclear particles.

A rather subtle piece of propaganda for the Hungarian communist party's *tolerenz*.

Before dinner I went for a walk with Engelbrecht and, under the shadow of vast and ghastly Soviet sculptures, we discussed our initial impressions. We both agreed that the atmosphere seemed far more liberal than we'd expected. A lot of the crowd walking about the grassy mounds above the Gelert were middle class and elderly. Some of them looked extraordinarily English, and one misheard pieces of their Magyar dialogue as scraps of English conversation.

The first night we were then taken to an enormous workers' social club with an entrance like a fortress and a shrine commemorating fallen workers. There was a dance and we were each provided with partners for a waltz. Mine giggled nervously. Then we were taken on to a rather sober nightclub in the Hotel Astoria and finally back to the Gelert. Lilian, the barmaid, one of those delightful sad central-European types, pretty and very wistful, told us that some of our friends had discovered the local colour. We hotfooted it round the corner to find them downing riesling at a prodigious rate, in celebration of the fact that this was a bar that stayed open till three in the morning. Such is the irrepressible Hungarian need to turn night into day.

The next day, being Sunday, we were hauled off to the Matthias Church, ex-coronation place of Magyar kings. That night there was a performance of Verdi's *Macbeth* (once again with the Hungarian State Orchestra). I sat with Engelbrecht. The performance was very fine; the production somewhat avant-garde, with a chorus of witches who crept about the stage like a massed army of black rags. In the first interval we noticed a tall, beautiful girl with a soft yet commanding face framed by long ringlet curls. She was looking in our direction and the stout-hearted Engelbrecht followed her to the bar. By the time I caught up they were already in conversation. She asked, in limited English, if we were part of a delegation. Her idea of Englishmen was over six feet with big teeth. She told us she was a law student and lived in the Karl Marx Hotel for Lady Students, in Lenin Street. It had been her turn for a student's free ticket to the opera. I asked her if she'd like to come out and dance and, after a little hesitation, she nodded, and said, yes, why not. She would meet me at the bar of the Gelert at twelve-thirty, and would I, please, be standing near the door. We went back for the last act and Engelbrecht made the expected comments.

I asked Lilian which was the most cheerful nightclub in Budapest because the Astoria had been a bit of a morgue. She said it was Pipacs, which means Poppies. Presently, Lantos Eva, for that was her name, arrived and waved to me rather shyly from the doorway of the bar. She had changed and was wearing a bright blue dress and pretty earrings. We set off in one of the indescribably uncomfortable Budapest taxis which were said to be a job lot from the Russians. They jolted hideously. Pipacs was quite a cheerful nightclub: small, plain, rather too brightly lit. There was an old runner in a peaked cap who spoke nearly perfect English and looked like that Hollywood actor who used to specialize in comic Viennese-Jewish parts. I asked him what life was like.

'Ach!' he said. 'It is not too bad but how can you run a nightclub when you are not allowed to make a profit?'

We stayed and danced until four. Lantos Eva drank cherry brandy fearlessly, while I stuck to the more conservative kind. The bill came to the equivalent of fifteen shillings. The band played 'Mac the Knife' and we danced acrobatically. I tied Lantos Eva's long corkscrew locks under her chin and she seemed to like it. I asked her if she'd come back to my room at the Gelert. She said she would. Lao Lederer, my *Observer* colleague, had told me that this kind of impulsive behaviour is absolutely characteristic of Hungarian girls. One can only wish it were more widespread.

We jolted back to the Gelert and I went on ahead to get my key. Eva stayed behind in the shadow. The general assumption was that the night reception staff were secret police. I asked for my keys and the man at the desk said, 'Mr Richardson, I'm afraid it is not permitted.' I tried to cajole him but he simply shook his head. So we drove back to the Karl Marx Hostel for Young Ladies. The driver seemed to be used to this sort of situation. He shrugged his shoulders and said in mixed German and English, 'It's very simple. You just wait until mid-day.' I kissed Lantos Eva goodnight and she agreed to come to lunch at two.

Next day, Monday, I abstained from visiting the collective farm and sat waiting in the Gelert. She never turned up. I sent for a taxi and one came driven by a huge fellow of about forty-five, with cheerful blue eyes and dusty fair hair. I summoned up my fragmentary German and told him more or less what had happened. He joined me in the quest for Lantos Eva with tremendous enthusiasm. At the Karl Marx Hostel he got hold of Eva's great friend Martha, a beautiful dark girl in a yellow macintosh. Would I not be satisfied with her, he suggested, with a wink, as if the hostel was a brothel. I said, 'You wait till you see Eva.'

Martha told us that Eva had slept late and had then gone, she thought, to one of the law libraries. She gave my taxi driver a list of about five. We set off full of optimism. 'We are going to find her. I know it,' he said.

The foreign visitor to a Budapest university library is treated rather like royalty. A procession formed up each time with my taxi driver taking the rear as a kind of bodyguard. We inspected library after library. No sign of Eva. At the last one a senior lecturer in law asked me very pointedly why I was so interested in this particular young student? I said that I represented the *New Statesman* and that she had asked me for some information on a point in English law. I heard a gigantic smothered guffaw behind me and looked round to see my taxi driver with his huge fist in his face. But the law lecturer was visibly impressed, and no longer seemed to doubt my intentions. Down by the Danube the taxi driver suddenly rammed on the brakes, so that his hideous metal box of a car jumped two feet in the air, and sprang out. He rushed over to another car and came back almost carrying a diminutive young Englishman who was a member of the British Council in Budapest. Of course, he was no more able to help us than anyone else. I drove back to the Gelert and my driver and I parted as brothers.

That night I had to go to dinner at the press club. I made a speech in which I reminded everybody that there had once been an insane plan to make the first Lord Rothermere king of Hungary. But, I said, there was only one Britisher in history who was a suitable candidate for this throne, and that was Macbeth. Why? Because 'Macbeth hath murdered sleep'.

The rest of that night was chaos and confusion. I remember a strange mélange of a loquacious Indian, one of the representatives of culture, whose particular forté seemed to be prostitutes' tariffs, and a tiny Hungarian tart in a monkey jacket and sailor's cap with tousled golden curls. We ended up in her flat in a working-class quarter, which alarmed her grandmother – she had not had time to take down a picture of the imperial family. It was all seen through a cloud of barasch – fierce Hungarian apricot brandy that tastes like hornets' piss. Yet such were the powers of the hot spring at the Gelert, that by ten o'clock next morning I was fully conscious and asking a kindly chamber maid to telephone the Karl Marx Hostel for Lady Students. Suddenly she shoved the receiver at me with a cry of, 'Lantos Eva kommt!' 'Stay where you are and don't move,' I told Eva. 'I'm coming right away.'

From what I remembered of our schedule, our plane was not due to take off till three-thirty. Eva was actually waiting for me and we walked to the Astoria for breakfast; poached eggs and brandy. Eva's explanation was simple: agonizing toothache coupled with slight trepidation at the thought of confronting reception again. We talked and talked, with the aid of her pocket dictionary. She told me her father was a judge in the town of Mikholcz. I said I expect he'd give me ten years. To compound the crime, I took her to Margit Island, a recognized retreat for lovers in the middle of the Danube. But sipping our brandy on the terrace of an ancient hotel and watching the drizzle drift by only made Eva restless. And understandably so. It was Eva who suggested we renegotiate the Gelert . . . But as we sprang up the hotel steps I was seized by the British Council.

'What are you doing here?' he spluttered. 'Your lot left hours ago!'

'What lot? Where?' I was still clinging on to Eva's hand. But it was no use.

'Can you pack in five minutes? If you leave now you'll just make it in time for the official send-off.'

This time no one stopped us. Eva stood over my bag, catching up armfuls of clothes and thrusting them in, as I hurled them across the room, doubled up with frustration and laughter.

Reviews

Ants

M. V. Brian: *Ants*

(Collins, *New Naturalist* series)

Unless one has had a rigorous scientific training, it is almost impossible to contemplate the social insects without indulging in anthropomorphism. Solomon, Aesop, La Fontaine are obvious examples, all to some extent misleading, if pleasing. A serious offender was Maeterlinck, who claimed that termites were more intelligent than men because they had found out how to digest wood and dissolve concrete, and could mould the bodily form of their citizens.

An amusing example of the over-complication involved in an anthropomorphic approach is the legend of the trumpeter bumble bee. This, A. D. Imms tells us, was first propounded by the Dutchman, J. Gordart, in 1700. He maintained that every morning a bumble bee roused the nest by sounding a reveille with its rapidly beating wings, like a bugler in the army. The legend persisted for more than two hundred years, until H. von Buttel-Reepen showed that the real function of the trumpeter was the same as that observed among the hive bees: to ventilate the nest by the air current it created.

With ants the temptation to indulge is almost overwhelming. Consider the notorious case of *Bothriomyrmex decapitans*, which is parasitic on another species, *Tapinoma*. After fertilization, the *Bothriomyrmex* queen enters the *Tapinoma* nest. The workers attack her. She crawls on to the back of the *Tapinoma* queen. By now it seems her foreign smell is masked by the *Tapinoma* smell, and, as Julian Huxley puts it, 'she spends more and more time on the back of her host queen, slowly but surely accomplishing her task of sawing her head off'. She is adopted by the *Tapinoma* workers, who rear up a brood of aliens, and the colony is converted from pure *Tapinoma* to pure *Bothriomyrmex*.

My first association to this performance is to liken it to some livid Jacobean drama of lesbian betrayal and murder; here is a plot for *Queens Beware Queens*, a collaboration by Middleton, Webster and Ford. But a moment's thought shows you that such behaviour is only possible among creatures governed by a very strict system of olfactory reflexes. However, a dash of the irresistible anthropomorphism may save one from going to the other extreme of mechanism. The insect world will always have its surprises. Ants, I believe, are still suspected of play activities. And an acknowledged authority on flies, Harold Oldroyd, has referred to the lesser house fly, *Fannia canicularis*, as 'to be seen . . . playing kiss-in-the-ring under a hanging lamp'. But the important thing when you go to the ant is to stick to the facts. This you can rely on M. V. Brian to do.

Dr Brian is the foremost authority on British ants and his monograph on them is a credit to the excellent *New Naturalist* series, in which it appears. Much of his text is based on his own investigations. His writing is lucid, on the dry side. He rarely hazards a metaphor and any hint of anthropomorphism is alien to him. When describing worker ants dragging big prey to their nests, he does not compare them to a gang of labourers; he gives exact, experimentally derived figures for their horse power:

> 'Single workers of *Myrmica rubra* developed 0.8×10^{-6} horse power and of *Formica lugubris* 3.2×10^{-6} horse power. When this [measurement] was tried for pairs of ants it proved difficult. However, in thirty per cent of cases the second ant contributed nothing at all.'

Dr Brian begins with a brief survey of evolution and life history. Ants evolved from a solitary wasp-type ancestor that took to terrestrial life – for which the modern ant's legs are magnificently adapted. Many varieties of ant had already evolved by the Eocene period, seventy million years ago. Ant societies are active in summer, hibernate in winter. Queen ants and males, collectively known as sexuals, congregate in flying swarms and copulate in the air. The queen, having picked a site for the nest, casts her wings, which are a handicap for earth-dwelling, digs a cell in soil or wood and lays the eggs. The first larvae may eat some of the eggs.

The first ants to metamorphose are small, relatively simple, wingless worker females. They relieve the queen of the care and defence of the brood and enlarge the nest and bring in food. Larger workers appear later. The queen needs to be fertilized only once and the sperm, enough to last for the rest of her life, are contained in a purse-like apparatus of which she controls the sphinctus. She is also able to control, in ways some of which are still unknown, the various castes of workers, queens and males into which eggs and larvae will develop.

Further, if somewhat irrelevant, complexity may be caused by the presence, as in other insects, of gynandromorphs, deformities that may be due to some abnormality of fertilization. In some of these one half is male and winged, the other half worker; in others one half is queen, the other half male. Of variations among worker ants, the most extreme are the honey-pots, found among *Brechygastra*, *Ptenolepsis* and *Myrmecocystus*. These happy Bessie Bunters develop enormously distensible stomachs and turn into living storage jars. They hang upside down from the roof of the nest and their fellow workers feed them by regurgitation.

The males, though they do not perish from total castration like the male bees and many copulate more than once, do not long survive the nuptial flight. Often on landing they are set upon by workers of their own species. Among some of the termites – more primitive insects related to the cockroaches – the male is forced to lead a monogamous life in a dark cell, repeatedly fertilizing the same queen. Perhaps some of the Duke of Edinburgh's prejudice against all forms of collectivism is now more understandable.

There are more than three thousand species of ants. The most spectacular inhabit the tropics. Among them are the driver ants of Africa, blind and insatiably ferocious, always restlessly moving on and devouring; the Huns of the ant world; and the so-called parasol ants of Central America, which carry back to their nests the pieces of green leaf they have cut out with their jaws, and hand them over to smaller workers to make beds for the fungus which is a staple food of the species.

But the social organization of the British ants is quite impressive enough; there are forty-seven species and four principal genera: *Myrmica*, *Leptothorax*, *Lasius*, and *Formica*. *Myrmica rubra,* a small brownish-red ant, armed with a sting, found in colonies of up to three thousand workers, is the one Dr Brian chooses for his beautifully detailed chapter on ant anatomy, one of the features of which is the special crop which Forel called the social stomach, in which food is stored to be given to other ants.

Lasius (the common black ant) and *Formica* have no stings but cant emit formic acid. *Formica* can shoot a jet to a distance of several centimetres and aim it. *Formica sanguinea*, a large red ant allied to the wood ants, raids the nest of *Formica fusca* and carries off the pupae. Some are eaten but others are allowed to hatch out and co-operate with the *sanguinea* workers. 'They have', writes Dr Brian rather austerely, 'misleadingly been called slaves.'

The large leggy wood ants make huge mounds of vegetable débris with galleries underneath and tracks leading to trees. *Formica rufa* is the commonest of them in southern England. I remember my awe as a small boy at coming on one of these huge nest mounds on the edge of a pine wood in east Devon, teeming with activity. Its population might have been three hundred thousand. You could smell the sharp whiff of formic acid on the heavy August air. An encounter between two *Formica rufa* workers making some sort of communication by interlocking their antennae – preparatory perhaps to an exchange of liquid food – is an unforgettable sight. Close relations of *Formica rufia*, inhabiting Wales and Ireland and the Scottish Highlands, have been subjects of some of Dr Brian's ecological surveys. Both the *Lasius* and *Formica* genera cultivate aphids, stroking them with their antennae to make them yield honey dew. There are some brilliant photographs, particularly one of *Formica rufa* taking a drop of honeydew from an aphid.

Habits of feeding vary greatly. Dr Brian traces them with minute care. '*Lasius flavus* is now known to eat seven species of myremecophilous aphids.' It also eats more of its own queens than the more aggressive and larger *Lasius niger*. All British ants fancy a mixed meat and vegetarian diet but only some species collect and store seeds.

How ants find their way has always been something of a mystery. Dr Brian tells us they use 'a number of environmental cues. The principal one is undoubtedly the light pattern of the habitat; but gravity, chemical patterns and, particularly with underground ants, shape are important.' The intensity of gravity is measured with special sense organs in the joints of the legs. Many species lay chemical trails from food areas to the nest. The complexity involved is shown by the fact that in *Myrmica rufa* the secretion from Dufour's gland has been found to contain twenty different substances.

A feature of modern myrmicology is the ingenuity required. 'It is not', says Dr Brian, 'easy to put a mark on ants. The only satisfactory method seems to be to narcotize them lightly and puncture their cuticle.' Radioisotopes can be used but only under strict surveillance.

Underground fighting can easily be studied by means of artificial plate glass nests. Dr Brian describes a series of battles of 'stings' versus 'jets': *Tetramorium* against different species of *Lasius*:

> '*Lasius alienus* rushed into the *Tetramorium* nest, grabbed any workers they could find and sprayed them with formic acid. The *Tetramorium* workers retaliated by trying to sting the *Lasius alienus* in the leg ... After this foray, *Lasius alienus* retired and started to build barrages across their main galleries and to extend the nest away in the opposite direction. *Tetramorium* advanced to these barriers and started to dismantle them. They got through and entered the *Lasius* galleries without resistance, walking about freely and ignoring both the workers and their brood. By this time quite a lot of workers had died, almost in pairs ... Against *Lasius flavius*, *Tetramorium* massed together in close order, plugging the entrance gap while other workers brought up soil to make a barrier. Later, they counter-attacked and pushed right into the *Lasius* nest.'

Among myrmophiles – the various invertebrates welcomed inside ant nests – the most popular of all are the caterpillar larvae of the large blue butterfly. These feed on thyme and secrete a liquid which the genus *Myrmica* find quite irresistible. In return they allow the caterpillars to eat some of their own larvae. Spiders are some of the most determined ant predators. Members of the *Therutdae* family sit in wait on the vegetation over the ant tracks and drop on passing workers, 'immobilizing them and enclosing them in silk, to be consumed later'.

Ants are eaten by specialist birds, notably green woodpeckers, wrynecks, and game birds, but not by general feeders. 'This', says Dr Brian, 'is thought to be because the toxins inside them have an unpleasant taste.' I am surprised, for as a boy I often ate ants. *Lasius*, I should think; I never dared try *Formica*. They tasted sharpish but not unpleasant. I was put on to them by an old man I met on Woodbury Common. He was spreading them on bread. He told me that in vagrant circles they were known as 'the tramp's caviare'. This is my sole original contribution to myrmicology.

Among other features of this splendid book are a complete section of distribution maps and a chapter on culture methods for the benefit of amateur ant fanciers. Some of these may already be visited in their homes by the tiny Pharaoh's ant, *Monomorium pharaonis*, most notorious and best established of indoor ants. Though sensitive to cold, it is very versatile in other ways and can establish small colonies of as few as fifty workers and fifty larvae in cracks and crannies. Dr Brian admits – reluctantly, one feels – that there is a strong case for controlling, if not eliminating it.

Rampant Obscurantism

Brian Inglis: *Natural and Supernatural*
(Hodder & Stoughton)

Rationalists who were perturbed by Bernard Levin's advance fanfare on his medium's trumpet in *The Times* can take a crumb of comfort. The book is less obscurantist than he made it sound, though judging by the way these case histories develop the prognosis is poor. Brian Inglis may not yet have caught up with the advance guard of miracle-mongers, the whirling dervishes like Stuart Holroyd and Colin Wilson; but he is getting dangerously near their dust cloud. The trouble with Inglis is that, though honest, intelligent and industrious, he is obstinate as his national animal the jackass – that noble beast whom Irishmen rightly revere. A few years ago in *Fringe Medicine*, he showed a lively Shavian propensity for enfilading the medical establishment; but the way he dug his heels in and refused to give reason the benefit of the doubt, even when confronted by such manifest paranoiac's contraptions as Abram's Box and Reich's portable orgone parlour, made me nervous.

Now, in *Natural and Supernatural* – a five-hundred-page 'History of the Paranormal from Earliest Times up to 1914', so a sequel may be expected – Inglis declared his partisan interest from the start. His argument, I take it, is that recent advances in parapsychology, including proofs of telepathy (and telekinesis), plus the evanescent and contradictory nature of matter as revealed by subatomic physics, have made hay of the old-fashioned mechanistic standpoint from which psychic phenomena used to be judged. So it is time to re-examine them in a new light. But of what?

It turns out to be a new nightlight of diminished scepticism, increased credulity – in fact of outright Belief. As for poor old Disbelief, whom we all agreed to leave up there, willingly suspended from the rafters in the psi lab, he has evidently been garotted. It reminds me of my communist days: when I expressed some faint doubts about the infinite moral and intellectual superiority of the international proletariat and its great Leader and Teacher. I was told that by saying such a thing out loud, so that it could be heard, I was influencing the world historical process in the counter revolutionary direction, guilty of bourgeois objectivism – as bad if not worse than bourgeois subjectivism.

And so, after a passing sideswipe at Geller-doubters, Brian Inglis takes off from the preface and begins at the beginning in the dark backward of the anthropological department, with divination, firewalking, shamanism. Inglis has read widely and writes nicely. He is a good hand with a traveller's tale and a lot of his book is fascinating, strongly to be recommended: as entertainment only. He has an eye for unfamiliar aspects of the famous, like Socrates and Cicero, and for interesting lesser-known figures such as Dr Elliotson, the mesmerist so highly thought of by Dickens and Thackeray. Yet, again and again, whether it's the Cana wedding feast, or Dr Johnson's favourite the Cock Lane Ghost, or the Phantom Drummer of Tidworth, you have to make a correction for viewpoint. The fact is that, with or without ESP and electronic indeterminism, most psychic phenomena as reported are just as contrary to the laws of physics and chemistry obtaining in the macrosphere, just as difficult to observe with any certainty, much less to measure, as ever they were. Of course, when he's on to one of the really good traditional things, Inglis plays it straight – for instance, our old friend St Joseph of Copertino, the seventeenth-century Flying Monk. The elaborate contemporary testimony to Copertino's feats of levitation has shaken even such a staunch sceptic as Dr E. J. Dingwall, albeit St Joseph lived in an age when witchcraft was generally accepted and a witchfinder had no difficulty in collecting sworn eye-witness accounts of infestations of hovels by black imps. (It was Dingwall, incidentally, who at a séance in Massachusetts could see none of the elaborate manifestations reported by the other participators, and was told he must be negatively hallucinated.)

An important part of the new nightlight attitude is the myth of a conspiracy over the centuries to suppress or distort the evidence of paranormal activities. It is perfectly true that some psychic investigators do suggest the Two Black Crows, comedians of the nineteen-twenties: when one made a joke the other said, 'Boy, even if that was good I wouldn't like it.' They can be crooked, too, like the late Harry Price, who faked the Borley Rectory poltergeist to get better publicity. Honesty seems to be the best levitator. But though I am dismayed to learn from Brian Inglis, following Andrew Lang, how flagrantly Anatole France rigged the sources for his biography of Joan of Arc, it doesn't alter my opinion about where Joan's voices came from.

The most significant part comes when we arrive at that 'whole mine of mysticism hatching beneath the scepticism of the nineteenth century', as the Goncourts called it. This is the period of the spiritualist wave that spread from America with the Fox sisters, the proliferation of mediums (most of them proved fraudulent), of the scientists Wallace, Crooks and Oliver Lodge who investigated them, and of the indubitably fabulous Daniel Dunglas Home (1833–86), medium extraordinary. Inglis's attitude to the fraudulent ones is characteristic. He doesn't for one moment deny the charges, but he does tend to play them down, and he is very ready to come to the rescue of the benighted scientists who, he feels, got an unfair deal from Victorian philistines. I find something rather equivocal about his attitude towards the mockers (Engels was one of them), of poor Russell Wallace, when his pet medium, Mrs Guppy, one of the fattest women in London, was alleged to have arrived in the middle of a séance at 69 Lambs Conduit Street, having been teleported there from Highbury Hill Park. Compare the testimony of Andrija Puharich, the American investigator who claimed that Yuri Geller was instantaneously teleported from down-town Manhattan to Ossining, a distance of thirty miles. However, Inglis's investigation of sources is extremely thorough and he doesn't restrict himself to those that support his side. Thus, when considering Eusapia Palladino, the famous Italian peasant medium who was caught helplessly cheating after some stunning manifestations, he digs up a Russian psychical researcher, Count Perovsky-Petrovo-Solovovo, who appears to have suffered from a strange state of investigator's indecision, oscillating between credulity and incredulity, like Freud in Jones's biography.

When he comes to D. D. Home (1833–1886), he is on to another of those traditional good things. The feats, of levitating both he himself and heavy Victorian furniture, of bell ringing, red hot coal handling, the entire psychic repertoire, attributed to this weird wispy individual (he was an illegitimate cousin of Lord Home), far surpass those attributed to any other medium. Despite Browning's indignation, expressed in the poem about 'Sludge', Home was never caught out. There is a story that he was exposed at a séance at the Tuileries in 1857, tweaking Napoleon III with his prehensile toes, but it was later denied by the Empress Eugénie and is generally dismissed as a malicious rumour. I don't think we can blame Brian Inglis for not mentioning it. I wish, though, he had paid more attention to the literature on conjuring, and especially to the books of the American John Mulholland. Edmund Wilson put me on to those. 'Many conjuring tricks,' wrote Mulholland, 'are perfect psychological experiments . . . A magician may, with mathematical certainty, rely on what any group will do during the process of a trick.'

Mulholland also, as Wilson remarks, 'affords a startling revelation of the common human incapacity to observe or report correctly.'

On Re-reading Firbank

Five novels by Ronald Firbank
(Gerald Duckworth)

When Firbank died, in 1926, aged thirty-nine, his witty, gossamer novels, with their unearthly neo-Byzantine climate, had already become the object of a cult. The spread of the Hemingway vernacular, and the reaction against aesthetic frivolity that came with the depression, distracted attention from him; but his devotees remained faithful. Now his tenancy of a rococo apartment in the House of Fame is established; however the prospect may dismay North Oxford, he had become compulsory reading for students of English Literature in the first half of the twentieth century.

The present omnibus volume gives us *Valmouth*, *The Flower Beneath the Foot*, *Prancing Nigger*, *Concerning the Eccentricities of Cardinal Pirelli* and *The Artificial Princess*. The first four are generally considered to be the cream of Firbank. *The Artificial Princess* belongs to an earlier period, before his style had developed into its final, firefly dance of inversions and elisions; it reads like a pastiche of one of several contributors to the Yellow Book. The publishers would have done better to have given us another of his books with an English background – *Vainglory* or *Caprice*. As it is, *Valmouth*, a dreamy fantastical comedy of negresses, centenarians, and Catholic ladies of approximately equal piety and decadence, is the only example here of how he treats a domestic rural scene. *The Flower Beneath the Foot* is a tragi-comedy of renunciation, royalty, and diplomacy in a Balkan capital. *Prancing Nigger* is a tale of love and loss among West Indian negroes. *Cardinal Pirelli* sketches the collapse of a most unsaintly prelate in Madrid and Seville. He is perhaps Firbank's only really successful male character.

It is difficult, without lengthy quotation, to convey an accurate impression of Firbank's work. He is, as Sir Osbert Sitwell points out in his entertaining introduction, the inspired amateur who writes because he must; we can almost hear him laughing hysterically at his own jokes. Some of his influences, such as Wilde and Beardsley, are easy enough to spot. His faintly blurred yet glowing word pictures, and his blend of moods and colours – 'the grey spleen of evening', 'the blue doom of summer' – suggest impressionist painting. His dramatic dialogue, with so much left unsaid, sometimes creates an extraordinary effect, as if Congreve, Angela Brazil, and Douglas Byng had become alchemically fused. He is, in fact, the oddest conglomeration of fantasy, satire, sentimentality, avant-gardism, naughtiness, silliness, delicious wit and beauty. It is no surprise to find that he inherited Irish traits, through his mother. What is almost alarming, and what Sir Osbert does not tell us, is that Firbank's Yorkshire grandfather, the founder of the fortune, was a one hundred per cent proletarian tyke, one of the roughest diamonds in the Midlands.

Eels

Christopher Moriarty:
Eels: A Natural and Unnatural History
(David and Charles)

It has taken two millennia to elucidate the main lines of the natural history of these wonderful fish. So much about eels, their serpentine appearance, complicated life-cycle and heroic migrations, seems mysterious and contradictory. Indeed, it is reported that Professor Übisch once exclaimed in a fit of exasperation that he did not believe the eel was a normal product of evolution at all; it was more like the subject of a special creation in the mind of Hegel on a wet afternoon.

The first landmark in the study of *Anguilla anguilla*, our familiar European species, was 350 BC when Aristotle established that freshwater eels migrate to the sea. He is also generally thought to have believed in the spontaneous generation of eels from mud, though the late Professor Bertin, that delightfully animated French ichthyologist, protests that the text is not altogether clear at this point. Be this as it may, it was not until 1684 that Redi observed both the exodus of the adult eels and the return of the young elvers to the rivers, and suggested there might be a spawning ground in the sea. Two more centuries were needed to discover the male and female sexual organs, and to observe the larvae form *Leptocephalus* and its metamorphosis into an elver. Finally, in 1922, the Danish marine biologist, Professor Schmidt, on the basis of a series of voyages beginning in 1904, announced his discovery that the Sargasso Sea, in mid-west Atlantic, was the eel's spawning ground. None the less, as Christopher Moriarty points out, the fully sexually mature eel has not been seen in the ocean to this day. Once in the Atlantic, eels elude observation. It is thought they do not survive the first spawning.

Christopher Moriarty entered the Irish Fishing Service in 1959 and was told: 'You'll do eels.' He has been doing them ever since and finds that every problem solved poses a hundred more. His book is racy but soundly informative, though it might have been more systematically arranged. It really does fill one of those long-felt gaps, for though eel literature is extensive – a bibliography in 1966 contained three thousand, four hundred entries – most of it consists of specialist papers, including a large quantity of mathematical statistics.

A remarkable feature of the eel's life cycle is the duration of *Leptocephalus*, which is ten millimetres long, shaped like a laurel leaf, transparent as glass, with a tiny head. Schmidt calculated that eel larvae take two and a half years to cross the Atlantic from the Sargasso Sea to Europe. Their food consists of micro plankton. Their metamorphosis to the agile elver, which has become adapted to life in brackish and fresh water, is a gradual process. Mortality must be enormous. Cannibalism plays its part. Moriarty found fifty elvers in the stomach of a female eel weighing five hundred grams. There are two further stages, the yellow freshwater phase lasting eight to eighteen years, and the silver phase when the eel is ready to return to the sea. The oldest eel on record (named Putte) lived to be eighty-eight. She was caught as an elver in 1863, and therefore was presumably born in the Sargasso Sea in 1860. She died in the Aquarium at Salsingborg in 1948.

The sexuality of eels is far from simple. Ninety per cent, according to Professor Bertin, 'pass successively through phases of neutrality, of precocious feminization and of juvenile hermaphroditism, before becoming definitely male or female'. The determining factor is thought to be environmental. Appropriately enough, one of the pioneer investigators here was Freud himself, as a young man in 1876. He was put on to it by Carl Claus, the Viennese comparative anatomist, who suggested he should check the work of the Polish zoologist, Syrski. In his paper *Über die Reproduktions-organe der Aale* Syrski claimed to have found the male eel's testis. Freud dissected some four hundred eels and confirmed Syrski's finding; his own paper was published in 1877.

Anguilla anguilla, when full grown, reaches a length of one metre, females being larger than males. The British angling record eel, caught near Bristol in 1922, weighed 3.85 kg (8½ lb) but, says Moriarty, eels of at least 5 kg (11 lb) have been recorded. Its fins are much reduced, but its internal anatomy is entirely piscine and at once distinguishes it from reptiles or amphibians. It breathes through gills and has a swim bladder for oxygen storage. It cannot live indefinitely out of water but it can survive longer on land than most fish, sometimes for as long as forty-eight hours. A limited amount of respiration can take place through the skin. Freshwater eels when migrating will leave the water if they meet a barrier and can make long journeys through wet grass. Elvers, confronted by a waterfall, will wriggle their way up through damp moss. Eels produce quantities of mucus which help to lubricate them. Many are great burrowers. Some species burrow backwards, diving into the sand, tail foremost.

Diet varies with size from insect larvae to shrimps, prawns, mussels, and a variety of fish. Flatfish are swallowed whole and found rolled up in the eel's stomach. Christopher Moriarty has developed a positive *tendresse* for *Anguilla anguilla*, expressed in phrases like 'eels are rugged individualists', and he is even inclined to defend it against accusations of scavenging, such as Günter Grass's account of eels devouring the corpse of a horse in *The Tin Drum*. His own observations of stomach contents 'point strongly towards a preference for living prey', though he does admit that eels in large numbers are found downstream from slaughter-houses.

Much work has been done on how eels orientate themselves during migration. They have been followed by releasing them with long-stringed rubber balloons attached, and tracked by means of ultrasonic tags. The straight course which they adopt supports the idea of some magnetic influence. They are known to be extremely sensitive to electric fields. Deelder, who has made a special study of eel movements, thinks that eels are continuously influenced by the moon and stars, also by micro-seismic activity. Silver (mature) eels in captivity display periodical restlessness. Some fishermen keep a few captives under observation to get a forecast of when the wild eels will begin to run in large numbers.

Ichthyology is possibly the most controversial and contentious of all branches of zoology, but it can be safely stated that the eels, *Order Anguilliformes*, comprise nineteen families and more than five hundred species. They branched off from some ancestral teleost – bony fish – during the cretaceous period. Other teleost fishes have developed eel-like forms. The most famous is the electric 'eel' found in South American rivers. It cannot be considered a true eel. There are several eccentric species among the true eels, such as *Avocettina*, with an immensely elongated body and obtusely curved jaws like an avocet's beak. Of the more sensational species, the best known in the British Isles is *Conger conger*. The record conger, according to Mr Moriarty, caught in 1904, measured 270 cm and weighed 72kg, a truly stupendous specimen. I wish he had told us rather more about the conger's ferocity and its habit of grunting like a badger when landed. Its life cycle in the Atlantic was traced by Schmidt, who found larvae between Gibraltar and the Azores. It also spawns in the Mediterranean.

The largest known eel is the giant moray, *Thyrsoidea macrura*, which is over three metres long. It lives in lagoons and shallow water over a wide range in the Indian Ocean. Its European cousin, the moray eel, *Muraena helena*, length 150 cm, though inclined to be sluggish is renowned for voracity. This is the eel which the Romans were reputed to feed with (fresh) slaves. The late Arturo Barea gives a vivid if rather highly-coloured account of catching one in Spanish Morocco on a hand line in *The Track*, the second volume of his autobiography.

Insatiable sensationalists are referred to Bernard Henvelman's *In the Wake of the Sea Serpent*. Here, Moriarty points out, the most tantalizing monster eel appears, but as a larva, a giant *Leptocephalus*. On January 31, 1930, the Danish vessel *Dana*, in search of eels between the Cape of Good Hope and St Helena, caught an eel larva nearly two metres long. 'Simple multiplication', says Moriarty, 'suggests that this might grow into a genuine sea serpent of seventy metres or so.'

An important section of the book deals with catching eels, from the primitive method known as 'bobbing', with a ball of worms threaded with worsted on which the eels catch their teeth, to various elaborate and sophisticated traps and nets. As a fisheries expert, Mr Moriarty goes into much useful detail about the various industrial aspects of intensive eel culture, including the vital questions of storage and stocking. Some figures are impressive; an average of twenty-six million elvers are taken up to Lough Neagh every year and the annual output of the lake is about seven hundred tons – perhaps two million eels. He also gives instruction in the difficult art of killing and skinning eels, and in the best and simplest ways of cooking them. Endearing, throughout the book, is the stress he lays on humane treatment whenever possible of a creature which is too often the victim of barbarous brutality.

The strange equivocal nature of the eel has inspired various legends. Oppian of Sicily, in the second century AD, relates an elaborate story of a mating between a female Roman eel and a male snake. The snake first undergoes a purification process, purging himself of his venom by vomiting into a hole near the seashore. Then he hisses his love-song. The eel darts towards land and he swims to meet her through the foam. 'Their mutual desire is satisfied. Panting with pleasure, the "she" eel draws the snake's head into her mouth.' There is a curious postscript to this idyll. The snake, on his way back to dry land, returns to his black vomit to reabsorb the venom. But if by chance a passer-by, having recognized the fatal liquid, has thrown it into the sea, 'then in desperation the snake bangs his head against the stone until he dies.' He cannot outlive his shame.

In Polynesian folk lore, the eel plays the part of Prince Charming. The eel-god Tuna appears to the maiden Ina, changes into a prince and becomes her lover. But the story ends on a sacrificial note. Ina had to decapitate the eel and bury its head. A coconut palm grows up over it and to this day every coconut bears at its tip the eyes and mouth of the eel god Tuna.

Pliny, as Moriarty notes, had a good deal to say about the high esteem in which the ferocious Roman eel was held by Roman matrons. One, which would answer the call of a bell, like a carp, was so beloved by its owner that she presented it with a pair of gold earrings (fin-rings or tail-rings?). Pliny, also, with characteristic wild exaggeration, writes of eels in the Ganges, three hundred feet long. However, his description of the wondrous eel balls in Lake Garda, where eels knotted themselves together in bunches, has been confirmed by modern observers.

An interesting medieval student of eels was Albertus Magnus, the Dominican philosopher and sage. He recorded eels leaving the Danube in search of food. Less likely is his account of eels during an exceptionally cold winter, shacking up together for warmth in a haystack. A strange fancy of eels, when on land, for garden peas is reported by Bock at the end of the eighteenth century, and by the Dowger Countess of Hamilton early in the nineteenth. The eels from Lake Hedenlunda, declared the Countess, wriggled into the fields at night and ate pea pods, making a smacking sound with their lips.

The proverbial slipperiness of the eel, combined with its vigour and tenacity, makes it an expert escapologist. And this, together with its phallic semblance, invests it with a special slapstick role in traditional popular humour. The Fool in *Lear* gives us an example: 'Cry to it, nuncle, as the cockney did to the eels when she put 'em i' the pasty alive: she knapped 'em on the cockscombs with a stick and cried: "Down, wantons, down!" ' I have myself witnessed a mass escape of eels in an East End restaurant when the atmosphere was very similar. Proprietor, staff and customers became convulsed. It was like an animated seaside postcard by McGill. Perhaps the most sensational eel break-out occurred in the nineteen-twenties when, owing to some idiosyncrasy of the PLM traffic controller, an eel tank on wheels was attached to the Blue Train en route for Monte Carlo. The eels escaped in large numbers and infiltrated the *wagons-lits* occupied by the customary clientèle of millionaires, ballet dancers, demi-mondaines, gigolos, and elderly lady roulette punters from South Kensington. The scene may be imagined.

Cornish Pixie

Daphne du Maurier: *Growing Pains*
(Gollancz)

Some of us Daph-fans are apt to be too obsessed with *Rebecca*. We fantasize about origins and psychodynamics like way-out Sherlockians. Apart from the affinity with the first Mrs Rochester, and the association of her surname, de Winter, with Dumas's 'Milady', the wicked nymphomaniac eludes us.

Can we detect in her any trace of the stage stars of the twenties who were always cluttering up Cannon Hall, the du Mauriers' Hampstead house, on Sundays? Hardly. Tallulah may have been a roaring nympho, but she didn't come from a Cornish county family. Maxim de Winter is easy, of course. That clipped throwaway style can only be taken from Gerald, for whom the husband-father role is a natural. But according to our depth-analysts, Mrs Danvers, the sinister housekeeper (whose brilliant impersonation by Flora Robson in the film is greeted every Christmas at fans' firesides with drunken shouts of 'Danny!'), is the key figure. She is the ugly witch-mother who metamorphoses backwards and forwards into her alias, the coruscating Rebecca, like the Queen in *Snow White* who made a deep impression on Daph.

But fans had better calm down because this autobiography stops in 1931 before *Rebecca* was written. The only thing immediately relevant to its genesis is Daph's Cornish craze, and a bit about Dr Rashleigh's house Menabilly, and its woods, near Fowey, which provided the imaginative base for Manderley.

1931 was a nodal point for twenty-four-year-old Miss du Maurier. Her first novel, *The Loving Spirit*, had not only been published but it found her the ideal husband. Boy Browning, a thirty-five-year-old major in the Grenadier Guards. To a friend he wrote:

0

'One of the best books I've read for ages . . . all about
Fowey in Cornwall. I'm determined to go down there
in my boat *Ygdrasil* . . . Perhaps I'll have the luck to
meet the girl who has written it.'

And he did. When Gerald got the news of the engagement he
burst into tears and said, 'It isn't fair.' But he couldn't really
disapprove of such a splendid son-in-law.

You don't need to be Freud to label Daph an Electra girl. That
daring profile of her father, *Gerald, a Portrait* (1934) was an
affectionate act of exorcism. (If she hadn't been able to get it off
her chest she might have turned into a Clytemnestra girl.) The
famous Georgian actor-manager's ego was wily as Proteus. You
feel he never stopped acting, whether over or under – even in his
sleep he vamped the Devil's grandmother. There is an extraordinary photograph of him (c. 1911) in this book, sitting in a tiny
kiddy-car, hunched up, looking as if, by some magical feat of
miming, he had shrunk, not into a dwarf but into a child dressed
up in its father's clothes. It was absurd that he should waste so
much of his great talents on vivifying zombies like Bulldog
Drummond.

Daph herself is no slouch when it comes to the essential
Thespian photogenesis (she was tested for Tessa in a silent film
of *The Constant Nymph*!). At thirteen she is challenging and tawny
but not in the least butch; a pretty girl with a deliciously
determined mouth, obviously a strong character and a bit of a
Tartar with the knack of making you feel a swine for having
Betjemanic thoughts about her. The most sensational illustra-
tion is a snap of her aged twenty-one, looking sulky and sultry in a
sou'wester, brandishing a boathook; in the background is a huge
conger eel which, as any surrealist would tell you, she has just
gaffed up out of the collective unconscious in the harbour. There
are also some stunning reproductions of artists' portraits, rich in
period value, school of 'Diana of the Uplands'. Her present day
image is that of a serene, prototypical, smart but not gaudy, Mrs
Exeter who has been through the mill.

I am sure she knows how much she owes to the du Maurier
genes carrying, through three generations, some mysterious
cluster of factors making for irresistibly compulsive entertainment. She subtitles her book 'The shaping of a writer'. I think
'the early years of a surprisingly normal woman' is equally

descriptive. She sails through all the difficult phases with an ease that's really rather remarkable in view of the background of her own obviously quite hefty temperamental load. A tomboy at puberty, she had daydreams which she shared with her sister, based on *Teddy Lester's Schooldays*, of being 'Eric Avon', an all-round athlete of genius. At her finishing school she had a powerful but not uncomfortable crush on Françoise, the elegant young directrice, later mysteriously sacked by the English spinster proprietress. Boyfriends were kept at arm's length by both parents. There was hell to pay if she came in after midnight. Gerald was especially jealous of his own nephew, Geoffrey, himself old enough to be Daph's father. Most fancied by her was Carol, who worked on Edgar Wallace films. She doesn't say so, but I think this must have been Carol Reed. After rumours – quite unfounded, just a few kisses in the bar – that she had been misconducting herself when staying with the Edgar Wallaces in Switzerland, she was sent on a Norwegian cruise, chaperoned by Viola Tree, who later fell into the drink in a picture hat, on the millionaire Otto Kahn's yacht. Her diary gets rather excited: 'This beauty is too much. It's defeating, utterly bewildering. Beauty most exquisite.' So does her sixty-six-year-old host. To cool him down 'springing to my feet . . . I stripped off my clothes and plunged naked into the water before his astonished eyes. A daring measure but it worked.'

Back home, determined to become independent, she buckled down to her writing. The house at Fowey was bought in 1927 and she entered on the sublimated pixie phase – with fuzzy old Quiller-Couch as mentor – that was to end with marriage. Meanwhile, a few miles away at St Austell, Rowse was starting to sun himself on the rocks of literature. Always a dangerous Duchy, Cornwall, But more please, Daph, and soonest.

The Marquis de Sade Consults Dr Freud

Ronald Hayman: *De Sade, A Critical Biography*
(Constable)

Ronald Hayman is a skilful biographer. He writes clearly and objectively and handles his – let's face it – none too easy subject without too much fashionable apologetics. Yet I am rather uneasy about his logic. The opening paragraph of his introduction reads:

> 'To explain evil', said Baudelaire in his *Journaux Intimes*, 'we must always go back to Sade – that is to natural man; Eluard was making the same point when he said that Sade "wanted to restore to civilized man the force of his primitive instincts. He wanted to liberate the erotic imagination for its own objectives." '

Now, in the first place, Baudelaire was wrong. Sade was not 'natural man'. He was a highly sophisticated product of tottering French feudalism. And in the second, Eluard was at least half wrong. Sade may have 'wanted to liberate the erotic imagination', but he couldn't possibly succeed. Why? Because it is in the nature of perversions to be addictive and from an addiction it is very difficult to escape. There is a rich variety of sexual perversions. Many of them are perfectly harmless. But it seems to be a psychological law that the more harmful, the more antisocial the perversion the more addictive it is likely to be because of the high degree of frustration involved. There is a direct analogy here with heroin, which is the most dangerous and rapidly addictive drug of all. Ronald Hayman seems to be at any rate partly aware of this, for he quotes from Rousseau's *Discours sur L'inégalité*:

> 'The less natural and urgent needs are, the stronger the passions and what is worse, the greater the power to satisfy them; so that after long prosperity, after having swallowed up

many treasures and ruined many men, my hero will end up by killing everything until he is sole master of the universe. Such is, in brief, the moral picture, if not of human life, at least of the secret aspirations in the heart of civilized man.'

This, of course, is a return to the infantilist solipsist position which Freud aptly labelled 'the omnipotence of thought'.

Now the principle of 'better out than in' is perfectly sound sense and good therapy, but in the case of the perversions it often doesn't work because of the addictive nature of perverse fantasies. One is reminded of poor Wilde's catch-phrase in *Dorian Gray*: 'to cure the soul with the senses and the senses with the soul', or of Aleister Crowley's novel *The Diary of a Drug Fiend*. In this the hero, a version of Crowley as seen by Crowley, haunting the Café Royal like a lifeguard to save souls, sets out to cure heroin addicts by taking their drugs away from them and taking them himself. Not surprisingly Crowley ended up on the Home Office list of heroin addicts.

When we come to the literary aspects of Sade I am also a bit foxed. Hayman writes:

'Barthes regards Sade's novels as great classics; Philippe Sollers ranks them "among the most varied and exciting texts in our literature". I do not rate Sade's novels as highly as this, but my view of his importance is extremely high. I think he is a key figure in the history of modernism, and, above all in the history of alienation. He was a nihilist, before the word nihilism existed, anticipating Dostoevsky and Nietzsche.'

We can dismiss the claims of Barthes and Sollers without a qualm. The dullness which even Hayman concedes to be present in *120 Days* and *Justine* is due to the Freudian repetition compulsion which is the very essence of addiction. In one sense everybody is an original, but I feel that Ronald Hayman is inclined to overestimate the originality of Sade. Before him were *inter alia* Gilles de Raies, who had intercourse with children and murdered them at the moment of orgasm, and the Countess Bathory who killed five hundred serving girls and drank their blood. You could say that Sade preached what they practised, though it would not be fair for, as Hayman points out, Sade's own 'sadistic practices were relatively mild and always stopped a long way short of murder'.

Nor is there anything particularly original in his nihilism. There have been nihilists of all sorts, some of them creative geniuses, like the unknown Hindu who invented Zero, others Taoist and Buddhist psychotherapists who laid stress on the Void.

Before I return to the main theme of sexual perversion, which Sade so powerfully illustrates, let me consider two types of ideological or religious perversion. One in the West is, of course, puritanism which, in the form of Calvinism, has done so much harm to the Scottish national psyche. A magnificent document here, far superior as a work of art to anything Sade wrote, is *The Private Memoirs and Confessions of a Justified Sinner* by James Hogg, the Ettrick Shepherd. And in the East there is or was the worship of Kali, the Hindu Goddess of destruction whose acolytes were the Thugs. Apologists of Kali, and of Sade, tend to use similar arguments, telling you that destruction is a form of creation. There you see man up to his old tricks making gods in his own image. Incidentally, Homer, possibly demonstrating the superior nature, even then, of Greek civilization, realized the nature of addiction. Achilles says:

'I wish that Strife would vanish away from among Gods and mortals, and of all which makes a man grow angry for all his great mind, that gall of anger which swarms like smoke inside a man's heart and becomes a thing sweeter by far than the dripping of honey.'

Now let us take Sade for a consultation with Freud. We must imagine the unfortunate Marquis arriving at 19 Berggasse, Vienna, not by coach but by Hispano-Suiza caravan, fitted up, I daresay, as a luxurious whackhouse on wheels. His valet Latour (one wonders if it was Latour Villiers de L'Isle d'Adam had in mind when he said: '*Vivre, nos valets le feront pour nous*') sets up the talking picture apparatus and Freud is a spectator of the scene in Marseilles, of which the following is an extract from Hayman's description:

'Latour came back with Mariette. Sade made her strip and

bend over the foot of the bed. He beat her with the broom and then ordered her to beat him. He counted the strokes given and received using a knife to carve the totals into the mantelpiece: 215, 179, 225, 240. Then turning the girl over he began to enjoy her. At the same time after starting to masturbate Latour, he let the man bugger him. This is the first evidence of practical experience in the simultaneous sexual penetrations that were to figure so prominently in his fiction.'

Freud takes down his paper 'Instincts and their Vicissitudes' and reads a few extracts:

'In considering the preliminary phase of the scopophilic instinct when the subject's own body is the object of the scopophilia, we must place it under the heading of narcissism; it is a narcissistic formation. From this phase the active scopophilic instinct, which has left narcissism behind, is developed, while the passive scopophilic instinct, on the contrary, holds fast to the narcissistic object. Similarly, the transformation from sadism to masochism betokens a reversion to the narcissistic object, while in both cases the narcissistic (active) subject is exchanged by identification for another extraneous ego.'

'Ha,' says Freud, 'it's curious you should have come here today. Only yesterday I was visited by a Polish Count Sacher-Masoch [Freud wasn't always as discreet as he ought to have been] after whom masochism was named. He had just come back from his honeymoon. He showed me some photographs of his wife in the arms of his valet. They were not very good photographs because he was under the bed when he took them, lying on his back on some drawing pins, and he had to reach up with one arm holding the camera. He asked if I could suggest any improvements. I replied that I was a psychoanalyst not a sensation provider.'

And in case this imaginary scene is thought too frivolous, let me quote from Freud's paper 'The Sexual Aberrations':

'No healthy person, it appears, can fail to make some addition that might be called perverse to the normal sexual aim; and the universality of his finding is in itself enough to show how

inappropriate it is to use the word perversion as a term of
reproach. In the sphere of sexual life we are brought up
against peculiar, and, indeed, insoluble difficulties as soon as
we try to draw a sharp line to distinguish mere variations
within the range of what is physiological from pathological
symptoms.'

How much light do the facts of Sade's biography throw on his
case history? If I find this difficult to answer it is no fault of
Ronald Hayman's. His account of them is admirably lucid and
he gives you a strong sense of period, of the exquisite decadence
of eighteenth-century France, and of that peculiar indefinable
something in the air which presaged the revolution. It might be
expressed as a dreadful coldness in personal relations. You find it
most notably in Laclos's novel *Les Liaisons Dangereuses*. But for me
the most horrifying story of all is about Louis XV and his pet
fawn. When it grew up and became a hind he shot it and
wounded it. It came limping to him for consolation. He shot it
again. Poor old Sade was never such a marble-hearted fiend as
that.

Sade's family were of Italian origin. His father was ambassador to the Court of Cologne where little Donatien-Alphonse-
François was born in 1740. He went to a Jesuit college, was
reputed to have a good heart, and was well liked by his fellow
pupils. He was not bad looking as a young man though somewhat pitted by smallpox. 'As with Genet,' writes Ronald Hayman, 'the soil in which perversion grew was habitual solitude
and constant frustration of the need to feel loved.' Sade became a
soldier and was commissioned sub-lieutenant when fifteen and a
half. A letter written when he was nineteen to his tutor l'Abbé
Amblet shows some guilt about various misdemeanours in Paris
and fear of his father. He wanted to marry the twenty-two-year-
old daughter of the Marquis de Lauris, even or perhaps most
especially after he had caught clap from her, but she chucked
him and he married Renée Pelagie, daughter of Mme de Montreuil, whose relationship with Sade seems to have been
strangely ambivalent.

His wife didn't excite him, although he had children by her,
and now, when he was twenty-four, he took a house in the rue
Mouffetard and set about his sadistic capers, one of his addi-

tional trimmings being to pollute crucifixes. We gather from Hayman's account (this isn't to my mind altogether clear at this point, as he seems to be possibly a trifle naïve in accepting Sade's own account at its face value), that he suffered from *ejaculatio retardata*. This according to Fenichel, is an hysterical conversion symptom and likely to be more deep-seated than its opposite, *ejaculatio praecox*. Whether this was due to beatings in youth, as Hayman suggests, or to what, if any, extent hereditary factors were involved, we shall never know. Hayman draws an interesting parallel between Sade and Stavrogin in Dostevsky's *The Possessed* (I wish people would stick to this, which is the correct title, and not call it *The Devils*), the key to whose religious dilemma was 'the combination of his pride with his lust for vileness'.

Sade's first arrest was for his performance with a twenty-two-year-old working-class girl Jeanne Testard, who talked to the police. The case was handled by M de Sartine, the Lieutenant General of Police, a strange thirty-year-old wig fetishist, who wore a special wig with curls like serpents to interrogate suspects. Sade was held in custody but allowed out after his family had petitioned the king. In April 1768 he was arrested again after an episode with a prostitute whom he whipped. He again regained his liberty helped by a petition from his wife, who presently gave birth to a daughter. Then, in June 1772, he and Latour indulged in the notorious orgy in Marseilles with four girls, one of whom was made ill by sweets containing cantharides. Mme Montreuil, Sade's mother-in-law, pressed for Sade's arrest. Sade and Latour were found guilty in their absence and faced a capital charge. In December 1772 Sade and Latour were arrested, but they escaped on April 30th much to the fury of Mme de Montreuil. After various complications, faithfully recorded by Ronald Hayman, including refusing to plead insanity, and another escape, Sade was to become a long-term prisoner.

It was in 1782 that he first became a writer (though he had written a play) with his *Dialogue entre un prêtre et un moribonde*, a story of a death-bed conversion. In 1784 he was transferred to the Bastille and began transcribing *120 Days*, his vast catalogue novel of almost every imaginable perversion, on an enormous roll of toilet paper. In 1789 he harangued the crowd through an improvised loudspeaker. In 1790 he was released and *Justine* was published. (The French revolutionaries were great releasers; they even released the animals in the Versailles zoo though the director warned them that, like men, many of these beasts were incapable of gratitude.) Sade was arrested and released several more times; he was transferred to the asylum at Bicêtre in 1803, then to Charenton where he organized theatrical performances. He died on December 2nd, 1814.

As a thinker, Sade's master was La Mettrie, one of the most radical of eighteenth-century mechanists who, while rejecting superstition, failed to appreciate that change and motion are the basic qualities of matter and life. Precisely what Ronald Hayman thinks I cannot be certain. At one moment he veers towards a Freudian position vis-à-vis perversion. The next he pronounces almost as if it were a slogan 'no-one is a sadist in the cradle'. This is contrary to one of Freud's most basic findings to the effect that we are all sadists in our cradles because the infant is a bundle of polymorph perverse tendencies. However, he has written a most stimulating and in many respects scholarly biography. If Sade's personality has eluded him, that was only to be expected.

Power House in Henrietta Street

Sheila Hodges: *The Story of a Publishing House 1928–1978*
(Gollancz)

In the spring of 1935, the Secretary of the Publishers' Advertising Circle, a small informal group of more or less junior 'executives', sent round a notice to say that the next monthly luncheon would be an occasion of extra special importance. Would all members make a point of attending and bringing with them a senior director of their firm?

Luncheon was held in one of the gilded mosaic masonic halls in the Holborn Restaurant. After the waiters had left, the doors were locked and the secretary got up and began to waffle about desirable and undesirable publicity techniques. He was cut short by Charlie Evans, the well-known managing director of Heinemann, a genial fellow not unlike C. B. Cochran. 'Let's get down to brass tacks,' he said with a wave of his cigar. 'We all know what we're here for. How can we down VG. Anyone got any suggestions?'

There was a faintly embarrassed silence. A foreigner might have thought he was calling for a volunteer Sparafucile or hit-man. (Actually, Evans had been on quite friendly terms with Gollancz; Sheila Hodges quotes an admiring letter congratulating Gollancz on his first list.)

The main reason for Gollancz's unpopularity was that at a time when trade was only just beginning to pick up, and profits, if any, were exiguous, he kept on taking large advertising spaces in *The Observer* and *The Sunday Times*. And not only did his advertisements, unlike publishers', sell books, but they put ideas into authors' heads. On Monday morning telephones would be shrilling with indignant lady novelists: 'Why on earth haven't you advertised *Spring Fever*? Gollancz has gone and plastered that bloody book of Esmeralda's all over both the Sundays again. How do you expect to sell me if you don't advertise me? I shall see what my agent has to say about this.'

Nobody had any practical suggestions. Michael Sadleir of Constable, with an expression of weary anguish on his handsome, ravaged features, treated us to a diatribe on the vulgarity of our times as compared with the gracious nineteenth century. He had recently completed his researches for *Fanny by Gaslight*, his novel of the Victorian underworld. 'We live', he said, 'in an age of plugged music, plugged films, and now plugged books. So let us combine together and take vast spaces ourselves and go on taking them, page after page after page, until we drive him out, out into outer darkness, out, out, out.' It might have been Dr van Helsing planning the exorcism of Dracula. Less than enthusiasm was shown for his proposal. Some of the smaller, specialist publishers shook their heads vigorously. 'Gollancz has got no back list,' they consoled themselves. 'He won't last.'

Soon after this the meeting broke up in desultory confusion. It was a unique, if left-handed, compliment to Gollancz. He had been publishing under his own imprint for only seven years and was so outstandingly successful that his competitors found him a serious menace. Publishing is still a very personal business and likely to remain so until the whizz computers take over. I doubt if any of them will whizz like Gollancz in his heyday.

Sheila Hodges, who worked for him for many years, has written a most interesting history, at the invitation of his daughter, Livia Gollancz, who now runs the firm. She gives you a strong sense of period and a lot of graphic detail about the technical as well as personal aspects of publishing. On the whole, hers is a good deal livelier and less conventionally pious than these celebratory exercises are apt to be; not all her geese are swans. Reactionary anti-Gollanczians, who would like to write off her hero, as a megalomaniacal, fellow-travelling Barabban paradigm, may find her a trifle hagiographical; but then nothing would satisfy them except a panning operation. In fact, she is quite reasonably objective and doesn't shrink from letting you know that VG could be dangerously infuriating at times. For Gollancz was one of those contradictory, hypersensitive extroverts who carry an exceptionally heavy temperamental load. Even so, at least eighty-nine per cent (a very high proportion for a professional man) of his benevolence was genuine, and it was impossible not to be fond of him when you got to know him.

Men become publishers for a variety of reasons. One I knew,

the son of a banker, suffered from eyesight so weak he couldn't read figures: his father bought him a publishing house. For Gollancz, despite his exceptional energy and ability, publishing was the only possible occupation. His schoolmastering – he taught for two years at Repton and was dismissed for radicalism by the headmaster, Dr Fisher, afterwards Archbishop of Canterbury and spiritual adviser to Princess Margaret – was a useful preliminary canter: didactic passion is essential for a publisher, more important than the moneymaking urge. Gollancz, says Miss Hodges, detested being called a good businessman. H'm, I wonder what that signified. But there's no doubt he was a born communicator and proud of it, a most unusual blend of pedagogue and entertainer. He could teach anything from civics to cigar smoking. Highly intelligent, widely educated but with none of the typical intellectual's inhibitions or literary exclusivity, he had a special nose not only for what would sell, but for what he could wrap his ego around and project on to the world.

In production and design he was advised by Stanley Morison, but also had his own typographical flair. He was at least partly responsible for the famous yellow peril jackets, and had a positive genius for advertising books, adopting a forceful but always friendly approach. His attention to detail was phenomenal. Sheila Hodges gives instances varying from thirty-page letters to booksellers, to handwritten notices about staff lavatories. He kept his overheads down to a minimum, grinned if wags compared his sparsely furnished office to Fagin's kitchen. And whenever his manic self-confidence threatened to get out of hand, there was always his charming and clever wife to apply the curb.

He started publishing on his own, after seven years with Benn, in April 1928, on sixty thousand pounds of borrowed capital. His first book was a novel, *Brook Evans*, by Susan Glaspell; his first bestseller *My Life* by Isadora Duncan. His list of sixty-four books included H. G. Wells's *The Open Conspiracy*, Guedalla's *Gladstone and Palmerston*, and a facsimile of Blake's *Book of Thel*. He showed a profit his first year and paid a dividend of fifty per cent his second.

He reached the peak of his bestselling phase in the mid nineteen-twenties with his novelists: A. J. Cronin, Phyllis Bentley, Daphne du Maurier, Eleanor Smith, Hervey Allen (whose *Anthony Adverse* was brought back from America by Norman

Collins, his assistant), and his autobiographies: Negley Farson's *The Way of a Transgressor*, Vera Brittain's *Testament of Youth*, Yeats-Brown's *Lives of a Bengal Lancer*. An emotional aura pervaded the entire list, including the intelligent detective stories of which the firm still keeps up a high standard. You can't even now think of some of his authors without him. Dorothy Sayers is a case in point. Though his opposite in many ways, she seemed – whether writing about Lord Peter Wimsey or Jesus, with whom in her mind Wimsey became closely identified – to have been specially created to be published by Gollancz. This was the period of the Book Society, which VG was alleged to have in his pocket along with the Lynd family and the popular novel reviewers. It was also the period of the Omnibuses and the Outlines. Miss Hodges recaptures it all very nicely. She points out, too, that there was more to Gollancz's list than middlebrow bestsellers: he published, *inter alia*, Kafka, Colette, Orwell, Elizabeth Bowen, Joyce Cary, Ivy Compton-Burnett, and Frank Harris's Shaw, which Shaw largely rewrote. She also recalls his unsuccessful paperback experiment, 'Mundanus'.

The most contentious phase, of course, was the Left Book Club, founded in 1936. The transition from Mr Gollancz, the publisher, to Comrade, or, as Low liked to depict him, leading his forces against a mass of Blimps, General Gollancz, was less abrupt than is sometimes supposed. Gollancz, who never made any secret of his socialist sympathies, had published a variety of left-wing books, including, in 1932, Strachey's *The Coming Struggle for Power*, a Marxist study of British politics which had great influence with the literary intelligentsia, and, also in 1932, *The Brown Book of the Hitler Terror*. In 1935, one of his advertisements was banned at the last moment from *The Observer* by its volatile editor J. L. Garvin, who declared: 'He shall not trail his pacifist socialist ordure over my son's dead body in my paper.'

Gollancz had been thinking about new methods of publishing left-wing books for some time; when the idea of a Left Book Club was handed him by Strachey and Laski he jumped at it. By now the threat of war if Hitler was not checked was obvious to anyone with a scrap of political intelligence. Gollancz embraced the Popular Front with religious fervour and put all his energies and organizational panache into the Left Book Club. At its peaks, it had nearly fifty thousand members. Its most popular choices were probably Orwell's *The Road to Wigan Pier* and Macartney's account of his prison experiences *Walls Have Mouths*. Relatively few of its books were propagandist, and Miss Hodges notes that as a popular political educator its admirers included Lloyd George and Violet Bonham Carter.

Two criticisms are still made: he is accused of using the Club to make money out of the Cause. Miss Hodges disposes of this: not only did it not make a profit, but Gollancz started neglecting the profitable side of his business for his political activities. He is also accused of having plunged into a reckless orgy of fellow travelling, turning a blind eye on Stalinism and lending himself to communist jesuitry. This he himself later admitted. But it must be remembered that the true face of Stalinism was still clouded by a thick veil of propaganda and optimism. A broad spectrum of fellow travellers and Communist Party members were totally convinced that – as Gollancz put it – only the Popular Front and an alliance with Russia could save the world. The Nazis were so manifestly vile, the appeasers so blatant and inept; the atmosphere was apocalyptic. At one pole of irrationality you had the Dean of Canterbury declaring that Stalin was building the Kingdom of God in Russia; at the other, Chamberlain announcing that Hitler's signature meant Peace in our Time. Miss Hodges deals adequately and faithfully with the episode and quotes some interesting Gollancz letters. I wish, though, she had gone into rather more detail.

Gollancz was perhaps never quite the same again after the Soviet-German pact. His political zeal was replaced by his own rather endearing mystical Judeo-Christianity, which dovetailed with his passion for music; he also agitated tirelessly for feeding the defeated Germans. He didn't lose his energy or flair, and he built up some interesting American connections. But wartime and post war publishing were, as Miss Hodges says, dull and restricted compared with the nineteen-twenties, when history was made in Henrietta Street. She carries the story on to the present-day world of publishing under inflation, and covers the firm's recent developments, such as the extension of the music list and the proliferation of science fiction. Most old book trade hands, when they reach for the pen, tend to write either blurbs or stamp catalogues, and few good or even readable books have been written about publishing. Hers is most certainly one of them.

Spanish Disciples of The Great Anarch

Murray Bookchin: *The Spanish Anarchists*
(Tree Life Editions)

I find the Great Anarch – Mikhail Bakunin, a huge effervescent
Russian of noble origin – a distinctly attractive figure. So, for a
time, does Marx. On November 4th, 1864 he writes to Engels:
   'Bakunin sends you greetings. I must say I like him very much
   and better than formerly . . . On the whole he is one of the few
   people whom after years I find to have developed forwards
   instead of backwards.'
Four years later he was carrying on about him like a paranoid
ward heeler. If only Marx had been more tactful . . . but that's
like wishing Cleopatra's nose had been an elephant's trunk.
   The reasons why anarchism caught on in Spain are made clear
by Murray Bookchin in this excellent study. This, the first
volume, takes you from 1868 to the eve of the Civil War in 1936.
(I look forward to reading him on various commentators from
Hemingway to Hugh Thomas, whom, already, he catches out in
a terminological inexactitude.) Why 1868? Because this was the
date – late October – of the Italian anarchist Giuseppi Fanelli's
visit to Spain. The tall, heavily-bearded Italian arrived at Barcelona from Geneva. It was the first time he had been in Spain
and there was every reason to suppose his trip would be a fiasco.
   Bakunin had raised barely enough to pay his fare. Fanelli
could speak hardly a sentence in Spanish and began by quarrel-
ling with Elie Reclus, the French anthropologist who was his
only acquaintance in the city. However, at his first meeting in
Madrid he established such a rapport with his audience – a gang
of workers of very 'advanced ideas' – that all barriers went down.
He stayed on for several weeks and scored a triumph. The
anarchist seed which he planted began to sprout almost
immediately. Fanelli never came back to Spain; he died eight
years later of tuberculosis.
   Bakunin's doctrine of anarchist collectivism, Bookchin points

out, must be distinguished from Kropotkin's anarchist communism. It was particularly suitable to the traditional collectiv-
ist aspects of the Russian village, between which and the Spanish
pueblo there is a clear affinity. Bakunin's stress on conspiracy
can be understood only against a Latin and a Russian background, where it was essential for survival. This was something,
suggests Bookchin, that Marx with his admiration for the
well-disciplined, centralized German proletariat could not
comprehend. I am reminded of the famous pub crawl by Marx
and Engels along the Tottenham Court Road, recorded in the
Memoirs of Wilhelm Liebknecht but omitted in English translations owing to communist priggery. Arriving at about the
fifteenth pub, Marx got into conversation with some men in the
saloon bar and started haranguing them on the superiority of
German culture. 'What music,' he demanded, 'has England
ever produced to compare with Mozart and Beethoven? Pah!'
Tempers rose high and the company nearly came to blows. Out
in the street Marx started throwing stones at lampposts. There
was a cry of 'Ware rozzers' and Marx, Engels and Liebknecht
had to run for it with the law at their heels. But Karl had showed
the Teutonic chauvinist cloven hoof.

The role of geography in Spanish history is at once apparent
when you fly over the Iberian peninsula, spread out like a lion's
hide. The contrasts between the arid treeless plateau of Castile –
freezing in winter, burning hot in summer, divided by mountain
ranges – the fertile coastal regions where rice is grown and the
great green plains of Andalusia with their latifundia surviving
from the Roman occupation offer a living history lesson. However, the uniformity of the main agricultural regions is more
apparent than real, as Bookchin remarks. Particularly suitable
to the anarchist doctrine are the mountain villages of Andalusia
and the smallholdings of Murcia.

Does he idealize? Perhaps a bit, but he makes no bones about
being partisan. It was a bit tactless, or disingenuous, to mention
Nestor Makhno as if he were someone to be proud of. Anyone
who has read the terrifying and fantastic description in Konstan-
tin Paustovsky's *In That Dawn* of Makhno's train, with its crew of
crazies shooting up a peaceful station, will feel he was a pretty
heavy liability to any movement or troop, unless it were the
Marquis de Sade's Irregulars. But this is by the way. In general,

as Bookchin shows, the moral tone of the Spanish anarchists was lofty indeed. This was especially true of the rural peasant anarchists. 'The anarchists of the sierras walked like unblemished prophets among the people.' But the Civil Guard made its own laws. You get the feel of it in the poems of Lorca. In the cities, proletarian anarchism drifted increasingly towards syndicalism. From 1882 the phrase 'anarco-sindicalistas' was heard more and more often. Meanwhile the misery of the poor continued to beggar description. As late as the nineteen-thirties, at an experimental pig farm in Andalusia, the peasants really were living much worse than the pigs.

A large part of the book describes the long series of little and not so little risings that went on throughout the nineteenth century and early twentieth, beginning – again in 1868, December – with the one in Cadiz led by Fermin Salvochea. One of the more sensational, 1909 in Barcelona, was known as Tragic Week because the police lost a total of eight men against a possible six hundred citizens.

Gradually we approach the birth of the Republic, via the abdication of Alfonso XIII, and the régime of Primo de Rivera, by far the least malevolent of dictators, just like a colonel in a Spanish musical comedy with the traditional *tonto* (half-wit) for a son. By the end we have met anarchist leaders of the nineteen-thirties, Divrutti and Garcia Oliver. A rather striking omission is the Spanish-American war of which I can find no trace, nor of the ideological ferment that followed it producing books like *Idearium Español* by the neo-Senecan Angelo Ganivet. But as a lesson in Spanish history it is delightfully stimulating. And what a relief to be free from both communist sectarianism and liberal trimming. Some of the conclusions seem universally applicable:

> 'The proletariat, in effect, became psychologically and sprititually part of the very social system it had been destined, according to Marxian precept, to overthrow. Proletarian socialism not surprisingly became an institu-onalised movement for the industrial mobilization of labour, largely economistic in its goals . . . Finally and most disastrously, it fused with capitalism's inherent historic trend toward economic planning.'

But at this point the reader wakes from his anarchist dream and asks: how the hell are you to feed, house, clothe and care for modern conurbations without planning?

Miscellaneous

Calling All Rats

Conservative Central Office molecular biologists have perfected a project for cloning Mrs Thatcher. That was my dream a few nights ago. I woke just as the first 635 of her came tripping into the House of Commons.

Improbable? No such word today. That afternoon I read that the Sussex University Students Union had made a grant of twenty pounds to the Men's Group for the purchase of two vibrators. They'll be canonizing St Onan next.

Seriously, how near are we to the End? In 1958 when I asked Bertrand Russell what odds he would offer, if he were a celestial bookmaker, on the human race surviving another century, he said: 'Not better than evens.' He wouldn't give you evens today. Isn't it time we looked round for a successor species?

Myself, I never forget that J. B. S. Haldane, in an essay published in 1932, wrote that, if we do finally become extinct, 'I venture to hope we shall not have destroyed the rat, an animal of considerable enterprise which has as good a chance as any other of evolving towards intelligence.'

Our nearest relations, the monkeys and apes, are already too specialized to develop into a master species. The rat retains a certain essential simplicity that makes him just the type, given the right mutation under the stimulus of a cataclysm or two, to turn into a crown prince. Already I can hear him squeaking:

Sewer rats of the World!
Unite!
You have nothing to lose but
your drains!

There are more than one hundred and thirty-seven species of the genus *Rattus*, of the great family *Rodentiae*. They include interesting characters like the Wood Rat, sometimes known as the

Trader Rat: he has a passion for bright objects and when he takes one to his nest he replaces it with a pebble. But our Heir is likely to be *Rattus norvegicus*, the Brown Rat. *Norvegicus* is a misnomer; nor did he come from Hanover with the Georges. He did arrive by sea, but he originated in central Asia.

He proceeded to dominate *Rattus rattus*, the Black Rat, who had reached Europe many centuries earlier. (Black Rats they were who plagued the town of Hamelin, c.1284, until the swinging local infestation and pests officer, in his with-it gear, piped them into the River Weser, later, when the local council defaulted on his bill, abducting the child population into the hollow Koppenberk.) Between them, the two species carry some twenty diseases, the Black Rat specializing in bubonic plague, the Brown Rat in typhus. Only a bigot will hold this against them.

The present lifespan of the Brown Rat is two to three years, but he lives dangerously and seldom dies of old age. Rats can breed at three to four months and produce three or four litters of six or more (record twenty-two) ratlets a year. Even Muggeridge, I'm told, hesitates before advising rats against contraception.

The rat population of the UK is about forty to fifty million. Each rat is credited with doing at least five pounds' worth of damage annually. Rats are omnivorous (Hagenbeck had to kill three elephants in his menagerie because rats had gnawed their feet), nocturnal and gregarious. There are eye-witness accounts of vast armies crossing roads by moonlight.

Like man, the rat has never achieved social, commercial or economic stability. 'Man and rat,' says Professor Hans Zinsser, 'are merely so far the most successful animals of prey.'

Rats are certainly no fools, but it is difficult to estimate their intelligence. Stories of two rats leading an old blind rat by a straw, or of one rat dragging by the tail another that is lying on its back, clasping a hen's egg between its forepaws, are (alas) unauthenticated. There is something about the rat which is very conducive to anthropomorphism. The heartrending way it squeals when cornered suggests some cockney old lag being nicked: 'Don't kill me, sir, fer Gawd's sake don't kill me. I swear I'll never do it again. Think of me wife and kids, sir.'

It's certainly true that rats, apart from a little cannibalism under stress, no worse than our baby-bashing, are good parents. And they seem to be capable of altruism. Rice and Grainer found that a lab rat would press a lever to lower a distressed rat hoisted above the cage, and would slow down its rate of pressing a lever for food if that lever also gave an electric shock to a nearby rat. In some situations one rat would exploit another, letting it do all the lever-pressing and snatching all the food, but rats which have been group trained will take it in turns.

Such behaviour, under the degenerative, concentration-camp conditions of the laboratory, is impressive. It points towards a moral code with a whiskered Polonius counselling some young clubrat: 'To thine own Rathood be true. Thou canst not then be false to any Rat.'

And if the rats do evolve to higher intelligence, I hope they will repair one serious omission we hominids have made: that is our neglect of the Foot, which we have allowed to degenerate into a mere means of locomotion, keeping it deformed in leather prisons. The possibilities of this wonderful organ for painting, piano playing, all forms of craftsmanship, have been demonstrated by handicapped armless persons. It may well be that the four-handed rodent civilization of the future will produce cultural achievements undreamed of.

In Search of Nib-Joy

The first fountain pen in my life was Nanny's stylograph, the Dwarf; a stumpy terracotta word tool with a fine point. At the nursery table with the blue cloth with bobbles round the edge, Nanny wrote letters to her sister with it. She wrote in neat mousey handwriting that I longed to imitate. My governess decreed that anything except a plain steel nib – but not the decadent sophisticated Relief with its oblique point – was bad for forming the hand.

In the early part of the Kaiser's war, England was still penholder-minded. Arriving at Brighton station en route for my prep school, I was greeted by a huge poster:

THEY COME AS A BOON AND A BLESSING TO MEN
THE PICKWICK, THE OWL, AND THE WAVERLEY PEN.

The inkpot was unsuited to trench life. The demand for fountain pens increased. A popular model was the Blackbird. It was advertised by a picture of a soldier writing home: 'Dear Mum, I hope this finds you as it leaves me, in the pink.' Shells were bursting overhead. I bought a Blackbird and was happy with it for a time. To fill it, you unscrewed the nib and its holder and injected ink into the barrel with a fountain pen filler. Apt to be messy.

More desirable, and more symbolically potent, were the self-filling makes; Swan, Waterman and Onoto were the best known of many. The Onoto was the first pen to give me real nib-joy. It had the advantage of a screw by which you could control the flow – always a problem. Its barrel was long, slender and beautifully balanced.

The perfectionist is never satisfied. A friend pointed out that the great penmen had written with quills. I began to experiment.

The quill was capricious: ecstasy one moment, despair the next, when you failed to cut a new point.

About this time I acquired a *Manuelle de Graphologie*. Being French gave it extra esoteric significance. I studied it with concentration. My aim, since handwriting was indicative of one's character, was to change my character, which was getting me into trouble just then, by changing my handwriting. It was simply a question of finding a suitable model. But the hand of those illustrated which seemed to suit me best was *Une Écriture Extrêmement Bizarre*; its writer, I gathered, had ended in a Maison des Fous.

Pen-fetishism lay dormant until I was sixteen. Then I went one winter with my sister to Gstaad, not so fashionable as it has become but even then sporting a crowned head or two. I collided with one, a plump olive-skinned little fellow, on my *luge* in the drive of the Palace Hotel. He was the Shah of Persia, soon to be deposed by the present Shah's father and retire to Paris where he kept a scent shop. In my hotel was a gambling machine, a sort of simplified roulette wheel. I discovered that if you banged the machine against the wall at the critical moment it would pay out whatever the pointer had stopped at. I came down very early one morning and won over five pounds before I was warned off.

In the window of a stationer's shop in the town was a fountain pen that had already aroused my passion. It was the largest pen I'd ever seen, a Continental Waterman, the kind of fountain pen you might expect to find one of the great villains of crime fiction signing his false name with, and now I could afford it. Its nib was retractile, worked by a screw at the hinder end. Capping and uncapping were major operations. If you didn't screw everything up tight you were in danger of leaking half a pint of blue-black.

'I can understand you getting ink all over yourself only too well,' said my sister. 'But how did you manage to get it all over that unfortunate girl you were dancing with?'

Time passed. Pens came and went and my passion ebbed and flowed with them. The ballpoints, like Nanny's stylo, returned on a higher plane of history's spiral, were wildly exciting at first but somehow too inflexible, too impersonal. The Parker 51 with its half concealed nib, which many an amateur psychoanalyst has compared to the uncircumcised penis, seemed at first to have enormous promise. But I could never, in spite of the patience of the girls at the nib-changing counter, get a nib that really suited me. One day I heard a girl say: 'Oh, Christ! Here's Old Nibby again!' It was time to pack it in.

But this year, something is stirring. Judging by the advertisements, there seems to be a renewed interest in fountain pens. Old Nibby prowls again from 'Pencraft' to 'Penfriends', trying them all: Parkers, Sheaffers, Watermans, and the German makes, Mont Blanc, and the Lamy. Which will he get first: nib-joy or the bum's rush?

Douceur de Vivre

'It's goodbye to luxury living, anyway,' said the local tycoon who has a light engineering factory and likes to let us know how well he's been doing. I was tempted to say: 'What do you know about it? Just because you've got a cocktail cabinet that lights up when you open it and plays the "Bluebells of Scotland" and you play golf at Marbella in the summer . . .' But I didn't want to hurt his feelings. Nevertheless, I'm right. Most of the present generation have no idea what real luxury means.

When was the peak? We can skip the oriental slave states and Rome. There can be no true luxury without comfort and the Romans had no feeling for this. Trimalchio's Banquet must have been sheer hell. For the top, we must turn to the Edwardian afterglow that ended in 1914. Most of the essential mechanical inventions had arrived. By 1911 the best motor cars were reliable enough to tour Europe in comfort; they were much roomier and more comfortable than ours.

Edwardian luxe was detailed and delicate. Everything was hand made, hand sewn. Food was delicious. French vines had recovered from the ravages of phylloxera. Smoking habits were civilized: Havana cigars, Turkish cigarettes. The barbarous whisky and soda might be becoming popular in the City but brandy and soda was still the gentleman's drink in between whiles. Prices, of course, bore no relation whatsoever to today. Between 1907 and 1941 my father lived in a house in Essex with sixteen bedrooms and eight acres with Jersey cows, pigs and poultry. He had eight indoor servants, two gardeners and a boy, a groom and a chauffeur, two hunters, a donkey, and two motorcars. All this he did on an income that never exceeded four thousand, five hundred pounds.

The Edwardian way of life persisted between the wars but only among the rich and the very rich. I have in my time stayed in the houses of millionaires and multi millionaires and have been lavishly entertained, even though I was kept awake all night by the bellowing of the Duke of Bedford's bison underneath my bedroom window at Woburn. But only once have I encountered that passionate attention to detail which true luxury demands. The host in this case was the late Ernest Mocatta, stockbroker and chairman of the Anglo-French Exploration Company. Not a millionaire, though he had enough to get on with. When he died in 1932, he left two hundred and forty-five thousand pounds.

Mocatta lived near Weybridge in an ugly but beautifully situated house with grounds sloping down to the river. I went to stay with him when I was in my last year at school. Everything here was perfection. The food – he paid his Scotch cook one hundred pounds a year – was exquisite, and absurdly profuse. At breakfast, old Ernest sat confronting a ring of boiled eggs like King Valoroso in *The Rose And The Ring*. On the sideboard were dishes of sole, salmon kedgeree, fried eggs, scrambled eggs, kidneys, a blushing York ham, a glazed tongue. This was for two of us only and Ernest never ate more than one boiled egg. Luncheon was relatively light: whitebait and wild duck pie. Nothing to speak of for tea; quite right – no gourmet wants to spoil his dinner.

Dinner was indescribable; seldom more than six courses. Ernest didn't believe in overloading, though Edward VII and his cronies went in for 24 courses with a sorbet in the middle to let you get your second wind; but he saw to it that there was nice balance. His was the only house where I have ever had enough of caviar. I was too young to appreciate his wine as it deserved, but he gave me a course of elementary instruction in the four great clarets, Latour, Lafite, Margaux and Haut Brion (Mouton Rothschild had not yet been admitted). He also instructed me in the champagnes and tended to deplore the Stock Exchange taste for very dry champagne. I learnt here lessons which I have never been able to afford to put into practice.

The servants were perfectly trained, their movements unhurried and soothing. I can hear now the voice of Ernest's butler, Nash, purring in my ear as I sat in the library after dinner reading a volume of rare Spanish eighteenth century pornography (Ernest, like some professional crammers, was a believer in erotic texts as short cuts to learning a language): 'Brandy and soda, sir, whisky and soda, sir, Vichy water, sir, Vittel water, sir, Malvern water, sir?'

It was summer, and every morning at noon a little procession would set out. First came myself. I was followed by Wright, the footman, carrying a tray with a crystal glass jug of iced white wine, and a box of one hundred fat Turkish cigarettes. We would halt at a little mock-Grecian temple overlooking the river. Wright would pour me out a glass of wine and depart.

Presently I would be joined by the aged Ernest who had been pottering about with his prize chrysanthemums. He was a small delicate looking man with a moustache and rather long white hair. He came from a well-known Portuguese Jewish family and there was a touch of wistful cynical melancholy about him that suggests the Portuguese national character. He came to a sad end, poor old fellow, suffering from an agitated depression. My father found him crawling on the floor counting gold sovereigns from a bag in his safe, muttering, 'This is all I've got. The rest is only paper.' I hope he never learned about my dreadful gaffe.

For there was one department where the Mocatta hospitality was too perfect. Coming up to bed, with a heavy thunderstorm lowering over the Thames Valley (the bedrooms were provided with volumes and volumes of light reading, Conan Doyle, W. J. Locke, etc., all bound in green morocco leather), I found the fire had been piled to a furnace. The room was stifling. I should never be able to sleep. Clumsily, for I had a lot of brandy on board, I took shovelfuls of fire and threw them out of the window. Next morning, I went down early and tipped a gardener to cover up the havoc among the chrysanthemums.

I Too Was A Fellow Traveller

My life with the British Communist Party started (of course) in the political thirties. I was then working for the publishers Routledge & Kegan Paul. The managing director was a dear little English Jew named Cecil Franklin. His father, who owned a private bank and discount house, bought him the firm because it was decided that Cecil's eyesight was not good enough to read figures. As a publisher he did not have to read anything.

I never made any secret of my extreme left political opinions. One of our authors was Ralph Fox, who edited a book of essays about dialectical materialism; most of the authors were later bumped off. I made friends with Fox and we arranged to collaborate on a life of Kamo, a fantastic Georgian Bolshevik adventurer who carried out the great Tiflis bank raid which Stalin masterminded from the party's Batum headquarters, for which a brothel was the front. Kamo later distinguished himself by feigning insanity when in a prison hospital in Germany, so as to avoid being exported to Russia. He pulled out all the hairs from one side of his head and arranged them in patterns on his pillow. He was a leading partisan in Georgia during the Civil War, but he found it difficult to get anyone to serve under him because of his habit of submitting them to stringent loyalty tests; he would divide half his band into Whites dressed up; these would spring out on the rest and say: 'Tell us where the Red brigand Kamo's headquarters are.' His end was an anticlimax. He fell off his bicycle in Tiflis in 1922 on the way to an adult education class.

Ralph Fox, brought up a Quaker, had become a communist after serving on famine relief in Russia during the aftermath of the Civil War. I asked him what he knew of Stalin because he had spent some time in Moscow. He said Stalin was very lazy and told me that at one time Stalin used to go to ground in the Kremlin and sit smoking his pipe underneath the kitchen table. This was almost the only endearing thing that I ever heard about the monster.

When the Spanish Civil War broke out Fox was called upon by the British Communist Party to be the political commissar of the British battalion of the International Brigade. At the same time another of my friends, but very far from a communist, Cyril Connolly, went to Spain, and I remember saying to my wife: 'It's not Ralph that I'm worried about. He will know how to take care of himself. But Cyril is so vague.' That shows you how green I was. Ralph was killed in action after only a few weeks. Cyril came back unscathed and wrote some excellent pieces for the *New Statesman* which were vilified by the communists for being simultaneously bourgeois, objective and subjective.

I spoke at a memorial meeting for Fox in Holborn town hall. Harry Pollitt was the principal speaker and let loose a tremendous blast of oratory. I had first heard of Pollitt from Andrew Rothstein, who was then *Tass* correspondent. I had had lunch with him in connection with a series of books that Routledge published. One of them was *Soviet Russia Neurosis* by Franklyn D. Williams, an American psychoanalyst of sorts, who declared that when he went round the mental hospitals in Leningrad they could not show him a single case of depression as they had all been cured by the communist social atmosphere.

I also met at this time Raji Palme Dutt, a founding member of the British Communist Party, who died last week, aged seventy-nine. I asked him to lunch, at Routledge's expense, at the Etoile in Charlotte Street. He arrived in a mackintosh and somewhat battered Homburg hat and endeared himself to me at once by saying: 'What a treat it is to have some decent food and wine for a change. I am afraid that it must be admitted that our English comrades have no idea of how to live.'

At Balliol, Raji got a first in Mods and was expected to be a safe first in Greats. In November 1917 he held a meeting, most orderly, he insists, to greet the Russian Bolshevik Revolution. Next morning he was summoned before the college authorities and told that he must leave Oxford and not set foot in either the university, or the town, until the time of his Schools the following summer. He got the first, and it seems likely that his first in Greats with fourteen alphas is an all time record. But when, thereafter, he applied for jobs he was invariably given a reference that read: 'Mr Dutt's academic qualifications are beyond dispute. However, his political opinions are so extreme and eccentric that you will have to make up your mind as to his suitability.' One wonders whether, now, in our more tolerant atmosphere, the Establishment might not have decided that it would be safer to give him a fellowship. It is rather piquant that the present (1974) Master of Balliol, Christopher Hill, is a Marxist historian.

All this time my old friend, Claud Cockburn, has been waiting in the wings. I did not know him then as well as I do now. At Oxford he was a generation older than me and I was much impressed by his worldly cosmopolitanism. I subscribed to the *Week* and was, like everyone, enthusiastic. Claud unquestionably had good sources of information, among them foreign correspondents, notably the Americans, who wanted to get stories printed which their own papers would not touch. He also had a wonderful gift for inventing a story that fitted the facts. A perfect example of this was his anecdote of Baldwin and the King's speech. It went, according to the *Week*, like this:

> 'The Attorney-General was much exercised when the draft of the King's speech was referred to him by the Prime Minister's office. In the margin there were constant references as follows: "Refer to AG . . . further references to AG . . . AG's intervention expected here . . . Everything left in AG's hands." The Attorney-General rang up the Prime Minister and said: "I don't know, PM, why you wanted me to vet all those passages in the King's speech, which, so far as I know, never ordinarily leaves No 10." To which Baldwin replied: "It has nothing to do with you, my dear fellow, it's simply that that silly secretary of mine mistook my references in my notes to Almighty God to you." '

The war in Spain dragged on. I went to Ireland for Christmas with my wife and stayed with the rich. Then, back in London in the spring, a slight misfortune befell me. Routledge had published Walter Citrine's book *I Search for Truth in Soviet Russia*. This was the book which maddened all party members and fellow travellers because it cast doubts on the integrity of the superb fortress of the proletariat. We were especially scornful of the way in which Citrine remarked on the absence of wash-basin plugs, and did not know in his ignorance that his was the traditional feature of Russian life from time immemorial.

One morning Qualcast, a firm of motormower manufacturers in Derby, asked if they could have a cheap edition of two thousand copies of Citrine's book to give away to their workers. I was having a drink that day with Ralph Wright, who was writing 'The Worker's Notebook' in the *Daily Worker* and I told him about it. 'That's a nice story for me', he said. I said he was welcome to it but he must keep it on ice until the event; then he could go to town on it. Some time later Ragge came into my room with a long face. Citrine had rung up to say there must be a communist in Routledge's office because the *Daily Worker* carried a story about the cheap edition. What had I to say about it? I admitted it appeared to be a breach of confidence – but soon afterwards little Cecil Franklin hopped into my room and said would I not like the opportunity to resign? I said fair enough.

There was a certain amount of sympathy for me in Left circles. Cyril Connolly sent me a message from Auden: the only practical expression came from Henry Parsons of Lawrence and Wishart, who asked me if I would like to earn a few guineas by subbing the proofs of the *Communist International*. I can remember now a very hot July during which I read the most inconceivably dreary pseudo-Marxist rubbish, much of which was concerned with Trotsky's plots and the iniquities of the POUM in Spain. It was in the same month that my wife and I got an invitation to a strange luncheon party. At Routledge I had met, over his children's stories, a young African, Prince Akiki K. Nyabongo, nephew of the King of Toro in the Uganda Protectorate. Nyabongo asked us to lunch with some friends of his in Pimlico. When we arrived we were told lunch would be later because the sirloin was too big for the oven and they were cooking it in the bath with a primus stove roaring underneath. It was a baking July day, as hot as Africa. Our host turned out to be Jomo Kenyatta and our hostess was his white help-meet. Also there was George Padmore, author of *Britannia Rules the Blacks*, which was condemned in orthodox communist circles for Trotskyism. I believed some Red high priest even branded George as the Black Bukharin. He afterwards became adviser to Kwame Nkrumah, the president of Ghana. At lunch he was lively as a lizard and kept twitting Nyabongo about his cossacks.

For a time I was actually a member of the Holborn branch of the Communist Party. The atmosphere was quite friendly. When I suggested that although Trotsky had become an enemy of the Soviet Union this should not have happened. and mistakes must have been made by other people than Trotsky, it was approved. I soon realized that the day-to-day work of a party branch, trying to promote the sales of the *Daily Worker* and 'leafletizing' the district, was dead boring – and not for me.

At the time of Munich I had 'flu. All through the summer Palme Dutt in his famous 'Notes of the Month' in *Labour Monthly* had been analysing the international situation and exposing the calculated policy of appeasement. On the afternoon of the day itself, Gilbert Armitage, an old Oxford friend and a barrister working for Sir Jonah Walker-Smith, father of Derek, at the Building Trades Employers' Federation, came to see me. He sat on my bed and said it was beginning to look very like war. I said: 'Nonsense. You'll see. They are playing it like a cliffhanger. They'll let it go till very last minute. Then there will be a message read out in the House.' That evening as I lay reading *Anti Dühring* and wondering why there was not any infallible dialectical method of teaching the calculus, the bell rang. It was Gilbert.

'How on earth did you know?' he said.

'I didn't,' I said. 'I just applied the philosophy of "As If".' It was as if there was a conspiracy in minute detail.

I next got caught up in the web of those numerous committees run by tireless Red ladies. This one was putting on a programme to celebrate International Woman's Day. My friend John Woodyatt, a keen fancier of sectarian Red ladies, was also involved. John was responsible for making sure that certain relics were in the hall. There was Karl Marx's wooden chair, in which he wrote, and which his daughter Eleanor had given to Will Thorne, and there was an urn containing poor ill-fated Eleanor's ashes. I caught John eating a pinch of these ashes; he did not display the slightest embarrassment. Sympathetic magic, I suppose.

The increasing menace of Hitler, abetted by the appeasers, made the Soviet purges and trials seem almost natural. There were meetings galore, and I remember one in particular at the Queen's Hall when that old buffoon the Dean of Canterbury raised both arms and chanted: 'Stalin is building the kingdom of God in Russia.' This I did think was overdoing it a bit.

In February 1939, I was offered a pleasant temporary job in Paris editing a report on the refugee situation for the World Youth Congress. We lived in the Hotel du Pavillon in the Rue de Verneuil just off the Rue des Saints-Pères. We had a perfectly clean double room with a bathroom on the same floor which cost, for the two of us, the equivalent of seventy new pence. I used to have my breakfast at the Gare d'Orsay: a dozen Arcachon oysters and a glass of Anjou wine for the equivalent of seven new pence. It was a delightful existence and I would gladly have gone on editing that report for years. But back in London the *Daily Worker* group of the Holborn party branch complained that I never attended meetings and took not the slightest interest in the group. Betty Reid, who afterwards married John Lewis, one of the most fervent of party ideologues and inclined to call any criticism of Russia 'slander', told me of the protests. So I quietly lapsed.

Czechoslovakia had been swallowed up and the question was whether there would be a further act of appeasement. We decided to have a holiday in France while the going was good. We went first to Arcachon and then to Port Vendres. In Collioure, the Spanish republican internees were quartered in an old tower that over-looked a triangular bull ring. Here we saw the most abominable bull fight with fourth-rate matadors and no picadors. The result was that the bulls' heads were never loxered and the *espadas* thrust at them like assassins. Blood spouted. French women screamed and all the time the band played a waltz tune. I had a strange sense of foreboding.

In Avignon we read of the signing of the German-Soviet pact and were confused. John Woodyatt, who was with us, said: 'I hope our master in Moscow knows what he's doing.' The English began streaming back from the Riviera coast. A young man asked me if I would allow his aunt, who had only one leg, to lie down in our room. I said: 'Yes, of course, but don't alarm her. Chamberlain will perform another act of appeasement.' We stayed on until the French mobilized. I went to be shaved and found the lady at the cash desk rather red about the eyes. She nodded when I asked if I could be shaved, and rang a bell. The bead curtain at the back of the barber's parted and an aged crone in a grey striped institutional dress shuffled forward. She began operations by thrusting a huge shaving brush up my nostrils. I expostulated. 'Ah, Monsieur,' she cackled, *'vous êtes le premier vif que j'ai rasé.'*

Looking back now, it seems absolutely incredible that I was able to to swallow the switch in the party line which condemned the war as 'imperialist'. One of the main arguments which party people used to support it was Clausewitz's famous slogan, often quoted by Lenin: 'War is politics carried out by other means.' I made use of this myself when I stood in for Randall Swingler at a Left Book Club meeting in Bayswater. Randall's astonishing optimism was best displayed at the end of September, when the Russians rolled across and occupied their half of Poland. I met him in Theobald's Road.

'What do you make of everything now, Randall?'

His friendly little face twitched and puckered. Then he said: 'I think it means capitalism is going to collapse without a shot being fired.'

A very few days before the German blitzkrieg in the West, I read the lead story in the *Daily Worker* by their diplomatic correspondent, Frank Pitcairn (Claud Cockburn's pseudonym). It ran something like this:

> 'Alarm and disquiet in The Hague and Brussels . . .
> Informed circles report a sudden and most emphatic
> climate of anxiety. Everything is utterly quiet on the
> German side of the line. The only conclusion, therefore,
> is that Britain and France are about cynically to violate
> the neutrality of Belgium and Holland.'

I did think my old friend Claud had been stretching it a bit.

It was getting near my call-up time, so I went to London and volunteered for the Auxiliary Fire Service. At the fire station in Soho I saw a dwarf fireman having a pillow fight with a pretty firewoman. This looked just the service for me. I was sent to a training station in Clerkenwell and arrived at my sub-station at Moreland Street School, off City Road, a week before the Blitz began. On the second night of a very active forty-eight-hour spell, I fell through a skylight on the top of a house in Emerald Street near Theobald's Road and dropped all the way down to the cellar – said to be about fifty feet. I did myself surprisingly little damage: a simple fracture of the left upper arm and a crack on the head which did not fracture the skull.

Budleigh Salterton, where my mother lived in the solid and comfortable mid-Victorian villa with a garden looking over the sea that my father had bought in 1917, was one of the least warlike places in England. My friend Joyce Evans told me: 'There is a man in this town called Wilfred McCartney, whom I am sure you will know of if you don't actually know him. He is staying at Eastcliff on the front just below your mother's house.' I did indeed know of McCartney. I first heard of him in 1927, when he was sentenced by that old beast Lord Chief Justice Hewart to ten years for having conducted a trifling inquiry into what the Foreign Office, with their usual traditional unwisdom, were doing in the way of supplying arms to the Poles with which to fight the Bolsheviks.

When it came to the abrupt change of line in September 1939, McCartney, who was writing his autobiography (it was never published), wanted to find some way of explanation or apology that would not seem critical. I devised a ludicrous phrase to the effect that the real intention was to surround Germany with 'a ring of peace'. This delighted him. I wonder whether it would have delighted Harry Pollitt, who had been dismissed from the secretaryship of the party when the line was switched at the beginning of the war.

I was beginning to receive call-up notices again and it was time to go back to London. In July I got an urgent message to go to Mr McCartney's suite at the Berkeley. I arrived after dinner and found Mac and Nye Bevan opening a bottle of champagne. 'Andy Rothestein is coming round', Mac said, 'to have a talk with Nye about how the Labour Party can best help the Russians.'

Presently Andrew arrived, looking, as usual, rather prim. He accepted a tiny glass of kümmel. Nye began in his usual expansive exuberant form:

'Now this is what we can do to start with, Andy. We can lay on a meeting in a committee room at the House of some fifty or sixty Labour members to be addressed by Harry Pollitt, or Willie Gallacher, or Palme Dutt, anyone you choose. I'd suggest that for a start.' Andrew looked down at his shoes and shook his head. 'There is one first step and one only,' he said, 'and that is to lift the ban on the *Daily Worker*.' Nye remonstrated that this would come later but it was premature to demand it right away. In a few minutes they were at it hammer and tongs and Andrew was reminding Nye of some opportunist course he had pursued in connection with a strike at Merthyr Tydfil in 1922. Poor Mac sat

looking like a political hostess whose lions had started fighting.
When Andrew departed, Nye exploded:

'That man!' he said. 'He's like a little priest, that's what he is.'

'Oh come, now,' I said, 'he's quite human, really, and he's got
the most delightful wife.'

'Wish to God she'd have come instead of him,' said Nye. 'Then
we might have got somewhere.'

In October I bumped into Andrew Rothstein, quite by chance,
and he asked me if I would like to work for *Soviet Monitor* as an
editor. This was a monitoring service of Russian broadcasts which
he had set up with the cooperation of the Soviet Embassy at
Whetstone, near Totteridge. It was arranged that I should start
on the Monday.

Next morning I received an urgent telephone message from the
Ritz where it appeared that McCartney had set up his banner
after being expelled from the Berkeley for making too much noise.
I arrived about eleven-thirty and found him lolling in bed in a pair
of scarlet silk pyjamas embroidered with blue tigers. Beside him,
on, but not in the bed, was stretched a nightclub blonde wearing
pink chiffon trousers. McCartney poured me out a glass of
champagne and asked me to drink to the health of the Red Army.
The nightclub blonde said:

'Fuck the Red Army.'

'Don't say that sort of thing, my dear,' said Mac, 'or you'll make
me cross.'

'Well,' she said, 'you've been drinking the health of the Red
Army for the last twelve hours and I'm getting browned off.'

'Then why don't you go home?' said Mac.

'I've told you sixty times,' said the blonde, 'that I'm not going
home in this ruddy fancy dress until it's dark.'

Life at the *Soviet Monitor* was on the austere side. One very Red
lady alarmed me by saying that cricket was a decadent bourgeois
game. In 1941, Maisky had taken offices in Grand Buildings,
Trafalgar Square, and installed a staff to produce *Soviet War News*,
a daily bulletin, and *Soviet Weekly*. The editor was Semyon Rostovsky. This interesting figure had been removed from Russia by
his mother at the time of the revolution when he was sixteen. His
education was finished in Germany; he joined the German
Communist Party and sided with the faction led by Ruth Fischer.
He wrote under the name of Ernst Henri a useful book called *Hitler*

Over Europe. As well as being editor, he also had to look after Soviet books and plays and he asked me to join his staff.

Apart from Rostovsky, who was in a state of burning zeal, there was one live Soviet Russian in the office. His name was Pavel Yerzin; he was some kind of assistant press attaché. He was of peasant stock from the Moscow region and had learnt to read when he was twelve, so as to help his mother dispose of buisness matters concerning the inheritance of his father's hut. He was an attractive fellow, with fair curls and a broad buttery mug, strong as a bull. He told me that he had wanted to be an engineer after leaving Moscow University but, being a party member, he had to do what he was told. I gathered that Stalin had decided that, as the diplomatic corps was invariably recruited from the flower of the ruling class, and as the flower of the proletariat was the engineer, that was that. Crises came when there were complaints that too many first-class engineers were going into the diplomatic corps not industry. The leader solved the problem in a flash: 'Second-class engineers for diplomatic corps.' Pavel was quite religious in his attitude towards communism. One day in February, I said: 'See you tomorrow, Pavel.' He shook his head. 'Not tomorrow,' he said. 'Tomorrow is the day our comrade Lenin died. We stay in embassy and hold meetings.'

Presently Rostovsky went, in a state of great excitement, to Moscow. He left Euston in the same train as Ludmilla Pav-lichenko, the girl sniper, who had been doing a propaganda tour of Britain. We went to see him off and Pavel called as the train left: 'Watch out for Stalin. He will bite you.' (How right he was. About the time of the Doctors' Plot, Rostovsky was sent to Siberia. He is back in Moscow now living in a special flat for the rehabilitated.)

The Russians had had one play put on, a rather crude affair by Simonov, no better and not much worse than the average run of war plays. They were very anxious to get another. One day I was rung up by Peter Ustinov. I asked him to dinner. He came in his private's uniform as he had just joined the Army Film Unit. His mother made a literal translation of a war play by Leonov, one of the most interesting Soviet novelists. Its plot was of a small town ne'er-do-well, who rose to the occasion during the German occupation and led the resistance movement. Peter was enthusiastic about it, and had nearly finished his adaptation. Presently Alec Clunes came to see me and said the Arts Theatre would guarantee the play a six weeks' run with a good chance that it might get a full-scale West End production.

At the Soviet Embassy, plays for some reason came under the jurisdiction of Zonov, the cultural attaché. He read Peter's adaptation and told me that it was absolutely all right, entirely faithful. The Holy Writ of a Soviet text had not been tampered with. I rang up Peter and told him. Then, like a bolt from the red, Rostovsky reappeared on the scene. He was a changed man, furtive and cynical. Something had frightened him. One of the first questions he asked me was: 'What's this about Peter Ustinov and Leonov's play?' I told him. He said it was impossible that Ustinov's name should appear in connection with any Soviet play or publication. Ustinov's father had been not only a White Guard, but also served in the Kaiser's army. I said what the hell had that got to do with it. Peter was born in 1922 and had never been inside Russia. Rostovsky shook his head. 'You don't understand,' he said. So when Alec Clunes came to see me I had to tell him that the play could go on in Peter's adaptation but his name must not appear. He said it was perfectly monstrous. I said I quite agreed. He said: 'Are these people mad?' I said: 'Undoubtedly.' Peter himself was typically sympathetic when I told him.

A remarkable woman translator who was allowed to work for us was Edith Bone. Bone was the name of one of those husbands *de convenance* who conferred British citizenship on political émigrés. Edith was Hungarian and a doctor. She had been to Russia just after the revolution, had taken part in the short-lived Bela Kun regime in Budapest. After that she lived in Germany. She was an interesting polymath, but devilish difficult. Once she came to dinner, stayed the night, got bitten by the cat (having boasted that all cats adored her), insisted on making coffee by a Hungarian method that included blowing down the spout of the pot. In the morning as I walked her to the bus stop in King's Road, she fell down and I thought: 'Holy Monkey Mother of God, this is the Man Who Came To Dinner.' The fate of Edith, when she went back to Hungary after the war, is well known. I saw her after her visit and she told me the regime was quite civilized. On her second visit she was arrested and kept mostly in solitary confinement until 1956. Is it surprising that she turned against communism or its operators, and that when I last saw her in the late fifties she was breathing a quite embarrassing amount of fire and slaughter?

By this time, 1946, I felt I'd had enough of professional Reds of any nationality, although I must say they'd never done me any harm. So I quietly elided from Grand Buildings. In the French pub Reg Bishop, the eighteen-stone editor of *Russia Today*, and one of the most genial of all British communists, said: 'Maurice, is it true you're deserting us?' I said I wasn't deserting anybody or anything but I'd had more than enough of working for the Russians. 'But we all know,' Reg said, 'the Russians are ghastly, only that's not the point.'

In 1966 I was living in Golders Green only a number two iron away from Palme Dutt. I was able to lend a hand in publicizing his late wife Salme Dutt's poems. (Salme Murrik was born in Estonia in 1888 and joined the Bolshevik party when young. She was a personal friend of Lenin, and when she asked him to send her to where the battle was toughest, he said: 'In that case you should go to England. That's the toughest place for communism.') I introduced him to Malcolm Muggeridge and Malcolm put him in his series of TV profiles alongside Sir John Reith and Leonard Woolf. They became very friendly; Malcolm used to call him the Red Doctor, and he used to call Malcolm, Savonarola. In 1970, Raji wrote to me: '[Malcolm's] personal lovableness always shines through whatever opinions he chooses to express. Personally I think he enjoys the dramatic aspect of his present bout of superintensive religious preaching; of course I have no doubt that he is completely convinced of what he is saying, but the pleasure shows through.'

Introducing Palme Dutt to Malcolm Muggeridge was my last political act. Soon afterwards I was having lunch with Henry and Virginia Bath at Job's Mill. Anthony Powell was there and we talked about people we had known at Oxford and what had become of them. I asked after Roger Hollis, who had been a great friend of mine my first two terms. We had even planned to abscond to Mexico. I had never seen him since Oxford and his brother Chris had been oddly evasive whenever I asked him. 'Oh,' said Tony, 'that's very odd. You may not believe it, but he's the head of MI5.' There he was in *Who's Who*. 'Sir Roger Hollis, seconded to the Ministry of Defence.' I tracked him down to Somerset and reintroduced myself over the telephone. He told me he had retired. (This was in fact due to the Profumo case; he died last year.) It was a sad disappointment. I had hoped he might show me my dossier.

The Accumulator

I was seventeen when I first backed a horse. Its name was Big Wonder. It was running in the Grand National, quoted at 100–1. In High Street, Budleigh Salterton, just after I'd seen the list of runners, I passed a man who must have been seven foot six if he was an inch. He wore a tweed cloak, and a wide green hat with those guy rope attachments you sometimes used to see on the homburgs of sophisticated bishops. I hurried to our local bookmaker to put one pound on.

Sportingly, he suggested I'd better have ten bob each way. I wasn't quite sure what each way meant, but even if I had been it wouldn't have made any difference, such faith had I in that huge, striding omen.

At lunch I told my father. 'Hope you lose,' he grunted. 'You're such a mug that if you win you'll think you can beat the book.'

Big Wonder fell at the second fence, but it was years before I could rid myself of superstition when betting.

My father was right, of course. It is dangerous to win. You think you're clever instead of lucky. You go on betting with the bookmaker's money. When you lose that you say: 'Bad luck, but I'll soon get it back.' And down you go.

In theory, it's easy not to be a mug. Never bet more than you can afford. Don't chase your losses. Follow form not fancy. If you do get a tip, however impressive the source, remember that in the long run tips cancel out, so don't raise your stakes. As a rule don't bet unless your horse has at least an even chance and the odds are better than evens. Learn which races not to touch, for example, selling plates and big handicaps. Be content with one win; the oftener you bet the more you stand to lose. Only bet when sober. If you can stick to these simple and obvious principles you won't lose much and, who knows, you may even win.

Why bet at all? Because rational betting is not only fun but valuable character training. Betting teaches you strict punctuality, instant arithmetic, one-pointed concentration, quick, decisive logical thinking and mental flexiblity. The scientific punter has to be one of those practical mystics who live in the eternal *now*. If Socrates were living today you'd find him and his mob at the tracks.

Here is a story to illustrate the presence of mind that racing can teach. A hardened racing man in Dublin, down on his luck, decided to fool around with an accumulator. Having picked the horses, some at long odds, and placed his bet, he thought no more about it. But on the course his choices started turning up. An accumulator can mount up astronomically. After the fourth race he was fifteen thousand pounds up. All this had to go on his selection in the fifth race. It won at 4-1. He looked at the card. Jenghiz Khan hadn't an earthly in the sixth and last race. But under the terms of the bet all his sixty thousand pounds must go on it.

Watching the horses parading in the paddock, he had an inspiration. He called out: 'George, I say, quick man. Will you take five grand for that horse?'

'Do you mean that? OK, it's a deal.'

'Thank God for that. Now I want you to come with me to the stewards and scratch him. We've just got time.'

Under the terms of the bet – the rules have been changed since – if a horse was scratched from a race the accumulator stood for the remaining races. Buying Jenghiz Khan had netted him fifty-five thousand pounds.

Ecstasy at Epsom

Race meetings, with their strange confused mingling, their agonising losings, joyful findings, and time-haunted intervals . . . race meetings are exactly like dreams.

Epsom is the biggest race meeting in the world. As well as the Downs, the Gipsies and the Derby, it has one of the prettiest paddocks and some of the nicest officials. On a blue, green and gold afternoon, with a whistling wind, Epsom is ecstasy.

The dream this year begins with some sharpish persecution by secret powers at Waterloo. No one to tell us, and no notice – we include many thousand visitors who have never been in London before – where to book for Tattenham Corner; and when we do find the hidden suburban station a determined attempt is made to send us to Hayes. This produces just the right touch of fever; perhaps it was intentional after all. As we reduce the Derby field to six runners, my delightful new train acquaintance presents me with the winner of the first race, which enables me to lose on the Derby with the bookmakers' money.

An Irishman remarked that to see the Derby properly and see it whole you need 'the brains of Mr Gladstone and the legs of a welsher'. My junior racing tutor, after inquiring about the state of my training, outlines his plan: after the paddock we watch them going up to the post, admiring Lester Piggott's elf-like seat on the abominable Zucchero, and rooting for Martin Molony. Then we dodge across the track, charm the crowd on the ropes into letting us through, and start on the uneven quarter-mile sprint to the yellow slide tower in the middle of the fun fair, between the dodgems and the 'naughty nineties.'

Here is the real strategic centre of the course. Here you can see nearly all the race except the start, all the crowd and the enormous stand. Here you realize that the Derby remains pre-1914; it is run in a country called Edwardian, where even the

Daily Worker sellers, hoping to proselytize on the strength of their famous red tipster, Cavton, look as if they were enjoying themselves: 'Smile, please, comrade. Remember this is a people's outing.'

Perfect Derby cross section of a dozen on top of the tower, includes professional racing gent from a proletarian quarter who tells me many unprintable – and I am sure, quite untrue – things about jockeys and trainers and owners; nice young SW3-type couple with boy who wants to slide down; Cockney lady in a check cap, and an Australian visitor who says it is all wonderful, but he thinks that the method of broadcasting a running commentary employed at Billabong might be adopted with advantage. When it is all over, we squat on our mats and slide down the spiral, like Chancellors of the Exchequer in reverse.

Enough about that race. Everybody was very sorry Ki Ming did not win, especially numerous clowns who had been busy practising their Chinese. But the dangers of premature celebration remined me to tell you the sad story of Bill Scott.

Bill Scott was due to ride, in the Derby of 1846, a wonder horse owned by Mr Hudson, a Yorkshire farmer, and renamed, no doubt for reasons of local patriotism, Sir Tatton Sykes. So confident was Bill that he started celebrating on the first day of the meeting. Twenty-four hours later, he arrived at the gate for the Derby in quarrelsome mood and had an altercation with the starter. The starter sent the field on their way, but Bill Scott remained behind to slash at him with his whip. Only when he realized that he was twenty lengths behind did he begin racing. Even so, he nearly caught Pyrrhus, the winner.

This year, 1951, the most exciting finish of the week is Thursday's Heathcote Stakes, when Rickaby on Lord Rosebery's Paradiso just manages to catch Charles the Bold Smirke on the Aga Khan's Eclat.

As Smirke, momentarily green as a lizard with concentrated effort, turns Eclat into the second's stall, he shoots the horse a look like a scorpion's sting, then darts past the grey top-hatted bucks lounging against the rail, into the weighing room. Several jockeys and others follow him.

It is on occasions like these that the witty Mr Smirke is particularly well worth listening to. Eclat, of course, is a brute. He changes legs, stops and starts, and generally behaves like the district nurse's Austin Seven. The bronze, benign Aga, looking more Buddhist than Muslin, waddles, with toes turned out, like a very unfussy penguin. 'Just a bit out of luck today,' he says. Nevertheless, he wins the Royal Stakes two hours later with Inshalla.

If, however, you really want to hear language which would make the utterances of seven dwarfs who have missed the nail seven times sound like 'Lilac Time', you must be in the weighing room after the Oaks. Whether Chinese Cracker could have won we shall never know; but an oriental firework who can arrive second with the rails painted on her flanks, and her jockey's boots gashed, is clearly some filly.

Blue evening comes down with wind still whistling through Epsom's red brick and white streets. And the air is still appreciably like champagne, though definitely dustier. My tour of the town reveals one of those rather surprising local reactions: Many Epsomites affect to detest Derby week. It dislocates life and paralyses business for all except those in the catering trade.

Nevertheless, gaiety extends in many directions. I find myself joining in 'I've Got a Lovely Bunch of Cokernuts', rendered by six Midland bookmakers, while a sad professional punter, obviously an ex-intellectual, reminds me that any racing man worthy of the name would skin his grandmother and sell her for cats' meat rather than do anything to shorten odds. Later, the three-and-a-half-year-old grandson of a veteran jockey is sparring with me vigorously. As I rise from my knees, he lands a foul blow, one which he has obviously been taught.

All this, though very nice and cheerful, is more or less what you might expect. Rather more of a turn-up for the book is the behaviour of the sprightly but – as she herself would be the first to admit – no longer young Scots waitress in the tea rooms. While serving four of her compatriots down for the day with poached eggs, she gives them excellent advice on the subject of ante-post betting, and then proceeds to describe the underground passage by which, according to some imaginative local historians, Nell Gwynne used to travel from the weighing room to the Royal Box.

De Mortuis Nil Nisi Bonum

The rational explanation for not speaking ill of the dead is obvious. We don't want to distress the bereaved, and the dead can't hit back. But, like many devices that prevent the truth, this particular convention doesn't really work. Cover-ups and euphemisms actually underline the real facts. 'Sir Mervyn returned from his studious retreat in the Isle of Wight refreshed and ready for the financial fray.' The obituarist who writes this is doing no good at all. Far better tell us straight out that Sir Mervyn served his sentence at Parkhurst as librarian and opened a new bucket shop as soon as he came out. Everybody smells a rat in a doctored obituary, even the widow. 'His office life was enlivened with many platonic friendships,' she reads, and snorts:

'Whoever wrote this insipid rubbish? Anyone would think I was married to a eunuch.'

There is also what is known in the trade as the acid drop. This breach of the convention occurs when the obituarist thinks he's been too free with the eulogistic clichés, so he sticks in a bizarre anecdote: 'Despite his brilliant conversational gifts, Prosper was not a popular guest. Sir George Rosenkrantz tells us this was because his hobby of taxidermy became, in later years, such a compulsion that he tried to practise it on his host's pets.'

In the academic world, of course, acid on these occasions is almost *de rigueur.* Two old dons, fellows of the same college and deadly enemies, were dining in hall one night when their disputes got out of hand. Suddenly don A jumped up, bowed his excuses to the master and dashed out. Don B sat enjoying his victory. But don A reappeared beaming over the port in the senior common room. 'I must apologize,' he said, 'for my sudden absence, but I wanted to make an alteration in the proof of my obituary notice for *The Times* of B, while the thought was fresh in my mind.'

Omission of vital facts always arouses suspicion. An interesting case of total omission is that of the Devonshire vicar some time in the last century who was burying the local ne'er do well. It was his habit at funerals to make a few valedictory remarks in the churchyard. This time he was stumped. Character and behaviour of the deceased had been consistently atrocious with not one redeeming feature. The vicar looked down at the coffin and shook his head slowly. ''Tis as 'tis. Cover 'un up,' he said to the gravedigger.

I'm not suggesting the ideal obit should read like a blend of Krafft-Ebing and 'Hue and Cry'. All I ask for is some scientific humanist objectivity to gratify that mildly affectionate curiosity which is what members of the same species should feel towards one another.

In these uncertain times, when people tend to lose their tempers with truth, the objectivist humanist needs to be vigilant. One can forgive Elizabeth Longford – she has a generous nature and is easily carried away – for writing a life of Winston Churchill from which he emerges like a cross between Little Lord Fauntleroy and St Francis of Assisi. But it was alarming to read, not long before his death, Auden, once the scientist's poet, dismissing psychopathological symptoms as irrelevant in the life of a writer. There can be only one motto here: Cromwell's instructions to his portrait painter: 'Warts and all.'

The Psychoanalysis of Ghost Stories

Mamillius:	A sad tale's best for winter:
	I have one of sprites and goblins.
Hermione:	Let's have that, good sir.
	Come on, sit down: come on, and do your best
	To fright me with your sprites; you're power-
	ful at it.

Shakespeare: (*The Winter's Tale*)

'Morbid dread always signifies repressed sexual wishes.'
(Freud)

You may think this is a rather ambitious subject for an amateur even though he holds the seasonal saturnalian licence, but I hope to show that some ghost stories are very suitable for psychoanalytical interpretation. These invented nightmares which we enjoy frightening ourselves with can be compared to little volcanoes that go straight down into primitive strata of the mind. The fantasy material that erupts through them is, to use an old-fashioned schoolboy's expression, red hot. It has been repressed and disguised by symbolism but, unlike higher forms of art and literature, it has not been rarefied and transformed out of all recognition either by sublimation or by contact with outer reality.

In this domain we can sometimes find unconscious motivations lying out in the open, like flint arrow heads on a path. One that occurs to me is a passage in the *Malleus Maleficarum* that confirms Freud's explanation – which he arrived at in the first place from a consideration of his patients' dreams and associations – of the fear of witches as being mainly due to their power as castrating agents. In the *Malleus Maleficarum* there is an account – it is told as if it were an eye-witness account – of a German witch who had a nest in the church steeple in which she kept the

purloined members of most of the men of the village, the largest
by far being that of the parish priest.

Freud himself deals with the subject of ghost stories in *The
Uncanny (Collected Papers*, vol. 4). It is difficult to do justice to this
paper, which includes a detailed analysis of Hoffman's story, *The
Sand Man*, in a short space. In abstract, it may seem like so much
psychoanalytical writing, unduly reductive; but Freud, with his
graceful style and strong feeling for literature, does justice to
Hoffman's fantasy at all levels. And his examination of the whole
genre is very thorough. He begins by defining the uncanny as
'that class of the terrifying which leads back to something long
known to us, once very familiar'. He then examines the etymol-
ogy of the German word *unheimlich* (uncanny) and concludes that
its 'meaning develops towards an ambivalence until it finally
coincides with its opposite'. He distinguishes between two main
types of uncanny element. One is the animistic; this relates to
'the omnipotence of thought, instantaneous wishfulfilments, the
secret power to do harm.' It is also bound up with man's attitude
towards death. The other proceeds from the return of the
repressed infantile complexes, and in particular the castration
complex. These, says Freud summing up, together with a
tendency to involuntary repetition, or repetition compulsion,
like that met with in dreams, 'comprise practically all the factors
which turn something fearful into an uncanny thing.'

Freud also points out the difference between fairy stories,
'where the world of reality is left behind from the very start and
the animistic system of beliefs is frankly adopted,' and ghost
stories in which the writer often pretends to move in the world of
common reality; he not only accepts all the conditions operating
to produce uncanny feelings in real life, but he can increase his
effects by so doing. 'He takes advantage, as it were, of our
supposedly surmounted superstitiousness.'

This is an important distinction and it helps to explain the
history of the literature of the uncanny; the waves of Gothic
romances at the end of the eighteenth and ghost stories at the end
of the nineteenth centuries, as reactions against rationalism,
which could take advantage of just that supposedly surmounted
superstitiousness.

Let me now see how I can apply these ideas to one or two old
favourites. In general, the less subtle and rarefied the ghost story

the more suitable it is likely to be for analysis. The writer who makes conscious poetic use of symbolism, like Poe with that crack in the wall in *The Fall of the House of Usher*, is showing insight into the working of the mind; he knows fear's address. The writer who is most suitable for my purpose is one who, in Edmund Wilson's words, 'uses the belief in evil spirits as things that come to plague us from outside.' I will begin, then, with perhaps the best known English ghost story, M. R. James's *Oh, Whistle and I'll Come to You, My Lad*, from the first collected volume of his *Ghost Stories of an Antiquary*, originally published in 1904. Before starting to interpret it I should like to make it plain that it is part of my thesis that the author of this kind of ghost story is likely to be completely unconscious of its inner meaning. We may take it for granted, I think, that the late venerable Provost of Eton was blissfully unaware of the latent content of his fantasies, though some of the biographical facts about him, such as his bachelordom, might help to confirm the diagnosis. Judging by what he himself wrote about ghost stories in his introduction to *Ghosts and Marvels, A Selection of Uncanny Tales from Defoe to Algernon Blackwood* he must have had a significant blockage at this point:

> 'Often have I been asked to formulate my views about ghost stories and tales of the marvellous, the mysterious and the supernatural. Never have I been able to find out whether I had any views that could be formulated. The truth is, I suspect, that the genre is too small and special to bear the imposition of far-reaching principles. The ghost story is, at its best, only a particular sort of short story, and is subject to the same broad rules as the whole mass of them.'

Oh, Whistle and I'll Come To You, My Lad is a particularly good example of M. R. James's style; urbane, dry, but slightly whimsical, and his quick laconic narration that goes straight to the point. He uses the commonplace device of opening in a cosy fireside atmosphere to heighten the effect of the horror when it comes. The haunted hero of the story is a youngish don, Professor Parkins, the new Professor of 'Ontography', a bit of a prig and old womanish, rather hen-like. We meet him dining in college. He mentions that he is going to Burnstowe (Felixstowe) for a golfing holiday. (James himself tells us he made the change in name. No doubt 'Burn' seemed more suitable than 'Felix', happy, as a locale for so terrifying an occurrence.) An archaeologist colleague asks him to look at the site of a Templar's Preceptory. Parkins mentions further that his room at the Globe Inn has an empty bed in it. Another don, Rogers, a bluff father figure, threatens to come and occupy it. He twits Parkins on his hyperrationalism.

Arrived at Burnstowe, Parkins meets another bluff father figure, a crusted colonel with whom he plays golf. On the way home from the golf course, he stops at the site of the Templar's Preceptory and, while probing about near what seems likely to be the base of a platform or altar, he unearths from a small cavity a 'cylindrical object – a metal tube about four inches long' – the baleful whistle.

Back at the inn he examines it and cleans out the dirt from it. It has two Latin inscriptions. One of these, *Quis est iste qui venit?* Parkins can translate. The meaning of the other which is a little cryptogram –

$$
\begin{array}{ccc}
 & \textit{Fla} & \\
 \nearrow & & \searrow \\
\textit{Fur} & & \textit{Bis} \\
 \searrow & & \nearrow \\
 & \textit{Fle} &
\end{array}
$$

– eludes him. Looking out from his bedroom window he sees a figure which he takes for a belated wanderer stationed on the shore in front of the inn. He blows the whistle and is startled yet pleased at its note, 'soft, yet with a quality of infinite distance in it.' Almost immediately a tremendous wind springs up. It is so strong that when Parkins tries to shut his window it is like 'pushing back a sturdy burglar'. The colonel is disturbed; he can be heard stumping about and growling in his room above.

That night Parkins has a waking nightmare in which he sees a man being chased along a seashore by a figure in pale fluttering draperies. He also hears rustlings from the unoccupied bed which he thinks are caused by rats. In the morning the bed-clothes are so disturbed that the chambermaid thinks Parkins must have tried both beds.

On the golf course the colonel remarks that the wind of the previous evening might almost have been whistled for. Parkins takes this opportunity of reading him a little lecture on superstition and coincidence, telling him about the whistle. The colonel, who has given significant indications of strong protestant leanings and severe disapproval of the local vicar's popery, is grave. Back at the 'Globe' they meet a boy who has been frightened by something flapping at Parkins's bedroom window. There is nobody in the room, but the bedclothes of the spare bed are in a state of tortuous confusion. The colonel is now quite sure Parkins is in for a nasty time. 'You know where I am if you want me in the night,' he says.

Parkins goes to bed. He is woken by the collapse of a screen that he has rigged up to keep the moon from shining on his face. He sees the bedclothes in the spare bed rise up and take shape. He rushes to the window. The shape, which he realizes is blind, gropes after him. He sees it has an 'intensely horrible face of crumpled linen'. It leaps towards him and next moment he is halfway through the window backwards, uttering cry upon cry. The colonel bursts the door open just in time. Parkins faints. On the floor at his feet is a tumbled heap of bedclothes. Next day the bedclothes are burned – with the help of Rogers, the second father figure who has arrived on the scene, and the whistle is thrown into the sea. Thereafter for some time Parkins is a very nervous man and 'even now cannot see a surplice hanging on a door quite unmoved.'

Most readers of M. R. James are agreed that this is his best story. It is one of what Edmund Wilson, who is otherwise apt to be too severe on him, calls his flashes of really fiendish fancy. It seems to have something personal in it. (James admits that the bedclothes taking shape was partly suggested by one of his own nightmares.) It is also more plausible than most of his stories, in too many of which, as Wilson says, the hobgoblins are almost parodies of themselves. The device by which the evil spirit is made to animate the bedclothes is very effective, the kind of thing that might almost happen to anybody. In its construction, with the *heimlich* and the *unheimlich* elements succeeding one another like an alternating current, it conforms very closely to the pattern which Freud outlines in his paper.

The uncertainty about whether an object is alive or not is another factor which Freud points to as helping to awaken uncanny sensations. And when you start examining it with a view to spotting repressed infantile complexes, it turns out to be almost embarrassingly rich.

In the first place there is the symbolism of the whistle which is both phallic and anal. The explanation of the myth of whistling for a wind is one of those points at which Jung, even now, has not diverged far from Freud. People may remember Jung's account of the schizophrenic who told him that it was the sun's (father's) phallus which was the origin of the wind, and how excited he was later to read in the German historian Dieterich's paper an almost exactly similar description of the Mithras liturgy. As a quondam pupil of Freud there was not really any need for him to have been surprised at such a widespread piece of symbolism.

A further indication in the story of the omnipresent castration complex to which a psychoanalyst would point is the blindness of the ghost, which has come to recover its purloined phallus. The evidence for the equation of blindness with castration is, as Freud remarks, 'plentiful in dreams, myths and fantasies, as well as in the analyses of neurotic patients.' It is not easy to demonstrate it to the satisfaction of the layman, who is inclined to reject it out of hand on rationalistic grounds, maintaining that the eyes are equally precious organs and it is only natural that they should be guarded by proportionate dread.

Significant, too, are the circumstances of the finding of the whistle. These are described in a wealth of detail. 'And when he introduced his hand it met with a cylindrical object lying on the floor of the hole.' It is almost as if Parkins is removing it from a living body. He himself continues to display an odd doubt about what it is that he has found. 'I suppose,' he says, 'I am a little rusty in my Latin. When I come to think of it I don't believe I even know the word for whistle.'

Then there is the ingenious dramatic device of the Latin inscription. Here for a moment, James, as narrator, is slyly gloating over the unfortunate Parkins's predicament, even though he must to some extent be identified with him. Parkins has enough Latin to translate *Quis est iste qui venit?* as 'Who is this who is coming?' But the little cryptogram defeats him. Add *biss* to *fur*, *fle*, and *fla*, and you have the second person singular of the future tense of the verbs *Furo*, I rage or go mad; *Flo*, I blow; *Fleo*, I weep or grieve. One of these verbs is wrong. I can't remember which. *De nada*. The arrangement in diamond formation allows one to translate it in any order. It can be rendered with a little licence as: You will blow. You will be sorry. You will go mad. You might expect a cryptogram to contain the key to the story. Does this one contain it? It is impossible to prove it, but the idea at once occurs to anyone with a little experience of psychoanalysis that blowing the whistle is an act in some way associated with masturbation, to be visited by the fearful penalities attaching to masturbation in the child mind. This squares with the attitude of the colonel, the heavy father figure. He knows perfectly well what Parkins has been up to. He as good as says to him: 'You've brought this on yourself, my boy, and you'll have to take the consequences.' The duplication of the father figures, with the reappearance of Rogers at the end, which is unnecessary to the story, is an example of the tendency to reiteration or repetition compulsion and duplication, as in dreams, to which Freud draws attention.

The final haunting of Parkins in the bedroom by the animated spare set of bedclothes has all the ambivalence which we have been led to expect in a ghost story. The attack which the ghost figure makes upon him is peculiarly intimate and takes on something of the nature of a sexual assault. It reminds one of Dr Ernest Jones's dictum: 'All the beliefs about the nightmare in whatever guise proceed from the idea of the sexual assault that is both wished for and dreaded.'

There is one more significant feature in the story which should not be overlooked and that is the Templar's Preceptory. The inference at the conscious level is that the evil spirit which is attached to the whistle is that of a Templar; what were the Templars notorious for, whether deservedly or not? Their homosexuality. That there should be a homosexual element in the story is not surprising, especially if you take into account the fussy hen-like personality of Parkins, which has a distinct hint of epicenity about it.

Few, if indeed any, short ghost stories are quite so rich as this one in evidence of repressed infantile complexes, yet it is remarkable how often a similar pattern can be discovered. It is certainly present in another well-known English ghost story that features in several anthologies, *The Beast With Five Fingers*, by William Fryer Harvey. This is a story of haunting by a severed hand that runs very true to Freudian form.

'Dismembered limbs, a severed head' (writes Freud) 'a hand cut off at the wrist, feet which dance by themselves – all these have something peculiarly uncanny about them, especially when . . . they prove able to move of themselves in addition. As we already know this kind of uncanniness springs from its association with the castration complex.'

There is no need to give a detailed synopsis of the story; it contains some irresistible features.

The source of the haunt is Uncle Adrian Borlsover (surely a significant name for a castrated displaced father figure), whose nephew, Eustace, inherits his library. Adrian, an eccentric bachelor, went blind at the age of fifty, but blindness was not quite so hard for him to bear as for most people as he had always had a peculiarly delicate sense of touch. He was an authority on the fertilization of orchids, and 'so marvellous was his sense of touch that when he was blind the mere passing of his long supple fingers over a flower was sufficient means of identification.' After developing powers of automatic writing with his right hand, of which he is quite unconscious, he dies and by a clause in his will his hand is sent to his nephew in a box. It comes alive and, although the story falls rather between stools, the account of Eustace and his manservant trying to trap the hand between books has some of the time uncanny vividness. I should mention that, like M. R. James, the author of this story, the late Dr William Fryer Harvey, was a man of the very highest character. He was a Quaker with a remarkable record of gallantry in the First World War and some of his friends called him a saint. It may be that the writers of uncanny ghost stories are persons of unusually good character. It would not be surprising if it were so. Poe might seem an obvious exception, but Poe's stories are not in quite the same category and go with a different symptom complex.

My next specimen is the popular favourite, *Dracula*, by Bram Stoker, the best known of all vampire stories, almost the last of the Gothic romances. It was published first in 1897 and it still sells at the rate of several thousand copies a year, so it must have preserved powerful horripilatory properties for all its crudeness. (In my own childhood's mind it is still linked with *Oh, Whistle And I'll Come To You, My Lad* by a nightmare I had after reading both the books at a very tender age, fairly soon after each other. An interesting feature of the dream was a sheep which played the traditional role of sacrificial victim, and used to give off a piercing whistle whenever a vampire was near.)

Dracula, I think, provides really striking confirmation of the Freudian interpretation. The source book here is Dr Ernest Jones's fascinating monograph *On The Nightmare*, which has a special chapter on the vampire superstition. (I strongly recommend *On The Nightmare* to anyone who wishes to read an example of applied psychoanalysis that does not demand any clinical knowledge; it is perhaps the most convincing written demonstration for the layman that there is.) The vampire superstition, as Jones points out, embodies a particularly complex form of the interest, both natural and unnatural, which the living take in the dead. In ghoulism the necrophiliac traffic is one way, as it were, but in vampirism 'the dead first visits the living and then drags him into death being himself reanimated in the process.'

These are surface considerations. The starting point from which to investigate the hidden content of the superstition is once again Freud's dictum that morbid dread always signifies repressed sexual wishes. In vampirism they become plainly visible. Here we enter a twilight borderland, a sort of homicidal lunatic's brothel in a crypt, where religious and psycho-pathological motives intermingle. Ambivalence is the keynote. Death-wishes all round exist side by side with the desire for immortality. Frightful cruelty, aggression and greed is accompanied by a madly possessive kind of love. Guilt is everywhere and deep. Behaviour smacks of the unconscious world of infantile sexuality with what Freud called its polymorph perverse tendencies. There is an obvious fixation at the oral level, with all that sucking and biting, also a generous allowance of anality. We are left in no doubt about the origin of the frightful smell, compost of charnel house and cloaca, that attaches to the vampire.

It is remarkable how in *Dracula*, Stoker makes use of all the traditional mythical properties and blends them with a family type of situation of his own contriving that turns out to be a quite blatant demonstration of the Oedipus complex. From a Freudian standpoint – and from no other does the story really make any sense – it is seen as a kind of incestuous, necrophilous, oral-anal, sadistic all-in wrestling match. And this is what gives the story its force. The vampire Count, centuries old, is a father figure of huge potency. He is planning, from his ancestral lair in the Carpathians, a raid on England to set up a contemporary vampire empire. He has summoned Jonathan Harker, a solicitor, to make the necessary arrangements concerning property. These, owing to the elaborate obsessional code of rules governing the vampire's existence, are extremely complicated. The vampire or 'undead' can only move about freely during the hours between sunset and sunrise. During that time he enjoys all the freedom of movement and change of a phantom. By day he is confined to his coffin.

Vampires are not very particular about their choice of object. When, on his first morning as a guest in Castle Dracula, Jonathan Harker cuts himself, the Count's eyes blaze with oral-sadism. He makes a sudden grab but just manages to restrain himself. That night when Dracula's daughters, who are themselves vampires, crowd into Jonathan's bedroom, the directly sexual nature of the phantasy underlying the superstition is revealed.

' "He is young and strong; there are kisses for us all!" I lay quiet, looking out from under my eyelashes in an agony of delightful anticipation. The fair girl advanced and bent over me till I could feel the movement of her breath upon me. I closed my eyes in a languorous ecstasy and waited, waited with beating heart.'

Later on in the story, which is told by the multi-narrational method – 'As I must do something or go mad, I write this diary' – used so successfully by Wilkie Collins – Dracula lands in England and the endogamous motif linking all the characters together as members of one family becomes apparent. Dracula's first English victim is Miss Lucy Westenra, beloved by a psychiatrist, Dr Seward. (He has in his care a 'zoophagous maniac' who is forced to become Dracula's agent. This is a rather impressive piece of characterization and one that seems to show an intuitive insight into the oral nature of the manic depressive disposition.) The second victim is Lucy's bosom friend, Mina Harker, as dear if not dearer to her as any sister. She is the wife of Jonathan Harker.

Dracula's onslaughts on Mina are not fatal, because they are interrupted. The language in which Mina describes them leave you in little doubt about their sexual character and the incestuous guilt attaching to it. Note particularly the extra-sanguinary symbolic significance attaching to blood:

'He placed his reeking lips upon my throat . . . I felt my strength fading away, and I was in a half swoon. With that he pulled open his shirt, and with his long sharp nails opened a vein in his breast. When the blood began to spurt out, he took my hands in one of his, holding them tight and with the other seized my neck and pressed my mouth to the wound, so that I must either suffocate or swallow some of the – Oh, my God, my God! what have I done? She began to rub her lips as though to cleanse them from pollution.'

Mina is saved and Lucy avenged by a noble brotherly band led by Dr van Helsing, Seward's old master, a Dutch psychiatrist. (If he were in practice today he would be a right-wing Catholic Jungian.) Van Helsing is up to all the vampire's tricks, though until the very end he is always a step or two behind. Apart from Van Helsing, who represents the good father figure, the set-up reminds one rather of the primal horde as pictured somewhat fantastically perhaps by Freud in *Totem and Taboo*, with the brothers banding together against the father who has tried to keep all the females to himself. Dracula himself seems almost conscious of this.

When nearly cornered in his house at 'Carfax' after several of his mobile coffins had been destroyed, he snarled:

'You shall be sorry yet, each one of you! You think you have left me without a place to rest; but I have more. My revenge is just begun! I spread it over centuries and time is on my side! Your girls that you all love are mine already; and through them you and others shall yet be mine.'

One was tempted to add: 'mine . . . in a vast polymorph perverse bisexual oral-anal-genital, sado-masochistic timeless orgy'. There are several more passages in which the symbolism and the underlying incestuous complex stick out a mile. Often, especially during some of Van Helsing's lectures to Seward on the Count's psychology, Stoker shows insight into the infantile nature of the vampire's personality. When the great struggle is finally over, and virtue has triumphed over polymorph perversion in a last minute Lyceum melodrama rescue situation, and the Count has been staked through the heart in his coffin, in the moment of final dissolution a look of peace comes over his face that is on a par for intensity with the raging fury that had preceded it.

I doubt whether Stoker had any inkling of the erotic content of the vampire supersitition. He himself was an Irishman, born in 1857, a younger brother of Sir Thornley Stoker, the Dublin surgeon who is familiar to readers of George Moore and Gogarty. Abraham Stoker was a formidable allrounder at Trinity College; he took a degree in mathematics, was President of the Philosophical Society, also athletic champion of the university; this should not surprise us; *Dracula* is plainly an athlete's fantasy. He was called to both Irish and English bars, entered the Irish civil service and became inspector of petty sessions. He was awarded the Royal Humane Society's medal for life-saving – something no true vampire would countenance. He wrote several other occult thrillers, but not one of them is a patch on *Dracula*. The list of his works begins with *The Duties of Clerks to Petty Sessions in Ireland* and ends with *The Lair of the White Worm* – about a noble family haunted by a monstrous snake, one hundred feet long, that lives in a well in the park.

There is some evidence in Stoker's life of an unusually strong father fixation. He was certainly a born hero worshipper. In 1878 he threw up his Irish career to become Irving's manager. He had met the great tragedian when he was playing in Dublin where Stoker was, among other things, dramatic critic for an evening paper. In an article which I wrote about *Dracula* in *The Observer*'s 'Best Sellers of the Centuries', I wrote that one is tempted to imagine that it was Irving's saturnine appearance and the savage hiss – audible sometimes all over the theatre – with which he told an actor to 'get further up stage!' that had inspired the character of Dracula. It may have played its part. Hero worship is often accompanied by ambivalence and has its obverse side. But there is, as Stoker himself indicates, an authentic model for Dracula. I was given a brief account of him by Mr G. Nandris, a philological scholar. Dracula, he tells me, is the nickname of the Rumanian Prince Vlad Tsepesh (born in 1456), who was also known because of his atrocious cruelty as 'The Impaler'. His reputation was spread through medieval Europe in a German pamphlet printed in Bamberg in 1491. This carried a portrait of him in which the features correspond exactly with Bram Stoker's description of Dracula's baleful aristocratic countenance in the novel. Stoker must have seen the pamphlet or a reproduction of it on his travels. He would have found the vampire superstition very active in the Carpathians in the nineties. It lasted well into this century. In 1909, twelve years after the publication of *Dracula*, some peasants in North Transylvania, where Stoker had located Dracula's ancestral seat, burned down the local landowner's castle because they said he was carrying off their children. A Marxist interpretation of the vampire myth might, with justice, make more of this aspect, viewing it as a perverted extension of the feudal *droit du seigneur*, based on a solid foundation of exploitation; he starves us and sucks our children's blood.

There we must leave *Dracula*. It is not the best-written vampire story. (That distinction should go to Lefanu's *Carmilla*, a tale in which the homosexual trend that accompanies the oral element in the myth takes charge and the central situation develops into a passionate lesbian affair between a female vampire and her girl victim.) But it is certainly the most inclusive. It had its imitators. The Edwardians had a distinct taste for the full-length occult thriller. One, *The Beetle Mystery* (1907), by Richard Marsh, may be of some slight significance. It has been republished as a paperback. Told by the multirational method, it is crude and jerky but has some period flavour. Its psychosexual motivation is scarcely concealed. The beetle is a metamorphosis of an avatar of Isis, sometimes ageless and sexless, sometimes pulsating with libido. It haunts Paul Lessingham, a Member of Parliament who in his youth was held prisoner, drugged, in a house in Cairo and forced to watch nameless orgies with pure English girl tourists as sacrificial victims. The symbolism by which insects, especially in obsessional sizes and quantities, are associated in myths and dreams with the female sexual organs, is made unmistakably plain; the author himself seems to be aware of it. In this rather dingy case the uncanny thriller can be seen verging towards a mild kind of ersatz pornography.

An example of an entirely different plane of the beetle theme being used by a real literary artist, as the foundation for an exercise in creative imagination, is Kafka's famous story, *The Metamorphosis*. In this a young salesman, Gregor, wakes up one morning and finds he has turned into a gigantic beetle. The consequences are worked out in fine detail and his beetledom is most realistically blended with the background of his everyday family *petit-bourgeois* struggle. He is fed under the door with bread and milk that he prefers to be very stale; when he tries to climb the wall he falls and cracks his carapace. Once you have accepted the initial miracle, you are more than satisfied by the situation as it stands. The horror is all in the present, pointed by allegory. You do not feel the need to dissect the latent from the manifest content to find out what the story is all about; they have become fused together into a whole. This fusion marks the distinction between a work of literary art and a dream or an invented nightmare such as our so Freudian ghost stories turn out to be. Even in that very superior literary ghost story, the admirably written *The Turn of the Screw*, by Henry James, we can see the dream work in action; we can also watch the author shying away from the full implications of the theme of child corruption on which the story is based.

And here, as we seem to have emerged from the volcanic underworld of the unconscious, is perhaps the moment to break off. I am very conscious how arbitrary and cursory my exercise has been, and how much I have left out; but if I had examined many more stories the catalogue of symptoms and symbols would have been interminable. I will end by quoting the shortest ghost story on record, one that defies analysis:

'A man went to bed in a haunted room. He hung his wig on the bedpost and in the morning it had turned white.'

London on All Fours

It is our day. National Animal Day. Collectors are out early with their tins and trays of flags. The agents of our Dumb Friends League and the Furry Fellowship solicit in the streets. In the clubs toasts are drunk: 'Here's to the Badger of bashful fifteen! And here's to the hedgehog of fifty!'

In a huge sad square in West Kensington, the square where agoraphobia started and whence it spread, an old lady in mauve totters up to a carthorse with a heavy moustache. She takes from her old-fashioned reticule a little silver box of violet cachous and proffers it tenderly. The horse inclines his head and mumbles. Suddenly he sneezes; the long wiry hairs of his moustachios crack like whips; the cachous spill and scatter in the dust.

Round the corner, in the slum at the foot of the hill, a cruel but plucky dwarf is trying to skin a conger eel much too large for him.

In the newspaper room at the public library, three hairy tramps like hearth-rugs jostle each other round the *Financial Times* and compute imaginary speculations on scraps of sandwich paper. One had a scheme for cornering the deposits left by the pigeons at the British Museum and St Paul's; he dreams of becoming the Guano King.

The Park at noon. A militant atheist is lecturing to an audience of dogs and strollers. Lightning and thunder clap. 'Hear that?' says the atheist pointing to the black sky. 'God has shot himself. He can't take it!'

Under a plane tree, beside his suburban miss, sits the last GI in London, placid and drowsy like a November fly. The member of the master race is putting her through a cross-examination about the love life of the islanders.

A shaft of sunlight strikes through a rift in the cloud and touches up the lips of the statue of the philanthropist. The old paranoiac who has been feeding the birds is delighted. The statue saluted him by nodding. He is having a good day. Presently he will shuffle along to Chelsea Embankment, feed the gulls and, when nobody is looking, throw earth at his enemy, Carlyle.

Twilight and evening bell. In the valerian groves of the bomb site, the alley cats are assembling for their Congress. A giant tabby known as Carver Doone, the terror of his neighbourhood, has the floor.

The paranoiac steals up to them and whispers: 'Hssst! Comrade cats! Lords and masters! I am an Animalian! Enrol me in your Fifth Column! I will work for the conquest of the human race and the domination of your species! I will serve you faithfully.'

The cats stare blankly back at him. No vacancies.

He snarls. He'll show them. Back in his lodging he embroiders a tiny banner for a mouse to carry in its fist: UP THE RODENTS!

Bats bring on the night.